D1526400

ORSON WELLES
ON SHAKESPEARE

Recent Titles in
Contributions in Drama and Theatre Studies

America's Musical Stage: Two Hundred Years of Musical Theatre
Julian Mates

From Farce to Metadrama: A Stage History of *The Taming of the Shrew*, 1594–1983
Tori Haring-Smith

Prophet of the New Drama: William Archer and the Ibsen Campaign
Thomas Postlewait

The Theatre of Meyerhold and Brecht
Katherine Bliss Eaton

Ten Seasons: New York Theatre in the Seventies
Samuel L. Leiter

Sam Shepard's Metaphorical Stages
Lynda Hart

The Letters and Notebooks of Mary Devlin Booth
L. Terry Oggel, editor

Carlo Gozzi: Translations of *The Love of Three Oranges, Turandot*, and *The Snake Lady* with a Bio-Critical Introduction
John Louis DiGaetani

The Critics' Canon: Standards of Theatrical Reviewing in America
Richard H. Palmer

Eugene O'Neill in Ireland: The Critical Reception
Edward L. Shaughnessy

Spotlight on the Child: Studies in the History of American Children's Theatre
Roger L. Bedard and C. John Tolch, editors

ORSON WELLES
ON SHAKESPEARE

The W.P.A. and Mercury Theatre Playscripts

Edited with an Introduction by
Richard France

Contributions in Drama and Theatre Studies,
Number 30

GREENWOOD PRESS
New York • Westport, Connecticut • London

Library of Congress Cataloging-in-Publication Data

Welles, Orson, 1915–85
   Orson Welles on Shakespeare : the W.P.A. and Mercury Theatre
playscripts / edited with an introduction by Richard France.
      p. cm. — (Contributions in drama and theatre studies, ISSN
0163–3821 ; no. 30)
   Includes adaptations of Shakespeare's Macbeth and Julius Caesar,
and Welles's Five kings, adapted from Shakespeare and based on
Raphael Holinshed's Chronicles of England, Scotland, and Ireland.
   Includes bibliographical references.
   ISBN 0–313–27334–0 (lib. bdg. : alk. paper)
   1. Shakespeare, William, 1564–1616—Adaptations. 2. Welles,
Orson, 1915–85—Criticism and interpretation. 3. Shakespeare,
William, 1564–1616—Stage history—1800–1950. 4. Shakespeare,
William, 1564–1616—Stage history—New York (N.Y.) 5. Theater—New
York (N.Y.)—History—20th century. 6. United States. Works
Projects Administration. 7. Mercury Theatre on the air (Radio
program) I. France, Richard, 1938– . II. Shakespeare, William,
1564–1616. Macbeth. III. Shakespeare, William, 1564–1616. Julius
Caesar. IV. Welles, Orson, 1915–85. Five kings. 1990. V. Title.
VI. Series.
PR2877.W45 1990
792′.09747′109043—dc20   90–32464

British Library Cataloguing in Publication Data is available.

Library of Congress Catalog Card Number: 90–32464
ISBN: 0–313–27334–0
ISSN: 0163–3821

First published in 1990

Greenwood Press, 88 Post Road West, Westport, CT 06881
An imprint of Greenwood Publishing Group, Inc.

Printed in the United States of America

The paper used in this book complies with the
Permanent Paper Standard issued by the National
Information Standards Organization (Z39.48–1984).

10 9 8 7 6 5 4 3 2 1

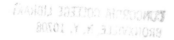

TO
LEON KATZ

Contents

List of Illustrations ix

Editor's Note xi

Acknowledgments xiii

INTRODUCTION 1

MACBETH 29
  Preface 29
  Production Credits and Cast 37
  Act One 39
  Act Two 62
  Act Three 81
  Notes to *Macbeth* 97

JULIUS CAESAR 103
  Preface 103
  Production Credits and Cast 108
  Playscript 108
  Notes to *Julius Caesar* 165

FIVE KINGS 169
  Preface 169
  Production Credits and Cast 174
  Act One 175

Contents

Act Two   231
Act Three   256
Notes to *Five Kings*   289

Selected Bibliography   295

List of Illustrations

Illustrations follow page 168.

Welles as Richard Plantaganet in *Winter of Our Discontent*.

Facsimile page for the 'Voodoo' *Macbeth*.

Ground plan and elevation for the 'Voodoo' *Macbeth*.

Coronation scene from the 'Voodoo' *Macbeth*.

Jungle scene from the 'Voodoo' *Macbeth*.

Costume parade for the 'Voodoo' *Macbeth*.

Facsimile page for *Julius Caesar*.

Ground plan and elevation for *Julius Caesar*.

Welles as Brutus, with Joseph Holland as Caesar and Martin Gabel as Cassius.

Welles standing over the Nuremberg lights.

Facsimile page from *Five Kings*.

Master Plans 1 and 2 for *Five Kings*.

James Morcom's sketch of the stage revolve in its first position.

Welles as Falstaff, with Edgar Kent as Shallow and Fred Stewart as Silence.

I,iv of *Five Kings*: Boar's Head Tavern.

I,x of *Five Kings*: a street outside of the King's council room.

III,xv of *Five Kings*: the French court.

Editor's Note

Orson Welles on Shakespeare is a fully annotated edition of Welles's celebrated Shakespearean adaptations—'Voodoo' *Macbeth* (1936), the modern-dress *Julius Caesar* (1937), and his compilation of the history plays, *Five Kings* (1939)—for the Works Progress Administration's Federal Theatre Project and Welles's own Mercury Theatre. With the publication of these playscripts, vital materials having to do with his contribution to American culture are available for the first time. While that contribution is a massive one, to date Welles is known mainly for his work in film. *Orson Welles on Shakespeare* reveals the seminal labor of his early years in the theatre, where he managed the seamless joining of art and popular culture—much sought after but seldom attained.

The texts of *Macbeth* and *Julius Caesar* that I have used are transcriptions of the stage managers' prompt copies, as prepared for the W.P.A. and Mercury productions by Elsa Ryan and Walter Ash respectively. *Macbeth* is now on deposit with the Institute on the Federal Theatre Project at George Mason University, while *Julius Caesar* remains in Ash's possession. No final version of *Five Kings* exists. Consequently, I have had recourse to the oldest surviving text, which, of the number of versions still extant, is the fullest and most inclusive.

The particular editions of Shakespeare and Holinshed that Welles used in compiling these adaptations are unknown. My sources throughout were *The Pelican Shakespeare* (Arthur Harbage, ed. Baltimore: Penguin Books, 1956–1960) and the 1965 reprint (by AMS Press of New York) of Volumes II and III of the 1807 London edition of Holinshed's *Chronicles of England, Ireland and Scotland*. All of the stage directions cited in the endnotes are mine.

Acknowledgments

I am grateful to Arthur Anderson and Thomas Anderson for their accounts of *Julius Caesar* and the 'Voodoo' *Macbeth* productions respectively; to Richard Wilson and William Alland for helping me reconstruct *Five Kings*; to Walter Ash for making available his Mercury prompt book for *Julius Caesar*; to John Keck for permission to reproduce James Morcom's sketches and ground plans for *Five Kings*; to Professor Lorraine Brown, Director, Federal Theatre Project Collection, George Mason University, for the W.P.A. prompt book for *Macbeth*; to Professor Vivian Perlis of the Yale School of Music for locating the few remaining fragments of Aaron Copland's lyrics for *Five Kings*; to Samuel Leve for (once again) allowing me to include his photographs and ground plans for *Julius Caesar*; to Stuart Vaughan, Associate Artistic Director, New York Shakespeare Festival; to Rebecca Campbell Cape, Lilly Library, Indiana University, and Dorothy Swerdlove, Theatre Collection, Library and Museum of the Performing Arts at Lincoln Center; to the late Frances Bordofsky of the Communist Party of America for directing me to the V. J. Jerome archives; to Dean Robert Corrigan of the University of Texas at Dallas, Dean Earle Gister of the Yale School of Drama, Professors Don Wilmeth of Brown University, Robert Carringer of the University of Illinois, and Oscar Brockett of the University of Texas at Austin; and, especially, to Max and Linda Tilton of Westbrook, Maine, on whose massive dining-room table this entire manuscript was assembled. But, most of all, I owe an incalculable debt to my wife, Rachel, and to Professor Leon Katz of the Yale School of Drama. They have been my sounding boards and, all too often, my unsung collaborators, not only on this occasion, but on practically everything that I have written during the past twenty years. No amount of thanks can even begin to approach the enormous contribution that they have made to my work, creative as well as scholarly.

ORSON WELLES
ON SHAKESPEARE

Introduction

We will never know exactly how George Orson Welles (1915–1985) was first introduced to Shakespeare. One especially fanciful story, told by Welles himself and repeated by almost all of his biographers, has him traveling to the High Atlas Mountains of Morocco with a satchel full of Elizabethan plays, which he studied while domiciled in the palace of an Arab sheik. A more recent legend involves Welles's mother, Beatrice, who we are to believe used *A Midsummer Night's Dream* to teach her son to read. But however Welles happened upon his favorite author, Shakespeare never had for him that deadening imprimatur— High Art. Instead, Welles became the quintessential groundling enjoying above all else that "passion torn to tatters, to very rags," split ears and all.[1]

The audience for his celebrated adaptations of Shakespeare (and Marlowe and Dekker) emulated, somewhat, the popular genius of the Elizabethans, all but the most destitute of whom were able, now and again, to afford a penny to stand in the pit of their favorite playhouse. Likewise, the price of a ticket to a W.P.A. production (the federal government's Works Progress Administration sponsored three of Welles's productions) was within the reach of most everyone. In addition, a federal mandate decreed that a certain number of complimentary tickets be set aside for people receiving Home Relief. As John Houseman, Welles's partner from W.P.A. days to the filming of *Citizen Kane*, promised in the pages of the *Daily Worker*, the Mercury Theatre when it succeeded W.P.A. sponsorship would follow its practice of charging only "popular prices."[2]

The theatre of Orson Welles thus became a place where workers and the hoi polloi met as equals and made for a very different ambiance from that of the commercial theatre. In the 1930s when, more than at any other time in our history, the intelligensia came to identify with the working masses, the exclusivity of Broadway seemed almost shameful. The egalitarianism of theatres like the W.P.A. and the Mercury quite naturally brought them within the orbit of the

Communist Party. Such was the party's influence in New York City at this time that only the most avidly anticommunist establishment theatres differed from its judgment. This meant abiding by the party's dictate to shun anything that might be construed as "elitest," "escapist" or "irrelevant." While this requirement might have been possible to follow, the concomitant demand for "socialist realism" was not.

Welles, being identified with a "people's theatre," came under the scrutiny of the party's cultural czar, V. J. Jerome, in whom adherents of the far left had vested sole authority to judge all cultural activities in New York City. Welles was amenable to working within these guidelines—for a while. The 'Voodoo' *Macbeth* (1936) earned enough credit with Jerome for Welles to follow it with two non-political productions, *Horse Eats Hat* and *Doctor Faustus*, which like *Macbeth* were done under the auspices of the W.P.A. *Horse Eats Hat* and *Doctor Faustus* met with only minor quibbles from party spokesmen, much to the relief of their creators.

With the possible exception of *Five Kings* (1939), which was produced in conjunction with the Theatre Guild, all of Welles's productions during the 1930s depended, at least in part, upon such left-wing organizations as the New Theatre League for their audiences. This left no doubt as to their political passions. Though not all were adherents to the party line, Welles could reasonably assume that his audience was, by and large, fervently liberal. As John Gassner has pointed out, the label of leftism "got attached to the entire serious-minded stage in America . . . and was not used pejoratively as it came to be used in the 1950s, but in a vaguely complimentary sense by proponents of liberalism and radicalism." In the 1930s, leftism (though not necessarily of the extreme Marxist variety) had become "the banner under which one fought *against* fascism and Nazism and *for* human decency, justice and social reforms to be incorporated into the law of the land without commitment to the overthrow of capitalism and the establishment of a 'dictatorship' of the proletariet."[3]

The adaptation of *Julius Caesar* (1937) reveals the way in which Welles was able to demonstrate the raw passion of his opposition to fascism and the world war it was about to unleash. Many who saw this inaugural production of the Mercury Theatre, including a number of prominent critics, came away more convinced than ever of the truth of Ben Jonson's adage, that Shakespeare was "not for an age but for all time." Without Welles's theatrical magic, however, *Julius Caesar* would never have echoed so effectively the fears of most Americans during this turbulent time in our history.

But in the 1920s and 30s, theatrical proponents of "justice" and "social relevance" in Europe and America often expressed mixed sympathies in their drama. Ernst Toller's *Man and the Masses* (1920), for example, produced in this country by the Theatre Guild, while calling for an end to capitalism, also demands that this be accomplished by means of a bloodless revolution.

As a result, the Communist Party set about to organize a theatre of unquestioned ideological purity. Thus the New Theatre Movement was launched. Judith

Read, writing in the *Daily Worker*, described its mission as that of bringing "the real problems of the American people to the theatre,"[4] and it was hoped that from these politically oriented groups would come a true revolutionary theatre in America. But the New Theatre Movement, which peaked in 1934, would just three years later already be in its decline.

Read lamented this failing. In glowing terms, she noted the high level of enthusiasm generated by plays such as *Peace on Earth* (1934), *Stevedore* (1934), and *Waiting for Lefty* (1935)—even those "wooden little one-acts because they called for solidarity and the end of war."[5] The "wooden little one-acts" of which she spoke were more the rule, however. Agit-prop (agitation and propaganda) dramas with one-dimensional characters and plots that led to foregone conclusions were churned out, and would soon bore even their most ardent supporters.

Party diehards remained convinced that the creation of a truly viable dramatic form was soon to be discovered, and, certain that propaganda need not be antithetical to art, supporters of revolutionary theatre labored on. (Some adherents of the New Theatre Movement were absorbed into the W.P.A., thus making them, ironically, government employees.)

It was against this backdrop that Orson Welles made his directing debut in New York with the 'Voodoo' *Macbeth*. He was in the right place at the right time to exploit thoroughly his particular talents. John Houseman (1902–1988) acknowledged the part that chance played in their success. "We had the enormous good luck to be working in the theatre at a time when it was possible to relate current events to the historical, sociological and economic events of the time."[6] In other words, Welles was supremely fortunate that, in using the theatre exactly as he wished, he was able to deal with matters of the gravest concern to his audience.

Yet the symbiosis that he formed with them was based neither on the socialist realism of the 1930s nor the propaganda contained in his own work. Rather, it was his vehemence of expression with its violent shocks—melodramatic and overwrought—that gripped his audience.

They were also invited to share in the knowledge that much of what was being done on stage was transparent theatrical trickery. So frankly engaged, their emotions were Welles's to command. Audiences, for Welles, were to be thrilled, frightened, and emotionally bruised, a perception of theatre that was very much at one with popular melodrama of a century before and also with the modernist movements of the 1920s and 1930s. But closer to Boucicault and William Gillette than to Meyerhold and Marinetti, Welles was unburdened by the overload of theory that dedicated followers of the avant-garde typically shouldered.

In fact, Welles seems not to have had the slightest interest in history. But he was innately sensitive to the central notion that animated most of the innovative theatre movements: namely, the realization that theatrical statement was not covered by rhetoric alone but by the totality of theatrical language. By subordinating text to inclusive effect, Welles created an expressive framework within which all the elements of production collaborated not to convey a statement, but, of themselves, to be the statement. And nowhere was this more in evidence than in his production of the 'Voodoo' *Macbeth*.

The rich and varied background Welles enjoyed as a child could easily have been the impetus for his casual eclecticism, open to any idea of theatre, no matter how radical or traditional. With his father, Richard Welles, he traveled extensively—in the Far East, in Great Britain, and on the continent. At home, his father's circle of acquaintances included playwright-humorist George Ade, at the time one of Broadway's most successful playwrights.

Ade was anathema to Welles's mother, Beatrice, for whom Richard's gang of fun-loving rowdies were, at best, aristocratic philistines. Her own salon was frequented by artistic and cultural celebrities who encouraged her to pursue a career in music. Local critics lauded her piano recitals of "interpreted music," during which she alternated keyboard work with short lectures on the background and aesthetic virtues of her Art.

Dr. Maurice Bernstein, who would eventually become Orson's guardian, was convinced that his young charge was a musical prodigy. Not altogether certain as to how such a gift could be made manifest, he gave Welles both a baton and a small violin. He also provided him with a puppet theatre, and it was under Bernstein's guidance that Welles began his lifelong study of vaudeville magic.

However fulsome his other experience, Welles's exposure to formal education was practically nil. Finally, and most fortuitously, he was enrolled in The Todd School for Boys in the Chicago suburb of Woodstock, Illinois, where he came under the tutelage of its headmaster, Roger Hill. Hill's philosophy of education consisted in the main of urging his students to do what is now known as "your own thing." Welles's "thing" was, of course, the stage and at Todd he experimented voraciously with all sorts of theatrical devices. At the time of his graduation in 1931, he had already formulated the basic concepts that would inform most of his W.P.A. and Mercury Theatre productions.

In addition to his duties as headmaster, Hill served as the director and guiding spirit of the all-male Todd Troupers, whose specialty was truncated versions of Shakespeare. He imbued his students with the notion that Shakespeare was meant neither to be studied nor dissected, but rather to be enjoyed and, above all, acted. A concern of Hill's was the audience before whom his students performed. He was quick to decide that this audience, consisting as it mostly did of parents and friends, was woefully uncritical and, therefore, worse than none at all. He solved this problem by taking his Troupers on the road.

Welles was an avid participant in the Todd Troupers—a star by the age of thirteen and co-director of the group in his final year. Their public performances, however, were keyed to meeting standards set by the Chicago Drama League, whose yearly competitions they entered and usually won. But Welles's passion for exploring new methods of production could not be satisfied by his work with the Troupers alone.

This was provided by the weekly unofficial productions done on campus. As these productions were also unheralded and unsung, neither were they taken seriously enough to be recorded in the Todd archives. This is all the more regrettable because, from 1928 to 1931, Welles had complete and undisputed control over these productions, and the scant detail that his fellow participants recall of Welles's activities during this period gives tantalizing glimpses of his artistic development.

The experience that Welles acquired at The Todd School for Boys would prove invaluable to his future work as a director. Less than five years after his graduation, and barely out of his teens, he showed the savvy and daring to make his professional debut in New York with his radically innovative adaptation of the 'Voodoo *Macbeth.*'

In 1930, a year before his graduation, Welles created an appropriately edited version of two of the chronicle plays for an unofficial weekly production. This was done expeditiously with crayon markings on a handy edition of *The Complete Works of William Shakespeare.*[7] To this compilation of *III Henry VI* and *Richard III* he gave the title *Winter of Our Discontent.* Of all the scripts that he must have prepared in a similar manner, this schoolboy antecedent for *Five Kings* alone is extant.

Winter of Our Discontent is not merely an important artifact; it is the paradigm for all of his future adaptations of Shakespeare, whether for radio, film, or the stage. His editing showed an almost preternatural familiarity and sureness in reshaping Shakespeare into productions which for all intents and purposes were entirely his own. Welles used Shakespeare's language as only one element within the conceptual framework of his productions. Thus the credit given him—''Production by Orson Welles''—was largely warranted.

At the tender age of fifteen, he was most interested in the fun of playing Richard Plantagenet. A photograph of him in this role shows a creature more gargoyle than human. With makeup that included an enormous nose, unlikely bald pate, and beetle brow, it is hard to believe that such a caricature was meant to be taken seriously. More than likely, Welles played the crooked-back king as he would later play Dr. Faustus—as the manifestation of a nightmare, inhuman and, therefore, all the more scarifying.

His intention was to make *Winter of Our Discontent* into a thriller, and everything that was not needed for the hour's worth of guile and treachery, murder and mayhem, was eliminated. If, as in all well-wrought melodramas, the villain was the most compelling role, so much the better for a young actor who would over the years frequently make such parts his specialty.

Winter of Our Discontent begins with IV,vii of *III Henry VI*. Of the original ten characters in this scene, Welles kept but seven. His method of elimination was simple: Montgomery is summarily banished when, across the bottom margin, Welles emblazoned ''FOR MONTGOMERY READ CLARENCE.'' Likewise, in V,v, Elizabeth is instructed to read for Margaret, thus leaving just one queen. In I,iii of *Richard III*, the long confrontation between the royal ladies and their king is cut and, thereafter, the only remaining female roles were that of Lady

Anne and, this time, Queen Margaret, who in V,iv is left to confront the fearsome Richard by herself, when Welles penciled in "FOR DUCH. AND Q. ELIZ. READ Q. MAR."

Act I of *Winter of Our Discontent* ends with Edward's unduly (for Welles's purposes) promising line from V,vii of *III Henry VI*, "For here, I hope, begins our lasting joy," to which is added the following cliff-hanger from V,v:

Edward: Where's Richard gone?

Clarence: To London, all in post; and as I guess,

      To make a bloody supper in the Tower.

Edward: He's sudden, if a thing comes in his head.

Thus does Welles foreshadow Gloucester's evil reign in Act II, which begins with I,i of *Richard III*. The future king, after reciting his famous catalog of woes, declares, "I am determined to prove a villain." As a rule, Welles was merciless in paring down lengthy speeches; but this one, which he delivered, was left intact.

As he had in *III Henry VI*, Welles freely rearranged passages in *Richard III*. After Gloucester's line from III,i, "Chop off his head," Welles's margin note reads, "SCENE ENDS WITH LINES ON 580" (reflecting the pagination of the Gollancz edition). The remaining thirty-four lines are taken from III,v and have Richard urging Buckingham to go to the Guildhall:

There, at your meetest vantage of the time,
Infer the bastardy of Edward's children;
Tell them how Edward put to death a citizen,
Only for saying he would make his son
Heir to the crown.

To which Buckingham replies:

I go; and towards three or four o'clock
Look for the news that the Guildhall affords.

By adding these few lines, Welles was able to provide the necessary exposition for III,vii, when the two men will again meet.

Minor roles often went uncast in Welles's version. The two murderers in I,iv, for example, were not the strangers that Shakespeare had written, but Catesby and Buckingham—logical substitutions, as they had been supporters of Richard since he was the ambitious Duke of Gloucester.

In Shakespeare's play the death of Edward is old news by II,iii. Welles's version, however, is edited in such a way that, prior to this scene, no mention has been made of the royal demise. News of a king's passing was too important for him to entrust to three anonymous citizens; instead, he assigned their speeches to Stanley and Hastings, who have cause to bewail the prospect of Richard's ascendancy.

Richard attains his throne, battles to keep it, and, with the desperate cry, "A horse! A horse! My kingdom for a horse!" meets his bloody end at the hands of Richmond. A scant seven years later, an infinitely more sophisticated Orson Welles would make of *Julius Caesar* a thriller whose emotional impact went well beyond that of the simple melodrama in *Winter of Our Discontent*.

Following his graduation from The Todd School for Boys, Welles left for a tour of Ireland, during which he was to occupy himself by painting "a lost Eden rich in romance and bounteous beauty." (During his stopover in New York during the summer of 1931, Welles attended a performance of *Alison's House* by Susan Glaspell at the Civic Repertory Theatre. It can be argued that from this play he gleaned the germinal idea for *Citizen Kane*.) For a brief (and depressing) time, he traveled about the countryside in a donkey cart, eventually finding work as "an assistant assistant scene painter" at the Dublin Gate Theatre. Founded in 1928 by Hilton Edwards and Michael MacLiammoir, the Gate emphasized the *art* of the theatre. As Welles described it: "Everyone works for the joy of working, the phrase 'nobody works for money' being *particularly applicable*. Salaries are of chorus girl dimensions. . . ."[8]

Edwards and MacLiammoir practiced a bravura and unrealistic style of acting that harkened back to the flamboyant actor-managers of the nineteenth-century English stage. Fortunately for Welles, his own performance skills at that time, while raw, jelled with theirs. Of his debut he wrote: "I performed a kind of J. Worthington ham Karl Alexander, with all the tricks of the trade that I could conjure up."[9]

Welles, the apprentice made good, performed the role of the evil Duke Karl Alexander in the Gate's production of *Jew Süss* with enough verve and gusto to excite even more kudos from the typically favorable Dublin press than usual. He trumpeted his auspicious debut in a letter to the Hills: "Step back John Barrymore, Gordon Craig and John Clayton. Your day has passed. A new glory glows in the east. I AM A PROFESSIONAL!"[10]

The reference to Edward Gordon Craig may have been offhand; yet Welles's own theatrical practices would come to resemble his to an astonishing degree. Primarily a designer, Craig in 1902 had published an essay "The Actor and the Ubermarionette," in which he recommended that a "divine puppet" be substituted for the all-too-fallible actor. Theatre people objected strenuously to this idea, among them his own mother, actress Ellen Terry. But nearly forty years later, that infamous ubermarionette was very much on Welles's mind. In his 1938 lecture "The Director in the Theatre Today," presented to the Theatre Education League in New York, he spoke of Craig as "a great visionary" who implied that "we must have no actors at all." And yet, Craig obviously fascinated Welles, who dwells on him through three long paragraphs. When he finally dispenses with "the great anarchist of the theatre," Welles has him suffering by comparison to "the truly constructive man, the crucified artist—Stanislavsky."

Stanislavsky, we are told, has been nailed to the cross by "his imitators, his students . . . the members of his apprentice theatre and the actual members of his company," all of whom, according to Welles, have done "immeasurable harm to the world theatre." But it is obvious that actors dedicated to the precepts of a Stanislavsky would be anathema to Welles. "A director," he begins, "is the *servant* of that aggregation of talent . . . which is a theatrical company. It is his responsibility to make everyone as good as possible *within the framework of his particular conception of a play*" (italics mine).

His tone of ersatz humility soon changes as he continues to define the role of the director:

The director, however, must be not only the servant but the *master*. . . . The composer, the light man, the scene designer, the choreographer and the actors . . . cannot all decide upon individual conceptions of the play. That would result in chaos. *The director must know what is right for that conception he has of the play* (italics mine).

Like Gordon Craig before him, Welles believed that a director ought to exercise absolute control over every aspect of a production:

The director must be better than his scene designer, better than his lighting—better than all of these people in the field of production; and it is his task to bring out of them the best talent and the finest results they can give.

He was especially perturbed with the designer who refused to accept his proper—that is to say, subordinate—function in the production. This anonymous "charlatan theatre craftsman" merely brings to his work "a knowledge of mechanics" according to Welles. The particular "charlatan craftsman" about whom he spoke so disparagingly was Samuel Leve, who designed the setting for both the modern-dress *Julius Caesar* and *The Shoemaker's Holiday*. Upon learning that his name had been omitted from the *Caesar* program and his considerable contribution absorbed into the credit "Production by Orson Welles," Leve appealed to his union, the United Scenic Artists, and this injustice was rectified.

Welles was unable to parlay his Dublin success into either a London or New York engagement; consequently, in March of 1932, some eight months after taking his leave of them, the disheartened seventeen-year-old returned to Chicago and the Hills. Roger Hill had just cut *Twelfth Night* for the Todd Troupers and offered it to Welles to direct. In addition to *Twelfth Night*, Hill had previously edited *Julius Caesar* and *The Merchant of Venice* for publication by the Todd Press. Welles was invited to illustrate these volumes and to write an introductory essay "On Staging Shakespeare and Shakespeare's Stage" that would be reprinted with each play. Originally known as *Everybody's Shakespeare*, a half-dozen years later and capitalizing on Welles's notoriety, this series would be retitled *The Mercury Shakespeare* and remain in print for over thirty years.

Set up in an apartment in Chicago's Old Town, Welles provided *Everybody's Shakespeare* with a great many deft and clever sketches—three per page, on average. His essay ends with an admonition to those of his readers who might afterward be moved to produce the plays to "try at least one of them without impediment. Fix up a platform," he entreats them, "and give Shakespeare a chance." In none of his own productions, however, did Welles follow his own advice.

During the fall of 1933, the Hills accepted an invitation to a faculty party at the University of Chicago. They took their young charge with them and, before the night was over, Welles had struck up an acquaintance with Thornton Wilder. Wilder, recognizing him as "the young American actor who had made such a success in Dublin" the year before, provided Welles with three letters of introduction to friends in New York—among them, Alexander Woollcott, who in turn introduced him to Guthrie McClintic and Katherine Cornell. They were also taken with Welles and invited him to join their upcoming national tour.

The tour began in Buffalo, New York, on 29 November 1933 and, after some 225 performances from coast to coast, was to have opened on Broadway the following June. It was in Wyoming that Welles learned that his "Manhattan opening" had been postponed until after Labor Day. Quickly he made plans for the interregnum. He would return to Todd and together with Roger Hill, produce a summer of repertory.

Welles was in his element that summer where, surrounded by starry-eyed disciples ("slaves" as John Houseman preferred to think of them), he could act out, at age nineteen, his long-held dream of being a great man of the theatre. It was amidst this riotous atmosphere that *Hearts of Age*, Welles's first film, came into being.

This silent ten-minute piece was shot during the last week of July on the Todd campus. Welles served as its star and director. Few (if any) of his collaborators, including his leading lady Virginia Nicholson, who was soon to become the first Mrs. Orson Welles, regarded *Hearts of Age* as much more than "cinematic fumerole." Now Virginia Pringle, she marveled at this interviewer's interest.

There was no script. Orson simply amused himself by thinking up totally unrelated sequences to be shot a la Grand Guignol. Bill Vance [another Todd alumnus] went around shooting reel after reel of happenings invented by Orson over a drink.[11]

Hearts of Age remained in Vance's possession until his death, whereupon in 1960, his widow, finding it among his effects, donated the film to the Greenwich (Connecticut) Public Library. It continued to languish for another ten years until the current film director Wayne T. Campbell simply happened upon it.

Virginia Pringle notwithstanding, for all its festival air *Hearts of Age* resembles nothing so much as expressionism's formless scream. Nicholson and Welles, both grotesquely made up, carry on a kind of slapstick-sinister flirtation. She alternately rocks back and forth on the massive Todd bell, scolds a human skull, and spins a world globe (precursor of the paperweight in *Citizen Kane*?). Welles, after slinking across the campus grounds, appears atop a fire escape, tips his hat to his future bride, and careens down the stairs followed by a disciple dressed entirely in white and carrying the globe. This is repeated several times, with Welles barely out of the frame before he reappears on the landing.

Finally, Welles, a lighted candelabra in hand, beckons us into a darkened living room where he sits at a piano and bangs away—all the while mugging for the camera. The last sequence shows a pair of hands sifting through a pile of tombstone-shaped cards until one bearing the legend ''The End'' is turned up.

The imagery is crude and overwrought, but the montage that Welles created from the various snippets of film worked to maximize the expressive force of very limited material. By accelerating the tempo of events, he provided the appropriate ambiance of dread and expectation, while the film's ending candidly, even gleefully, admits that a joke has been played. But it is Welles's private joke.

In viewing *Hearts of Age* we are caught up by its silly gothic trappings, which elicit from us the same undefined responses that make horror movies both ridiculous and exhilarating at the same time. And Welles, realizing this, laughs right along with his audience. Pauline Kael singled out this characteristic in *Citizen Kane*.

I think what makes Welles's directorial style so satisfying is that we are constantly aware of the mechanics—that the pleasure *Kane* gives doesn't come from the illusion but from our enjoyment of the illusionist and the working out of the machinery.[12]

Welles, basking in the glory of his summer's accomplishments, rejoined the Cornell tour in the belief that he would again be playing Marchbanks in *Candida*, Mercutio in *Romeo and Juliet*, and Octavius in *The Barrets of Wimpole Street*. Much to his dismay, he discovered that another actor had been hired to replace him as Mercutio and that his Broadway debut would be in the lesser role of Tybalt. But it was while wearing the black and scarlet of the Capulet nephew that Welles caught the eye of his future partner and mentor, John Houseman.

Houseman's importance to the career of Orson Welles remains inestimable. His only sustained success in the theatre, as well as his major achievements in radio and film, occurred during his association with John Houseman. Still, even Welles's most recent biographers, relying on their subject's own wishful thinking, seek to diminish Houseman's role. The result is to render much of Welles's work inexplicable.

It was Houseman's decision ''to risk my whole future on a partnership with a twenty-year old boy, in whose talent I had unquestioning faith but with whom I must increasingly play the combined and tricky roles of producer, censor, impresario, father, older brother and bosom friend."[13] Only someone of Houseman's particular genius and complex background could have pulled this off.

Born in Bucharest, and one of the most successful grain merchants in North America by the age of twenty-five, Houseman was bankrupt at twenty-seven. At thirty-one he became producer-director-impresario of the Virgil Thomson–Gertrude Stein opera *Four Saints in Three Acts*, winning Thomson's confidence for the job, according to Houseman, on no other credentials than his having been European bred, the product of both a French lycée and an English public school—and a willingness to work without pay. But the extraordinary *succès d'estime* of *Four Saints* left Houseman only with a reputation in certain circles for creative collaboration, "but with no immediate professional credit in the commercial world of Broadway."[14]

The conditions of his meeting with Welles, however, which he describes as "ineluctively shaping themselves," had nothing whatever to do with Broadway. They were, instead, the result of a partnership that he formed with Nathan Zatkin in the short-lived Phoenix Theatre. By announcing without prior approval that *Panic*, a verse play by Archibald MacLeish, had been selected as the Phoenix's opening production, the eager press agent had unknowingly induced his theatre's premature birth and Houseman's inevitable encounter with the nineteen-year-old wunderkind.

Regardless of MacLeish's demurral, the Zatkin announcement cannot have been all that untoward. No other management had expressed interest in *Panic*, an anti-capitalist tract written after the manner of a Greek tragedy. Critics of every political stripe had been unanimous in finding objectionable MacLeish's previous dramatic offering, *Frescoes for Mr. Rockefeller's City*, with the left-wing being positively rabid in its denunciation.

For John Houseman, who found himself "unable to function within the patterns of the existent commercial, social or art theatre set-ups,"[15] *Panic* was the perfect vehicle, and with its production he hoped to step in where others feared to tread. Zatkin's cooperation made it certain that the opening of the Phoenix would be a major theatrical event.

Only then, if Houseman is to be believed, did he realize that his production was taking shape without an actor to play the all-important role of McGafferty. Whereupon he embarked on an apocryphal talent search for that certain someone, as yet unknown to him, who could assume a role that "like Lear [was] almost impossible . . . to cast in the American theatre." Needless to say, his hunt for "a formidable J. P. Morganesque figure in his late fifties, the leading industrialist and financier of his time"[16] turned up none other than Orson Welles. McGafferty, in fact, with his "almost legendary greatness" sounds like no one so much as Charles Foster Kane.

Realizing its limited audience appeal, Houseman scheduled only three performances of *Panic*, the last of which was immediately bought up by the left-wing magazine *New Theatre*. *New Theatre* and *New Masses* both organs of the Communist Party in this country, fervently supported *Panic* and pressed the sale of tickets on their subscribers. Likewise, their reviewers praised the Phoenix management for having championed so worthy, if unmarketable, a play. This, in turn, established for Houseman exactly the sort of reputation that he wanted.

He also came away from this production on remarkably good terms with his temperamental young star. Already in the thrall of that famous voice, Houseman initiated a series of conversations with Welles, whose theatrical acumen was a constant source of amazement to him. These conversations not only taught the two "each other's language" but also set "the form and tone of our future collaboration."[17]

In 1935 Houseman became, in effect, head of the Negro Theatre Project for the W.P.A. with a mandate that included producing Shakespeare in Harlem. His chief concern was that the project's work be of exceptional quality, which necessitated finding "a director in whose imagination and power I was completely confident."[18] That is to say, Houseman neither could nor would have taken the job without Welles.

By virtue of its very existence, the Negro Theatre Project was a political hotbed in Harlem, where it was housed, as well as in Washington, D.C. Houseman's talent for ingratiating himself made him as well suited for this job, fraught with the racial tensions that would plague it, as anyone—black or white—could at that time have been. Its potential for giving work to upwards of eight hundred people made the Project a major topic of conversation throughout the black community. The talk was serious; at times, angry. And earlier in the year, Harlem's chronic unemployment had contributed to the numerous acts of violence that had erupted north of 125th Street.

Not surprisingly, the color of whoever was to manage the Negro Theatre Project became an important issue. Of equal moment was that this person also be acceptable to the Communist Party. The Party had no particular candidate in mind but demanded that "a Negro name" with connections to the United Front (against war, fascism, and censorship) be chosen.

Rose MacLendon was acceptable to all concerned. MacLendon, who unbeknownst to anyone had cancer, insisted that "a suitable white associate" be hired to share equally in the management of the Project. The person she had in mind was her good friend, John Houseman.

The actress succumbed to her illness before her company could mount its first production, *Walk Together Chillun!* by Frank Wilson. Her death only strengthened Houseman's resolve that the Negro Theatre Project be the first federally supported group in New York City to open its doors to the public. *Walk Together Chillun!* premiered on 6 February 1936 at the newly renovated Lafayette Theater. The play and its production met with a cordial, if unenthusiastic reception, but for the Harlem community it was enough that the Project's debut was "neither a disaster nor an 'Uncle Tom' piece."[19]

Brooks Atkinson concluded his review by noting that "Mr. Wilson is talking to his comrades. He is not appealing for Times Square applause."[20] As if in response to this slur on Harlem audiences, Roi Otley, after praising Welles's "magnificent and spectacular production" of the 'Voodoo' *Macbeth*, warned white audiences that the work of the Negro Theatre Project was "purely for Harlem consumption."[21]

But when Houseman and Welles began their collaboration at the Lafayette Theater, they had also to contend with the "ugly rumors" that were circulating throughout the Harlem community. Houseman, it was alleged, had spent so much money on his "boyfriend's folly [*Macbeth*] as to jeopardize the future of the Negro Theatre Project." Early rehearsals, closed even to Houseman, gave rise to the omnipresent rumor (revived to suit the circumstances) that what Welles was preparing "was, in reality, another vast burlesque intended to ridicule the Negro in the eyes of the white world."[22]

As black actors were seldom seen by white audiences other than in certain stock roles, such rumors could not be dismissed as merely the expression of a collective paranoia. Neither was the reception accorded black actors who had performed Shakespeare in the past cause for optimism.

The W. E. B. DuBois essay "Can the Negro Serve the Drama?" laments the treatment of black actors in America:

Take, for instance, *Comedy of Errors*, as given by the Ethiopian Players "a la jazz." To a modern audience the Ethiopian Players tried a new thing. They set the scene in a circus tent [with] very simple scenery, a matter of clowns and light and jazz music. . . . The beautiful Edna Thomas gave an interpretation of Shakespeare which could scarcely be bettered. If this [production] had come out of France with a European imprint . . . New York would have gone wild in praise. As it was . . . three white gentlemen insulted the actors with their gestures and comments.[23]

Against such odds, the 'Voodoo' *Macbeth* was a stunning success.

Attracted by a brass band and ballyhoo befitting a Broadway premiere, 5000 residents of Harlem turned out Tuesday night [14 April 1936] for the opening of the Negro version of *Macbeth*. . . . Lieutenant Samuel J. Battle, the first Negro to be appointed to the Police Department, said it was the largest crowd at a Harlem premiere that he had ever seen.[24]

No first-night audience, thus attended by the sixty-five-piece band of the Mitee Monarchs, Elks Lodge No. 45, which paraded up Seventh Avenue to a temporary grandstand erected for the occasion (by the Parks Department) in front of the Lafayette Theater, could have been expected to take the "Voodoo" *Macbeth* seriously. The pervasiveness of racism was also bound to affect adversely critical judgments of *any* production, Shakespearean or otherwise, performed by blacks.

Welles had not planned his production so as to mitigate against such factors. The expressionist setting of a dark jungle world, from which voodoo celebrants emerged, virtually begged comparison with Eugene O'Neill's *The Emperor Jones* (1920). Certainly, Welles did nothing to give his *Macbeth* either the look or the feel of a patently sober-sided Shakespearean adaptation. To have done so would have worked against his intention, which was to adapt the play so that it would live for his audience as it once had for the Elizabethans.

Hecate, as a voodoo priest surrounded by his priestesses and celebrants, touched a common nerve. Even the most rational members of Welles's audience shared at least some ambivalence about the putative powers of voodoo. This Hecate not only deprived Macbeth of his free will but did so as but one step on the way to world domination. No sooner was Macbeth dead, and his severed head tossed to the crowd, than it became clear that Malcolm would serve next as terror's agent. This idea of an all-pervasive, steadily impinging, and never-ending evil had, by 1936, become a commonplace of contemporary horror stories, political as well as cinematic. It was by such means that Welles sought to capture the imagination of his contemporaries.

In her book, *The Negro in American Theatre*, Edith J. R. Isaacs looked back upon the 'Voodoo' *Macbeth*, which, by 1947, had become legend. "A jungle tragedy of black ambition," she enthused, "*The Emperor Jones* gone beautifully mad."[25] It is not surprising that the O'Neill play should loom large in people's minds. Audiences at that time were unaccustomed to seeing black performers in serious roles, and, in all probability, Brutus Jones was the first major character played by a black to be widely seen.

While not entirely disapproving of Welles's *Macbeth*, Brooks Atkinson, none-theless, found it chiefly "a voodoo show inspired by the Macbeth legend." He noted how difficult the witches' scenes had been to stage in conventional pro-ductions: "But ship the witches down to the rank and fever-stricken jungles of Haiti . . . and there you have a witches' scene that is logical and stunning and a triumph of theatre art."[26]

His imagination was captured by what struck him as the idealization of Negro extravagance: "The pageantry is pretty heady spectacle. With an eye to the animalism of the setting [Welles] turned the banquet scene into a ball at a barbaric court."[27]

But missing the verse and narrative of the original play, the *Times* critic was adamant that the 'Voodoo' *Macbeth* not be considered Shakespearean: "Although the staging by Orson Welles is uncommonly resourceful in individual scenes, [the production] has missed the sweep and scope of a poetic tragedy."[28]

Atkinson had very definite opinions as to the capabilities of black actors. Deviating further from Shakespeare's text, he reasoned, would have allowed Welles to use their talents to even better advantage: "When the play falls within their *Emperor Jones* caprice, they have the artists and actors who can translate supernaturalism into flaring excitement."[29] Given the pervasiveness of racial stereotyping, it was not unusual to exploit what was believed to be the unique characteristics of black performers.

John Mason Brown also thought that Welles had not used his cast advanta-geously: "Divorced from Scotland and its thanes, with its language simplified or restated in vivid racial idioms . . . [the 'Voodoo' *Macbeth*] should be a tale of Black Majesty besides which even *The Emperor Jones* would seem tame."[30]

The idea of setting *Macbeth* in Haiti and using a black cast appealed to Brown. But Welles, he felt, had failed both Shakespeare and his audience with a version of the play that was "not only overly orthodox but far more inept than are most revivals."[31]

"This *Macbeth* seems to have a cast full of Emperor Joneses," declared Arthur Pollock, obviously amazed by the sight of black performers in such a drama. "They play Shakespeare as if they were apt children who had just discovered the Bard."[32] Childishness and simplicity were, to Pollock's way of thinking, innate characteristics of the Negro race; his racial bias was so intense that he was unable to see beyond it. Welles had populated the Lafayette stage with "simple people full of wonder as they go about the business of the tragedy, simple and full of wonder as the characters in such a tragedy should be."[33]

Robert Garland was even more condescending. "*Macbeth* is colorful, exciting—a good colored show." He declined to go further, advising his readers, "It mightn't be a bad idea to forget Shakespeare entirely."[34]

Burns Mantle agreed that the production was not Shakespearean. "It's a little as though O'Neill's Emperor Jones had re-established his kingdom in the South Sea Islands and staged a monster fete."[35] But unlike so many of his colleagues, Mantle did not object to the use of black actors. Headlining his column, "Negro Theatre Creates Something of a Sensation in Harlem," he went on to describe Welles's production as "colorful" and "startling."

Percy Hammond did not review the production so much as he excoriated its sponsor: "The Federal Government gives an exhibition of deluxe boon-doggling at the Lafayette Theater in Harlem presenting *Macbeth* with considerable pomp and circumstance."[36]

The cast also fell victim to Hammond, who expressed surprise at "the inability of so melodious a race to sing the music of Shakespeare."[37] Such criticism was less inspired by their acting abilities than by the fact that they were beneficiaries of the W.P.A. As further proof of money ill spent, Hammond complained that "despite this large army of federal officials, *Macbeth* could not get its curtain up until 9:30 last night, an hour late."[38]

Hammond was as politicized by the right wing as most of Welles's audience was by the left.

Black critic Roi Otley hailed it as "a magnificent and spectacular production of a Haitian *Macbeth*."[39] There was much in the words of his white colleagues that bore out his assertion that "the presence of Broadway and Park Avenue could hardly be considered a particularly sympathetic audience. . . . Nor were they cognizant of the implications of such a production."[40] Almost a decade after W. E. B. DuBois had written about the problems faced by black actors, precious little had been done to solve them.

For Welles, the 'Voodoo' *Macbeth* was a personal triumph, but the elation that followed was as brief as it was transitory. The Negro Theatre Project offered no further challenge to someone whose horizons now seemed boundless, and, having contracted for only one show, Welles saw no reason to remain.

Houseman's position as head of so prominent a unit made it possible for him to command his share of the still-considerable resources of the Federal Theatre Project. To maintain their partnership, he indicated to Hallie Flanagan, head of the Project, that he and Welles wanted to form their own production unit. Within days, permission was granted.

Not only were they to have their own unit, but the Maxine Elliott Theatre, at 39th Street and Broadway, was also made available to them. Flanagan's acquiescence was not surprising as her mission from the outset had been to create a national theatre of the highest artistic merit. And unlike Houseman and Welles, most of the people with whom she was required to work had proved unequal to this task.

Privately, Houseman was cautioned to set up his unit with all deliberate speed because funding for the Federal Theatre was already being threatened in Congress. Barely two years later, Representative J. Parnell Thomas of New Jersey would denounce the Project as both ''a link in the vast and unparalleled New Deal propaganda machine''[41] and a branch of the Communist Party, thus sounding its death knell.

In 1936, when Houseman and Welles acquired their own production unit, there were still three years of life left in the Federal Theatre Project. This newest venture, they decided, should be named for its W.P.A. designation—Project 891. After mulling over such possibilities as a modern-dress *Julius Caesar*, Jonson's *The Silent Woman*, and Webster's *The Duchess of Malfi*, Houseman and Welles chose instead to launch Project 891 with Labiche's *The Italian Straw Hat* and Marlowe's *Doctor Faustus*.

Forced to justify the presence of a nineteenth-century French farce in a classical repertory, Houseman explained that farce was ''taught in schools.'' Having satisfied the authorities, the title was forthwith changed to *Horse Eats Hat* and the play completely rewritten by Welles and Edwin Denby. The setting was now the American Midwest and Welles exploited the humor of prudish reactions to libidinous goings-on.

Horse Eats Hat opened 26 September 1936 to generally unfavorable notices. There was, however, some rather passionate support, notably from *New Theatre Magazine*.

On 8 January 1937, *Doctor Faustus* opened to a far better response. It ran for five months, playing to over eighty thousand paying customers.

Thus far, Project 891 had kept faith with Flanagan. They had produced as promised works that, though after passing through the prism of Welles's imagination bore little resemblance to their origins, could still be termed classical drama. Houseman's assertion that ''ever since its belated formation as a 'classical theatre' Project 891 [has] been the most purely theatrical, the least social minded or politically involved of the New York Theatre's five major theatrical units'' was, strictly speaking, correct.

All this was soon to change, with Project 891, according to Houseman ''caught between repeated, demoralizing rumors of reduction and liquidation.''[42] He and

Welles knew that a presentation of Marc Blitzstein's *The Cradle Will Rock* would give a powerful boost to morale. They also knew that the Federal Theatre was a sinking ship. By producing the Blitzstein opera, with its social (i.e., anticapitalist) message, Houseman and Welles were making certain that they did not go down with it.

Due to Project 891's defiance of a routine government directive that called for the postponement of all cultural events until the start of the next fiscal year (in approximately two weeks), federal marshalls padlocked the Maxine Elliott. Anticipating such a response, and the attendant publicity, Houseman had previously arranged for another theatre, and *The Cradle Will Rock* was sung into history. As Houseman had anticipated, the music also reached the ears of those who were to become his and Welles's next angels—the Communist Party and its supporters.

By the summer of 1937, the Federal Theatre's days were numbered. Over sixteen hundred pink dismissal slips were distributed in New York City alone. Welles resigned his position with Project 891 on August 15th, the same day that Houseman received notice of his dismissal (due, in fact, to a new regulation that permitted only American citizens to work for the W.P.A.). Before the month ended, the Mercury Theatre had been registered and incorporated in Albany, New York, with John Houseman and Orson Welles as its president and vice-president, respectively.

"The Mercury Theatre was at first just an idea bounded North and South by hope, East and West by nerve,"[43] wrote *Time*. If one were to take Houseman's memoir *Run-Through* at face value, the Mercury flew into town "on a wing and a prayer." On the strength of "a paid-up capital of one hundred dollars" Houseman and Welles were able to rent the Comedy Theatre at Broadway and 41st Street, assure themselves of Brooks Atkinson's benediction, and announce their coming season.

Houseman, a magnificent storyteller, does nothing to detract from the fairy-tale atmosphere with which he has surrounded the Mercury Theatre—waiting, as Cinderella, for her fairy godmother to appear. In his account, the waiting ended with the advent of seven investors. While their names are unfamiliar, six are characterized lovingly: one has "a cultured voice"; another, "warmth and enthusiasm"; a third is a "gentle, shrewd, sincere, white-haired gentleman"; he is followed by the "heir to a New England carpet manufacturing fortune"; and lastly, a Harvard law student "who had a passion for the theatre." A seventh, neither named nor characterized, gave "one final cash contribution." The Mercury, almost magically, had thus acquired a capitalization of "ten thousand five hundred dollars."[44]

The amount of each contribution is also given and, according to strict arithmetic, the total is, in fact, fourteen thousand dollars. As Houseman has implicitly requested that his readers suspend disbelief about so many things, one has to assume this applies to the Mercury's funding as well. Even without its opening triumph, the fascist *Julius Caesar* with its seamless joining of art and politics (made possible only through the existence of a Mercury Theatre), Houseman's incredible saga of that organization's birth would still be a good read.

He details the help that he and Welles received from some of the finest young theatrical talent in New York: among them, Samuel Leve, the lighting designer Jean Rosenthal, and composer Marc Blitzstein, who provided *Julius Caesar* with an original score. Noticeably absent is any explicit reference to the Communist Party, which not only supplied theatre parties well into the following year, but almost certainly was a financial backer of the production itself.

The Party's domination over much of the intellectual life of the 1930s offered Welles the challenge of satisfying its demand for a drama that was artistically viable as well as socially relevant, politically responsible, and inspirational. This was in accord with his own thinking about theatre.

Even if it had not been, Houseman had already committed the Mercury to following the Party's cultural mandates. If, as he claims, in writing their manifesto he attempted "to avoid the line of vague, verbose grandeur generally associated with the announcements of embryo, indigent artistic groups,"[45] judging by the two drafts printed in *Run-Through*, Houseman uncharacteristically failed to do so. In any event, neither the manifesto nor his "PLAN FOR A NEW THEATRE" published in the *New York Times* had anything like the impact of the article that Houseman wrote for the September 18th issue of the *Daily Worker*, a date concurrent with the distribution of a quarter of a million handbills announcing

JULIUS CAESAR
!! DEATH OF A DICTATOR !!

Emblazoned across the top of the paper's theatre page was the banner headline:

AGAIN . . . A PEOPLE'S THEATRE;
THE MERCURY TAKES A BOW

In the fine journalistic prose of his first paragraph, Houseman makes the commitment that with the Mercury "another step will have been taken towards a real people's theatre in America." With bows to agit-prop companies, such as the Theatre Union, the Theatre of Action, and "other socially conscious groups" he pledges that, in entering the field of "popular priced theatre," plays that the Mercury presented, while representative of all theatrical periods, would be chosen for their "contemporary significance."

From there, Houseman segues gracefully into an announcement of the Mercury's opening production, *Julius Caesar*, which is described as "the most contemporary of Elizabethan plays." The emphasis, he tells his readers, would be on "the social implications inherent in the history of Caesar [and] the atmosphere of personal greed, fear and hysteria that surround a dictatorial regime." "The modern parallel," he asserts, "is obvious."

Welles evoked passionate reaction to highly charged political issues with this production. Simultaneously, *Caesar* received critical accolades as a Shakespearean adaptation. Thus John Mason Brown could declare, "What Mr. Welles and his associates at the Mercury have achieved is a triumph that is exceptional from almost every point of view."[46]

This successful juggling of art and politics was accomplished, in part, because Welles superimposed no rhetorical statement of his own. Rather, his message was embedded in the theatrical devices that had shaped the production and provided his audiences with the means for inspiring their own passions. As intended, *Caesar* was filtered through the prism of each spectator's own particular knowledge and experience.

Certain critics judged it prudent not to concern themselves with how the production may have fit into the context of contemporary politics. Brooks Atkinson advised looking at *Julius Caesar* simply as "an exciting excursion into stagecraft." Caesar was personally ambitious: in his opinion that was reason enough to assassinate him. However, Atkinson also expressed concern that a wrong may have been done by killing a ruler, who, though a dictator, seemed at least a benevolent one. This led him to conclude that it was a mistake to draw parallels between Shakespeare's play and current events. "When *Julius Caesar* is presented as a play of action, Shakespeare sounds like a Fascist, and perhaps he was without knowing it."[47]

On the other hand, Stark Young had not doubts about classifying the production's noble protagonist by modern standards: "The idea of state that Brutus holds and represents leans rather more towards that of fascism than of democracy."[48] Young's definition of fascism is equally applicable to Plato's vision of the ideal state: one governed by an elite that is well suited for the job.

While admiring in Welles's production "a certain boldness of outline and freshness of technique," Young remained focused on the text, and, in his opinion, the production was no more capable of exploring the dictator theme than was Shakespeare's play. "In the end all we get is a new dictator praising Brutus' martyrdom," a grievous flaw in the eyes of this critic, who was convinced that Welles had edited the text "with the intention of increasing its modern application and making it a dictator play."[49]

Joseph Wood Krutch's review appeared four days earlier than Young's and diametrically opposed it. For Krutch, the modern accoutrements of *Julius Caesar* had much the same effect as a recent modern-dress production of *Hamlet*. He even suggested that Welles might have gone further in "helping to suggest a parallel between the dying republic of Rome and the world of today . . . but there is no forcing of the parallel and no distortion of Shakespeare's play to point to a modern moral."[50]

Grenville Vernon found the attempt to draw a modern political equation based on the production futile: "It is idle to ask whether the play is meant to be pro-Fascist or anti-Fascist. . . . Shakespeare's tragedy offers no perfect parallels to modern events, although there are strange likenesses to what is happening in

Europe today."[51] He concluded that "Those who see the Mercury's *Julius Caesar* must see it without preconceived notions as to how it should be played or what its meaning is."[52]

This was also the approach of critics who, like Sidney Whipple, were impressed by the Mercury production simply because it had "dared to throw off every past convention."[53] The popular tabloids were similarly open-minded. "They have tossed convention down the air-shaft," cheered Burns Mantle. Robert Coleman's review exemplified the gut-level response for which Welles was, after all, reaching. The production had been so directed, Coleman wrote, "as to emphasize the timelessness of its observations upon tyranny and freedom, dictatorships and demagoguery," and he applauded Welles for sweeping "the classroom dust off *Julius Caesar*."[54]

Thus, when Heywood Broun commented, tongue-in-cheek, that "Shakespeare has written so timely and provocative a piece that the critics were actually arguing whether he favored fascism or communism or was perhaps a Trotskyite,"[55] he may well have had the tabloids in mind as participants in this apocryphal debate.

Writing in the *Daily Worker*, Eric Englander left no doubt that Welles had seen in *Julius Caesar* "an analogue to modern fascism"; however, the parallels were "desperately strained" for Englander.

The anarchistic assassination of Caesar is shown favorably because it means the death of a tyrant. The climatic [sic] death of Brutus is pictured with equally approving emphasis because liberals cannot survive a period of civil strife.[56]

In depicting Caesar as a tyrant, Welles's interpretation was in keeping with Marxist dogma. Brutus, though, was played incorrectly, since Shakespeare emphasized "only his passionate patriotism, his heroic struggle for freedom."[57] This divergence of Welles's was not of major import, however.

What the left found most offensive in Welles's production were the aspects of experiment and stylization. Shakespeare, the "humanist ideologist of the bourgeoise of the time,"[58] was not to be defiled by "formalism," the term used to condemn all departures from realism. "Welles . . . edited the text and supervised the lighting and directed the actors [who] partake of the same intense sensationalism as the literary treatment."[59] In other words this *Julius Caesar* was an example of the despised formalist antirealism.

The USSR declared socialist realism (realism that reflected approved ideology) the only proper style for all art in 1934. By 1937, the pressure against experimentation was given new weight, with the *Daily Worker* echoing the party line. However, theatre in America was not taken seriously, either as a medium of ideas or the integral part of society that it was in the Soviet Union. So, the *Daily Worker* could blast Welles for formalism while summing up its review with "Merits Attendance."

Julius Caesar was officially condemned, while privately the radical left organized theatre parties for it. They had reason enough to maintain friendly relations with the Mercury. One inducement came in the form of a promise by Houseman to showcase plays from the contemporary social scene, notably a revival of *The Cradle Will Rock*.

On New Year's Day, 1938, *Julius Caesar* was joined in repertory by Dekker's *The Shoemaker's Holiday*. Though Welles's direction exploited the most bawdy elements he could invent, V. J. Jerome saw fit to overlook *Shoemaker's* "escapist" tone. The fact that the worst of the lechers were members of the proletariat seems to have been the mitigating factor.

By November, the love affair between the Mercury Theatre and its left-wing comrades was over. It ended with the Party's angry denunciation of Buchner's *Danton's Death*.

The relevance of *Julius Caesar* to the politics of the 1930s was far from explicit. Welles could, therefore, choose whatever parallels he wanted to draw. The parallels between the Jacobean revolution, as depicted in his production of *Danton's Death*, and the Marxist revolution, on the other hand, were both blatantly obvious and unflattering to Stalin.

Houseman mythicizes the demise of *Danton's Death* by once again feigning an ignorance that is hard to believe of men as intelligent as he and Welles. He alleges in *Run-Through* that it was not until ten days prior to their first scheduled preview that they were finally made aware of the difficulties that lay ahead. It was Blitzstein, the self-appointed political advisor to the Mercury, who told them that "in producing *Danton's Death* [they] were all guilty of a serious and dangerous error." So egregious was that error, Blitzstein suggested the production's immediate cancellation. Instead, Welles met with Jerome; the changes that ensued from that consultation only succeeded in ruining the production as he had conceived it without having made it the least scintilla more pleasing to Jerome.

Danton's Death opened on 14 November 1938, and lasted a humiliating twenty-one performances. Whereupon the doors of the Mercury Theatre closed, never to be reopened.

In *Run-Through* the Mercury's fallen president points to several of the "if-only's" by means of which the theatre might have been restored to its devotees. But in the denouement, it was discovered that the Mercury had, in fact, outlived its usefulness for both Houseman and Welles, who were Broadway bound as the result of an alliance with the Theatre Guild to produce *Five Kings*.

In Philadelphia our patience and our money ran out, as did the audience. So, *Five Kings* came to an untimely but not ignominious end. In spite of all its drawbacks this contact with youth provided a refreshing interlude.[60]

To the contrary, the Guild's collaboration with Houseman and Welles was anything but refreshing. While pretending to recall the episode humorously as "one of our wildest adventures,"[61] finally what Lawrence Langner conveys is the prevailing sense of bitterness and rancor that soured the relationship. He begins by describing what was, ostensibly, the saga of a confrontation between well-meaning professionals and irresponsible amateurs.

The Guild approached Houseman and Welles in May of 1938. Realizing that their steady diet of light comedies was eroding their subscription base troubled Langner and the other aging board members. An alliance with the Mercury offered hope of a much-needed rejuvenation; so the Guild readily acquiesced to Welles's suggestion that it underwrite his "agglomeration of Shakespearean plays."[62] Although *Five Kings* was, for all intents and purposes, still pretty much a pig-in-a-poke, the Guild agreed to make a collaborative investment in it.

Furthermore, they agreed not to interfere in the all-important matter of artistic decision making. The Guild's ability to advise—without it seems, Welles having to heed their suggestions—appears to have been their only hedge against "merely supplying our dwindling funds to youth."[63] Such an arrangement proved to be the height of folly.

Langner explains the Guild's blatant lack of judgment thus: "I let myself be beguiled into the belief that I would, in some mysterious manner, recover my zest for the theatre which, at the moment, had been dulled . . . by a long series of failures."[64] Despite this, and the Mercury's recent succession of hits, Langner implies that Welles's refusal to take advantage of the wisdom of age was ultimately responsible for *Five Kings* never becoming viable enough for the risk entailed by a New York opening.

Given a modicum of good faith the Guild might well have brought *Five Kings* to Broadway. The notable lack of candor in Langner's snide account of Welles's foibles during the brief life of this production makes clear that there was no faith at all in it. There is also evidence that the Guild may have written off *Five Kings* even before it reached Boston. According to Langner, his "first intimation of danger" came shortly before *Five Kings* went into rehearsal, whereupon he suggested that Welles revise his production scheme, especially since touring was such an essential part of it. This was advice that Welles chose to ignore, thus dooming *Five Kings*—certainly, in Langner's mind—to artistic and financial disaster. The only way the Guild had of cutting its losses was to close the production out of town.

However, their dissatisfaction with the Mercury in general, and Welles in particular, did not begin with production problems on *Five Kings*. In her article, "Theatre Guild and Welles May Go Phfft," Katherine Hillyer reported that the ill will went back

as far as the beginning of the 1938–39 season, when the Guild thought Welles would direct a pair of plays for production in their regular subscription list. Somehow nothing materialized until *Five Kings* was put into rehearsal, too late to go on the road as anything but a subscriber's "dividend."[65]

And an earlier article in *Variety* noted that the Guild had been "backward in getting its production schedule into swing this season."[66]

   The Guild was dependent on a subscription audience, which it promised five
new productions each season. By purchasing their tickets in advance, subscribers
essentially underwrote the productions they were to see, and each offering on
the regular schedule was assured of at least breaking even. Langner's assertion
that in only two years of its history did the Guild turn a profit might well be
true. But, by the 1930s, their struggle was to avoid losing money. Welles
wounded Langner and his fellow board members when, through seemingly blatant improvidence, he endangered their shaky financial structure.
   But the wound cut more deeply than just an assault on their fiscal planning.
The Theatre Guild had been founded in 1919 by former members of the Washington Square Players, a prominent art theatre in New York City. It set as its
goal to be a fully professional company dedicated to the production of plays of
artistic excellence that were generally shunned by commercial managements.
After a long and distinguished history, the Guild had, of late, found itself
producing standard Broadway fare. Thus, the same people who in 1922 had
championed the likes of Kaiser's *From Morn Till Midnight*, now looked ex-
pectantly to Orson Welles to return them to the forefront of innovative drama.
   This would explain why the Guild, for a time, had willingly suspended its
disbelief concerning the Mercury's method of operation. While not averse to
experimental drama with its predictable hazards, Guild board members over the
years had become attuned to practical considerations as well. The generation
gap between the Guild and the Mercury made it impossible for Langner to
sympathize with Welles's excesses. James Morcum, the designer of *Five Kings*,
idolized Welles. Yet he described "fights over money that would curl your
hair."[67] John Houseman, who was equally devoted to Welles's genius, stuck
by him. Langner, however, was neither willing nor able to do likewise.
   From his first sight of a Boston dress rehearsal, Langner realized, as did his
wife, Armina Marshall, that *Five Kings* "was something that was interesting
and provocative, but also gave you the feeling that it wasn't going to work."[68]
The fact that *Five Kings* might not even succeed artistically angered Langner,
who was sufficiently irate that in his autobiography, written over a decade later,
he remembered the critics being no more optimistic about the show's chances
than he had been. "The opening performance . . . took place before the elite of
Boston, who came to pray but remained to scoff."[69]
   According to Peggy Doyle of the *Boston Evening American*, however, this
was decidedly not the case. She described an unusually large and varied audience,
which, except for a handful of suburban customers, stayed until the final curtain
rang down at 12:30 A.M. For Doyle, this was "a considerable Boston tribute."[70]
   Like most of the other Boston critics, Doyle was bending over backward to
be supportive of Welles. His work in New York had given him precisely the
sort of aesthetic cachet that first brought the Theatre Guild to prominence. And,
since "The War of the Worlds" broadcast of the previous Halloween, when the
Mercury Theatre on the Air had apotheosized into the Campbell Playhouse,
Welles himself had become a national celebrity. As a corporate spokesman, he

assumed the role of sophisticated world traveler and gourmet (who, nonetheless, preferred Campbell soup). All this worked to give him the aura of someone who was to be taken seriously, and "the audience waited for the curtain to go up on what might be anything in the way of theatre."[71] For Doyle and her fellow critics, this might even be a nascent *Julius Caesar*.

The exception was John E. Hutchens, who commented wryly, "When it was all over, you found yourself wishing that they had done one play."[72] Yet, a more approving reviewer, while noting that the audience was "regaled alternately with lusty comedy, grim tragedy, light humor and poignant pathos,"[73] also noticed lighting errors and mistakes in the timing of the revolving stage. It was all very well for audiences to have stayed, as Doyle pointed out, until after midnight; but, clearly, this should not have been necessary.

Elliot Norton, the dean of Boston critics, found *Five Kings* to be "an extraordinary and exciting adventure in theatre," but followed this plaudit with a caveat. "Eventually, after an enormous amount of touring and rehearsing, they will turn up in New York with two evenings of Shakespeare."[74]

Another distinguished Bostonian, Elinor Hughes, thought *Five Kings* "the most impressive and ambitious undertaking of the Mercury's short and exciting career." While acknowledging that Welles had "an arduous task before him to bring it within reasonable compass," Hughes declared, "We have sufficient confidence in Mr. Welles and his company to believe that everything needful will eventually be accomplished."[75] Unfortunately, her faith was not shared by the Theatre Guild.

The production's major problem appeared to be length. Houseman was optimistic when forty minutes were cut during the Boston run. "Slowly, the show was finding itself." But in its second stop, Washington, D.C., this problem reappeared. "A vital, living drama. And it is that, despite the fact that it runs long and tends to have cumbersome spots."[76] Once more, it became typical for a reviewer to comment, "The genius of Orson Welles was demonstrated in the theatre last night," only to point out that the demonstration was conducted "before an audience that was held in its seat long past midnight."[77]

Katherine Hillyer of the *Washington Daily News* felt, as most everyone involved in the production may also have,

There's no reason why *Five Kings* shouldn't be boiled down to fit the conventional running time of other productions. The strength of the show is in its cast . . . in its bravura as an experiment . . . but not, alas, in its structure.[78]

Welles continued to make cuts, but these worked not so much to shorten the production as to lower its quality.

The Philadelphia reviews were savage. "A richly impressive facade behind which one hears reverberations of emptiness,"[79] wrote Edwin H. Schloss of the *Record*. J. H. Keen ridiculed the production. "As a stage colossus, it is something to gape at, as one might a prehistoric creature brought back to earth."[80]

Exercising its power over a production that was greatly over budget, and lacking an assured audience, the Theatre Guild withdrew its support of *Five Kings*. It was not so much a lack of funds on their part as a loss of faith. Some four years later, the Guild experienced similar difficulties with an unwieldy musical entitled *Green Grow the Lilacs*, and once again they were advised to cut their losses out of town. In this case, however, they kept faith with the production and, changing the title from the Lynn Riggs play on which it was based, *Oklahoma!* opened on Broadway in 1943 for a run of 2,248 performances.

While losing the support of the Theatre Guild, less than four months after the demise of *Five Kings*, Welles received "the most glorious deal ever given, up to that time, to an individual by a major Hollywood studio."[81] Houseman continued to stand by Welles through the filming of *Citizen Kane*, after which their increasingly tenuous relationship came to an end. For Welles, certainly, the good times were now behind him.

"Orson Welles: There Ain't No Way" is Pauline Kael's lament on how the vicissitudes of Hollywood filmmaking prevented him from achieving his full potential. She beings by saying "What makes movies a great popular art form is that certain artists can, at moments in their lives, reach out and unify the audience—educated and uneducated—in a shared response."[82]

One is again reminded of the Globe Theatre, where Shakespeare, with his popular art form, accomplished much the same thing; and of Orson Welles, who, by exploiting his favorite author nearly four hundred years later, would for all too brief a while do likewise.

NOTES

1. *Hamlet*, III,ii,10–11.
2. Except for a surcharge of $.50 on Saturday nights, prices at the Mercury Theatre ranged from $.55 for a seat in the balcony to $2.20 for the boxes and orchestra.
3. John Gassner, *Dramatic Soundings* (New York: Crown Publishers), pp. 449–50.
4. Judith Read, *Daily Worker*, 18 September 1937.
5. Ibid.
6. Personal interview, New York, 6 June 1972.
7. Israel Gollancz, ed. (New York: Gossett and Dunlap, 1911).
8. Letter to Roger Hill, undated, probably early October 1931.
9. Ibid.
10. Letter to Roger Hill, October 1931.
11. Letter to author, 22 October 1972.
12. Pauline Kael, *The Citizen Kane Book* (Boston: Atlantic Monthly Press, 1972), p. 78.
13. John Houseman, *Run-Through* (New York: Simon and Schuster, 1972), p. 207.
14. Ibid., p. 128.
15. Ibid., p. 148.
16. Ibid., p. 149.
17. Ibid., p. 170.
18. Ibid., p. 184.

19. Ibid., p. 187.
20. *New York Times*, 6 February 1936.
21. *Amsterdam News*, 18 February 1936.
22. Houseman, *Run-Through*, p. 191.
23. *Theatre Magazine*, July 1923.
24. *New York Herald Tribune*, 15 April 1936.
25. Edith J. R. Isaacs, *The Negro in American Theatre* (New York: Theatre Arts Books, 1947), p. 47.
26. *New York Times*, 15 April 1936.
27. Ibid.
28. Ibid.
29. Ibid.
30. *New York Evening Post*, 15 April 1936.
31. Ibid.
32. *Brooklyn Daily Eagle*, 16 April 1936.
33. Ibid.
34. *New York World-Telegram*, 15 April 1936.
35. *New York Daily News*, 15 April 1936.
36. *New York Herald Tribune*, 16 April 1936.
37. Ibid.
38. Ibid.
39. *Amsterdam News*, 18 April 1936.
40. Ibid.
41. *New York Times*, 27 July 1938.
42. Houseman, *Run-Through*, p. 244.
43. 27 January 1938.
44. Houseman, *Run-Through*, p. 280.
45. Ibid., p. 288.
46. *New York Daily News*, 13 November 1937.
47. *New York Times*, 12 November 1937.
48. *The New Republic*, 1 December 1937.
49. Ibid.
50. *The Nation*, 27 November 1937.
51. *Commonweal*, 3 December 1937.
52. Ibid.
53. *New York Sun*, 12 November 1937.
54. *New York Daily Mirror*, 12 November 1937.
55. *The New Republic*, 29 December 1937.
56. Eric Englander, Review of *Julius Caesar*, *Daily Worker*, 13 November 1937.
57. A. A. Smirov, *Shakespeare: A Marxist Interpretation* (New York: The Critics' Group, 1936), p. 58.
58. Ibid.
59. Englander, Review.
60. Lawrence Langner, *The Magic Curtain* (New York: E. P. Dutton and Company, 1951), p. 273.
61. Ibid., p. 269.
62. Ibid.
63. Ibid., p. 270.

64. Ibid.

65. *Washington Daily News*, 18 March 1939.

66. 14 December 1938. The season had begun with a box office disappointment, *Dame Nature*, which Langner would memorialize as the production that led the Guild to seek revival from Welles.

67. Personal interview, 7 June 1972.

68. Personal interview, 19 September 1972.

69. Langner, *The Magic Curtain*, p. 271.

70. 28 February 1939.

71. Ibid.

72. *Boston Evening Transcript*, 28 February 1939.

73. Helen Eager, *Boston Traveler*, 28 February 1939.

74. *Boston Post*, 28 February 1939.

75. *Boston Herald*, 28 February 1939.

76. Jay Carmody, *Washington Evening Star*, 14 March 1939.

77. Nelson Bell, *Washington Post*, 12 March 1939.

78. 14 March 1939.

79. *Philadelphia Record*, 21 March 1939.

80. *Philadelphia Pictorial*, 21 March 1939.

81. Houseman, *Run-Through*, p. 432.

82. Kael, *Kiss Kiss Bang Bang* (Boston: Atlantic Monthly Press, 1968), p. 196.

Macbeth

PREFACE

In fashioning his text for the 'Voodoo' *Macbeth*, Welles, at the tender age of twenty-one, already showed himself to be a true descendent of the noblest tradition of Shakespearean adaptation. John Houseman attributed this to Welles's education. "Welles was led by his inspirational headmaster [Roger Hill] to feel very strongly about the virtues of Shakespeare. He was educated in the great classical tradition of Shakespearean performance, and knew exactly how Booth had behaved, and Kean and Macready."[1]

Welles's own work would have satisfied John Foster Kirk, whose essay "Shakespeare's Tragedies on the Stage" critiques a part of that tradition. While approving of Kean, Garrick, and Mrs. Siddons, Kirk found fault with Macready because "he had somehow failed to do what they had certainly done . . . capture the imagination of his contemporaries."[2] Even Welles's harshest critics could not fault him on that score.

Brooks Atkinson congratulated him for the way in which he handled the often sticky problems of the witches.

They have always worried the life out of the polite tragic stage; the grimaces of the hags and the garish make-believe of the flaming cauldron have bred more disenchantment than anything else that Shakespeare wrote.[3]

Yet the witches had not been entirely problematical for nineteenth-century theatre artists. William Hazlitt faulted Macready's beknighted production, feeling that "the ideal and preternatural" had evaded the actor-manager. Whereupon Hazlitt went on to complain that there was "not a weight of superstitious terror loading the atmosphere, hanging over the stage."[4]

In laying his emphasis upon these agents of preternatural barbarism Welles was "working within and developing a tradition of *Macbeth* stage interpretation."[5] While a 1921 production, designed by Robert Edmond Jones, had also emphasized the supernatural—three great tragic masks were hung over the stage, high above the action, through which shafts of light poured down upon the events below—by the 1930s, a new critical orthodoxy discouraged such interpretations. In 1934, for example, Tyrone Guthrie eliminated the witches from the opening scene of his London production "for fear the audience might conclude that they are the governing force in the tragedy."[6] And the year before, again in London, Vera Komissarzhevsky had tried to humanize the witches by depicting them as three scavengers looting the bodies of dead soldiers. Welles (and others) reacted against this tendency to make understandable that which might well have lain beyond human comprehension.

However extreme Welles's rearrangement of *Macbeth* may have been, it remains within an eminently sensible guideline recently articulated by Daniel Seltzer. Much as Antonin Artaud urged that the theatre be something more than a museum for old plays, so Seltzer is grateful for whatever energy can be brought to the mounting of Shakespeare. He is thus hospitable to the notion of "reconstituted" Shakespeare (as Welles's adaptations certainly were), but with the caveat that such productions be based "so far as possible . . . on clues within the text."[7]

So strong is the textual grounding of the 'Voodoo' *Macbeth* that its production was not only a reconstitution of Shakespeare but a distillation as well. Signs of the preternatural inundate Shakespeare's play; to the witches' "supernatural soliciting," Macbeth says,

Shakes so my single state of man that function
Is smothered in surmise and nothing is
But what is not . . . (I,iii,140–42)

The play's universe is drenched in magic. In Welles's hands the natural world ceases to exist entirely, and all is pure sorcery.

"Thunder and lightning. Enter three Witches." Thus does Shakespeare begin his play. The exposition illuminating that initial encounter between humanity and the divine occurs during the relatively banal encounter played out by Duncan and his followers in I,ii. Macbeth and Banquo confront their destinies in I,iii and, thereafter, what is corporeal and what is not are dissoluble.

For Shakespeare to have placed so heavy an emphasis on necromancy is understandable. At the time *Macbeth* was written, such matters were very much in vogue. Several people suspected of witchcraft had recently been executed, and while their efficacy could be argued, the dark arts were, nonetheless, to be reckoned with. Shakespeare had yet another reason for writing *Macbeth*—to curry favor with James I, his new sovereign and patron of the King's Men. So,

even if magic had not been *au courant*, Shakespeare could hardly have treated this subject lightly.

Alfred Harbage debunks this notion of royal pandering, nothing that, if it had been Shakespeare's intention to do so, "he might have dramatized more credible episodes in Scottish history [and] might have drawn a more flattering portrait of Banquo."[8] However, the interest of James I to which Shakespeare appealed was not his lineage.

As the author of a pamphlet on witchcraft himself (the results of a three-month sabbatical from royal duties during which he conducted his investigation), James was seriously concerned with such matters. His findings, that these tales of witchery could not be substantiated, came after the production of *Macbeth*. Prior to this, however, James was known to believe that the ship carrying his Scandinavian bride-to-be had been scuttled by sorcerers bent on preventing this Protestant princess from reaching her Catholic intended. It is this sort of superstitious terror that also haunts *Macbeth*.

But it is the very structure of Shakespeare's play, not the phantasmagorical, which does the most violence to realism. *Macbeth* follows the order of a fairy tale, along the lines of those age-old folk myths recorded by the Brothers Grimm. True to form, *Macbeth* begins with the premise on which its narrative is based. In folklore, it would be worded thus: "Once upon a time, a man was promised by three witches that he would be king." As any wise child knows, and Macbeth will shortly learn,

Oftentimes, to win us to our harms,
The instruments of darkness tell us truths,
Win us with honest trifles, to betray's
In deepest consequence. (I,iii,123–26)

In Shakespeare's play the covenant of the witches is the ultimate reality. Their prophecy is not a blessing but damnation, a curse that extends beyond Macbeth, who has been condemned to sin, and this evil, like a plague, taints the entire natural world.[9] Macbeth, embroiled in the fear of what he is about to do, cries out,

Now o'er the one half-world
Nature seems dead. (II,i,49–50)

By this time, his lady has already declared,

The raven himself is hoarse
That croaks the final entrance of Duncan. (I,v,36–37)

The atmosphere has been charged with portents of disaster. Immediately before Duncan's body is found, Lennox describes the "unruly" night just ended.

Lamentings heard i' th' air, strange screams of death,
And prophesying, with accents terrible,
Of dire combustion and confus'd events. (II,iii,52–54)

Nature's order has been disrupted. The behavior of all creatures, bird and
beast, no longer conforms to natural law. Nowhere is this expressed more con-
cisely than in the short exchange (of nineteen lines) immediately following the
discovery of "the great doom's image" (Duncan's body). This unnatural state
is limned in the lines that begin II,iv. "Enter Ross with an Old Man." This
anonymous ancient speaks:

Threescore and ten I can remember well;
Within the volume of which time I have seen
Hours dreadful and things strange, but this sore night
Hath trifled former knowings. (1–4)

To which Ross replies,

Thou seest the heavens, as troubled with man's act,
Threatens his bloody stage. (5–6)

The Old Man continues:

                                        'Tis unnatural,
Even like the deed that's done. On Tuesday last
A falcon, tow'ring in her pride of place,
Was by a mousing owl hawked at and killed. (10–13)

It was to "th' selfsame tune and words"[10] that Welles chose to play out his
own production. His concept may have devolved from elements implicit in
Shakespeare's play, but the working out of it as a tapestry of sight and sound
made the 'Voodoo' *Macbeth* a discrete and original work of art.

Welles's text provided a narrative shorn of everything redundant to its main
conceit—witches dominating the world work their will through Macbeth. For
Welles to have included any more of Shakespeare (which a number of critics
found wanting in his production) would have deviated from its essential impact.
Welles sought a totality of sensual experience through the use of sight and sound,
employing rhetorical content as a structural device, inextricable from that construction of which it was a part.

The production began with a pounding of jungle drums. That sound, along
with the tropical setting, defined the locale: Haiti, circa 1820. The almost constant
beat of the drums underscored the importance of events and accentuated the
mounting tragedy. Thus was created a primitive aural violence that went beyond

mere ethnicity to speak of an immemorial evil that has existed since the fall of man.

Visually, the jungle and palace were counterpoints to each other, eventually blending in the final scene when the jungle's encroachment on civilization was complete. The jungle was represented by a luridly painted backdrop, but the palace setting was solidly three dimensional and provided for a fluidity of movement—up and down, through and around—that afforded the utmost flexibility. The most prominent feature of this expressionist structure was a multi-storied tower crowned by a practical roof. The tower was connected to the palace by a bridge, which could be used either for a passage or as a gateway over the center entrance. When in place, the portable throne faced the courtyard, flanked by the great arched gateway. This setting was, however, preeminently a habitat for the witches, who, like so many insects, infested it, immune from all repellents.

The most extreme alterations that Welles made of Shakespeare's text concerned the witches. Their lines were drastically reduced and none of their scenes left intact. In the 'Voodoo' *Macbeth*, what dialogue remained was used over and over again, with the witches' sounding indistinct and from afar to signify their constant presence. Welles's repeated use of the line ''All hail Macbeth!'' provided ironic counterpoint to the miserable state of this man who would be king.

Finally the witches alone prevail, with Hecate, their voodoo master, attaining the dramatic status of co-protagonist. In six of the production's eight scenes, Hecate and his communicants play some part. It is Hecate who bids Macbeth kill Macduff's family. He himself joins in the murder of Banquo. Malcolm is shown the way to Birnam Wood and advised to cut it down by Hecate, while the three witches are attendant on Lady Macbeth in her madness.

Music was an integral part of the transition from one scene to the next. During the ballroom scene (Welles II,i), while the lords and ladies of Dunsinane danced to a medley of Josef Lanner waltzes, drumbeats began to intrude quietly on these genteel proceedings. They reached their crescendo after the transition from the dancers within the palace to Hecate standing silhouetted against that ''strange light'' let in after the palace gates had swung open.

Welles employed lighting as a means of making scene changes. Simultaneously, lights were lowered on one of the set's numerous playing areas and raised on another, in a manner reminiscent of the film dissolve. Aural and visual effects were imbedded in the framework of his production so that their utilitarian and emotive functions were as one.

Despite its many unfavorable critical notices, the 'Voodoo' *Macbeth* was an overwhelming popular success. The same cannot be said of Welles's film version of this play. His audience has been almost nil, with critical opinion, at best, mixed (although the film's enormous technical difficulties, many of them of Welles's own making, were generally acknowledged).

The sagacity of the few Welles's partisans viewing the film sympathetically sheds light not only on this *Macbeth*, but, by extension, his 1936 stage version as well. The film's detractors express many of the same reservations—Shakespeare's characters are treated in a cavalier fashion, Macbeth's existence as a moral being has been ignored, the original text has been egregiously violated, and the like—as those who attended the 'Voodoo' *Macbeth*.

In 1948 Republic Pictures, a studio generally known for its grade-B westerns, approached Welles with an offer to film *Macbeth*. For a budget of $700,000 (modest even at that time), Welles agreed to make the movie in three weeks. According to Charles Higham, "Welles' intention in making *Macbeth* as a compact, engrossing melodrama at a cheap studio was to bring the play to the world of the small town, the half-educated . . . of the American hinterlands."[11]

The film was released later that same year, and almost immediately withdrawn after receiving universally bad notices. It again "premiered" in 1949 with a similarly disastrous reception. The film's most horrendous and continuing problem lay in the quality of its sound track. The cast first recorded their lines, then in performance tried, with dubious results, to synchronize the sound track with their lip movements. After successive re-recordings, the results were still wanting.

Despite the chaos surrounding the production, the film that emerged is remarkably cohesive. Its setting is a still-barbaric early Christian Scotland, dominated not by voodoo but by Celtic witches. The drama begins as these druidical creatures plunge their arms into a steaming cauldron and emerge holding the partially moulded clay figure of Macbeth. Using this figure, on whose completion they cackle "The charm's wound up," the witches direct the luckless Scot much as Hecate had manipulated his Haitian counterpart. At the film's end, the figure is decapitated, to a repetition of "The charm's wound up." The final image has the witches holding aloft Y-shaped poles silhouetted atop a rocky crag and overlooking a Scotland whose natural world lies rife with confusion.

Welles repeated the concept of Shakespeare's text from his 1936 stage production with but one significant amendment in the film. The power of necromancy retains primacy, with Macbeth still its creature. Evil continues to permeate the world, but here Welles has added an elementary Christianity as its counterpart. As Jack J. Jurgens has perceptively noted, "Christian values, symbolized by the Celtic cross, constitute a fragile man-made order which is powerless before the natural forces of chaos embodied in gnarled trees, swirling fogs and witches."[12]

Despite their similarity of concept, in appearance the 'Voodoo' *Macbeth* and Welles's film of the play varied markedly, this aside from the inevitable differences when works are rendered in different media. The stage version had revealed a lush and fervid jungle, replete with the magic of voodoo whose forces inexorably impinged on an elegant and civilized court. Instead of two opposing worlds, the film, which was made in Utah, displays an atmosphere of unrelieved primitiveness.

This was accomplished, in part, through the use of suggestive or impressionistic backgrounds—namely, a half-dozen large, multifaced set masses. There were distant echoes of the tower, winding stairs, parapets, bridges, and ramps that formed the setting for Macbeth's Haitian palace; however, these same shapes in the film are muffled and indistinct. Craggy and crudely jagged, they appear hewn out of solid rock.

In such surroundings, all semblance of courtly manners is replaced by a violent eroticism. The sexual tension between Macbeth and his lady is palpable. The passionate embrace with which he first greets her makes bodily lust seem as one with the urge for power. Contemplating future deeds, Lady Macbeth writhes erotically, engulfed in the fur that covers her nuptial bed. Afterward, she is awakened from her walking sleep by her husband's lusty embrace. And finally, bosom heaving, she throws herself from the tower into the engulfing arms of death.

The power of such moments lies in the film's most crucial design element: a constant, sometimes vibrating display of light and shadow. Welles also achieved stark and heroic effects by silhouetting figures against a cyclorama of light. Sequences that take place in the film's exterior world are played against gigantic walls of rock, whose depth and texture were defined by means of illumination, which at the same time created an environment different from that of the interior scenes.

Harold Leonard has suggested that "production stringencies may even be made out to be responsible, in part, for the overall unity of style . . . the monotone austerities contribute to the atmosphere of sheer 'stonehenge—powerful unrelieved tragedy' that Welles said he was after."[13] Another possibility is that Welles may have found it true that "movies do most everything better than the stage."[14]

Welles, for whom the rhetorical content of a work was not its most important feature, functioned best with the sort of aural and visual effects that were possible only on film. The editing in *Macbeth*, as it exploits both effects, was strongly derivative of Eisenstein. Nowhere was this more evident than in the scene depicting the execution of the erstwhile Thane of Cawdor—a scene that is not to be found either in Shakespeare or in Welles's script for the 'Voodoo' *Macbeth*. Vertical, spaced staves carried by horsemen wearing circular horned head-dresses are intercut with crowded round drums and that haggard traitor forever isolated from his fellows. A final thundering beat of the drums signals that the axe has fallen.

Critics of the film often shared the preoccupations of those who reviewed the 'Voodoo' *Macbeth*. Harry Raynor found it "worse than oversimplified. [Macbeth] does not struggle against the idea of evil but is only superstitiously afraid of it . . . To watch the film with a clear memory of Shakespeare's play is to be infuriated beyond measure at the destruction of a noble and moving work of art."[15] For Parker Tyler, "the play in its 'native' barbarous milieu, alien to the refined court verse . . . puts certain lines of Shakespeare into a ridiculous light by framing them with lusty bits of staging."[16]

Pauline Kael, in her deeply felt lament for Welles, makes the viable claim that he "might have done for American talkies what D. W. Griffith did for silent film.'' It is her contention that ''when Welles went to Europe, he lost his single greatest asset as a movie director: his sound.''[17] Higham ends his discussion of this film by saying, ''It is impossible to deny that *Macbeth* is a failure; but its concept is a noble one. It remains an authentic film *maudit*, worth re-seeing today.''[18]

Examined together, these two works—the film and Welles's text for the 'Voodoo' *Macbeth*—provide insight into the way in which he conceived and realized his ideas. Any reassessment of the Welles oeuvre must take both into account.

NOTES

1. Personal interview, New York, 18 April 1972.

2. *Lippincott's Magazine* (May–June 1884), quoted in Arthur Colby Sprague, *Shakespearean Players and Performances* (Cambridge: Harvard University Press, 1953), p. 87.

3. *New York Times*, 15 April 1936.

4. *The Examiner* (25 June 1820), quoted in Sprague, pp. 94–95.

5. John S. O'Connor, ''But Was It Shakespeare: Welles' *Macbeth* and *Julius Caesar*,'' *Theatre Journal* (October 1980), p. 344.

6. Ibid.

7. ''Shakespeare's Texts and Modern Productions,'' in Norman Rabkin, ed., *Reinterpretations of Elizabethan Drama* (New York: Columbia University Press, 1969), pp. 97–98.

8. from his introduction to the Pelican *Macbeth*, p. 19.

9. Shakespeare's near-contemporary Cornelis Jansen (1585–1638) theorized that even the most devout were not immune from predestination. Racine, invoking tenets of this Jansenist heresy, would show in *Phaedre* (1677) a protagonist who, like Macbeth, is powerless not to transgress against her own better self.

10. I,iii,88.

11. Charles Higham, *The Films of Orson Welles* (Berkeley: University of California Press, 1970), p. 128.

12. *Shakespeare on Film* (Bloomington: Indiana University Press, 1977), p. 151.

13. *Sight and Sound* 19, no. 1 (March 1950), p. 16.

14. *Modern Screen* (April 1940), quoted in Higham, p. 125.

15. *Sight and Sound* 22, no. 1, (September 1952), p. 13.

16. ''Orson Welles and the Big Experimental Film Cult,'' *Film Culture* 29 (Summer 1963), p. 33.

17. Kael, *Kiss Kiss Bang Bang*, p. 199.

18. Higham, *The Films of Orson Welles*, p. 134.

MACBETH

Adapted and directed by Orson Welles
Music orchestrated by Virgil Thomson
Sets and costumes by Nat Karson
Lighting by Feder

Lafayette Theater, New York, 14 April 1936

CAST

Duncan	Service Bell
Malcolm	Wardell Saunders
Macduff	Maurice Ellis
Banquo	Canada Lee
Macbeth	Jack Carter
Ross	Frank David
Lennox	Thomas Anderson
Siward	Archie Savage
First Murderer	George Nixon
Second Murderer	Kenneth Renwick
The Doctor	Lawrence Chenault
The Priest	Al Watts
First Messenger	Philandre Thomas
Second Messenger	J. B. Johnson
The Porter	J. Lewis Johnson
Seyton	Larrie Lauria
A Lord	Charles Collins
First Captain	Lisle Grenidge
Second Captain	Gabriel Brown
First Chamberlain	Halle Howard
Second Chamberlain	William Cumberbatch
First Court Attendant	Albert McCoy
Second Court Attendant	George Thomas
First Page Boy	Viola Dean
Second Page Boy	Hilda French
Lady Macbeth	Edna Thomas
Lady Macduff	Marie Young

Hecate	Eric Burroughs
First Witch	Wilhelmina Williams
Second Witch	Josephine Williams
Third Witch	Zola King
Court Ladies	Helen Carter, Carolyn Crosby, Evelyn Davis, Ethel Drayton, Helen Browne, Aurelia Lawson, Margaret Howard, Lulu King, Evelyn Skipworth
Court Gentlemen	Herbert Glyn, Jose Miralda, Jimmy Wright, Otis Morse, Harry George Grant, Merritt Smith, Walter Brogsdale
Voodoo Drummers	Abdul, McLean Hughes, James Cabon, James Martha, Moses Meyers, Jay Daniel
Voodoo Men	Ernest Brown, Howard Taylor, Henry J. Williams, Louis Gilbert, William Clayton, Jr., Halle Howard, Albert McCoy, Merritt Smith, Richard Ming
Voodoo Women	Lena Halsey, Jean Cutler, Effie McDowell, Irene Ellington, Marguerite Perry, Evelyn Davis, Essie Frierson, Ella Emanuel, Ethel Drayton
Witch Men	Archie Savage, Charles Hill, Leonardo Barros, Howard Taylor, Amos Laing, Allen Williams, Ollie Simmons, Theodore Howard
Witch Women	Juanita Baker, Beryl Banfield, Mildred Taylor, Sybil Moore, Nancy Hunt, Jacqueline Ghant Martin, Fannie Subert, Hilda French, Ethel Millner, Dorothy Jones
Cripples	Clyde Gooden, Clarence Porter, Milton Lacey, Hudson Prince, Cecil McNair
Soldiers	Benny Tatnall, Herman Patton, Emanuel Middleton, Ivan Lewis, Thomas Dixon, Albert Patrick, Chauncey Worrell, Albert McCoy, William Clayton, Jr., Allen Williams, Halle Howard, Amos Laing, William Cumberbatch, Henry J. Williams, Louis Gilbert, Theodore Howard, Ollie Simmons, Leonardo Barros, Ernest Brown, Merritt Smith, Harry George Grant, Herbert Glyn, Jimmy Wright, George Thomas, Richard Ming, Clifford Davis

The production was preceded by an overture, "Yamekraw," by James P. Johnson, arranged by Joe Jordan. ''Yamekraw,'' which was made up of spiritual, syncopated, and blues melodies, is thought to be the first Negro rhapsody.

ACT ONE

Scene One

First trumpet boom. Second trumpet. Low roll of thunder. Rain up and down. Thunder fades. Silence.

The curtain rises on a jungle.[1] Pause. Enter Macbeth[2] and Banquo.

MACBETH
(to Banquo, as he pushes aside the leaves and tall grass.)
So foul and fair a day I have not seen.[3]
(seeing Hecate[4]; to him)
How far is't called to Forres?[5]

(Hecate does not answer. Macbeth and Banquo are suddenly aware of the ring of women[6] and the Three Witches. Lightning flashes.)

BANQUO
What are these,
So withered and so wild in their attire,
That look not like th' inhabitants o' th' earth
And yet are on't?

(Thunder up and down.)

BANQUO
(to the Witches)
You should be women,
And yet your beards forbid me to interpret
That you are so.

(Pause. Thunder up and out.)

MACBETH
Speak, if you can. What are you?

FIRST WITCH
All hail, Macbeth! Hail to thee, Thane of Glamis!

(At this, Macbeth starts on his way.)

SECOND WITCH
All hail, Macbeth! Hail to thee, Thane of Cawdor!

(This stops him.)

THIRD WITCH

All hail, Macbeth, that shalt be King hereafter.

(Cut thunder. Cut voodoo drums.)

MACBETH

By Sinel's death I know I am Thane of Glamis,
But how of Cawdor? The Thane of Cawdor lives.
A prosperous gentleman; and to be King
Stands not within the prospect of belief.

WITCHES
(in rotation)

All hail, Macbeth! Hail to thee, Thane of Glamis!
All hail, Macbeth! Hail to thee, Thane of Cawdor!
All hail, Macbeth! That shalt be King hereafter![7]

(Choir)[8]

BANQUO

Good sir, why do you start and seem to fear
Things that do sound so fair?

(Voodoo drums in again. To the Witches.)

To me you speak not.
If you can look into the seeds of time,
Speak then to me, who neither beg nor fear
Your favours nor your hate.

FIRST WITCH

Hail!

(Cut voodoo drums again.)

SECOND WITCH

Hail!

THIRD WITCH

Hail!

FIRST WITCH

Lesser than Macbeth, and greater.

(Choir)

SECOND WITCH

Not so happy, yet much happier.

(Choir)

THIRD WITCH

Thou shalt get kings, though thou be none.

FIRST WITCH

So hail, Macbeth and Banquo.[9]

SECOND WITCH

Banquo and Macbeth, all hail![10]

MACBETH

(turning wonderously to Banquo)
Your children shall be kings.

BANQUO

You shall be King.

MACBETH

And Thane of Cawdor too. Went it not so?

(Enter Ross)[11]

BANQUO

To th' self-same tune and words.

*(One beat, then voodoo drums in. Roll of thunder. Star-
tled as he sees Ross)*

Who's here?

ROSS

The King hath happily received, Macbeth,
The news of thy success.
As thick as tale came post with post,
And every one did bear
Thy praises in his kingdom's great defense.
And for an earnest of a greater honour.
He bade me, from him, call thee Thane of Cawdor;
In which addition, hail, most worthy Thane!

ALL THE WOMEN

All hail, Macbeth! Hail, Thane of Cawdor![12]

BANQUO

What, can the devil speak true?

MACBETH

The Thane of Cawdor lives.

ROSS

Who was the Thane lives yet;
But under heavy judgment bears that life
Which he deserves to lose.[13]

MACBETH

*(after a moment, turns to the
Witches)*

Tell me more.[14]

THIRD WITCH

All hail, Macbeth! Hail, King![15]

MACBETH
(partly to the Witches, mostly to him-
self)

This supernatural soliciting cannot be ill.
I am Thane of Cawdor. If good, why do I yield
To that suggestion
Whose horrid image doth unfix my hair
And make my seated heart knock at my ribs
Against the use of nature?
My thought, whose murder yet is but fantastical,
Shakes so my single state of man that function
Is smothered in surmise and nothing is
But what is not.[16]

BANQUO

Look how our partner's rapt.

MACBETH
(to Banquo)

Do you not hope your children shall be kings,
When those that gave the Thane of Cawdor to me
Promised no less to them?[17]

BANQUO

'Tis strange: and oftentimes, to win us to our harm,
The instruments of darkness tell us truths,
Win us with honest trifles, to betray's
In deepest consequence.

MACBETH
(aside)

Come what come may,
Time and the hour runs through the roughest day.
(turning back to Banquo and Ross)
Pardon, kind Ross, your pains are regist'red where
Every day I turn the leaf to read them.
(starting off with them)
Let us toward the King.

(Exit Macbeth, Ross and Banquo.)

FIRST WITCH

Why, how now, Hecate! You look angerly.[18]

*(Hecate suddenly draws out a great bull whip and lashes
out at the three Witches with it. Confusion. Screeches.
The low undertone of chanting stops. "The Circle"[19] is
in disorder.)*

HECATE

*(to the three Witches over the si-
lence)*

Have I not reason?
How did you dare
To trade and traffic with Macbeth
In riddles and affairs of death;
And I, the master of your charms
The close contriver of all harms,
Was never called to bear my part,
Or show the glory of our art?

*(The sound of retreating hooves. As the sounds grows
dimmer, Hecate speaks again.)*

And, which is worse, all you have done
Hath been for a wayward son,
Spiteful and wrathful; who, as others do,
Loves for his own ends, not for you.

(Sound out.)

But make amends now; Go about!

*(At this command, "The Circle" is reformed, the chant-
ing resumed.)*

ALL

Round, around, around, about, about!
All ill come running, all good keep out!
About! About! ABOUT![20]

WITCHES

Thrice to thine, and thrice to mine,
And thrice again, to make up nine.

(All of the Women repeat this.)

HECATE

Weary sev'nights, nine times nine,
Shall he dwindle, peak, and pine.[21]

(The Witches repeat this.)

ALL

Thrice to thine, and thrice to mine,
And thrice again, to make up nine.

HECATE

I'll drain him dry as hay.
Sleep shall neither night nor day
Hang upon his pent-house lid.
He shall live a man forbid.[22]

ALL

Thrice to thine, and thrice to mine,
And thrice again, to make up nine.

HECATE

Peace! The charm's wound up.[23]

(Blackout)

Scene Two

*A tower (right) is connected to the palace (left) by a
bridge, making a gateway entrance in center stage. A
ramp over the palace battlements leads to a door in the
tower. The tower has a practical roof, and, under it, a
throne faces the courtyard.*

Late dusk. Distant thunder and lightning.

*A Porter is asleep at the gate. Enter Lady Macbeth
reading a letter.*

LADY MACBETH

What is your tidings?[1]

(reading)

'I have learned by the perfect'st report they have more in them than mortal
knowledge. Whiles I stood rapt in the wonder of it, came missives from the
King, who all-hailed me Thane of Cawdor, by which title, before, these weird
sisters saluted me, and referred me to the coming on of time with "Hail, King
that shalt be!" This I have thought good to deliver thee, my dearest partner of
greatness, that thou mightst not lose the dues of rejoicing by being ignorant of
what greatness is promised thee. Lay it to thy heart, and farewell.'

'Hail, king that shalt be!'
Glamis thou are, and Cawdor, and shalt be
What thou art promised. Yet do I fear thy nature.
It is too full o' th' milk of human kindness.
To catch the nearest way. Hie thee hither,
That I may pour my spirits in thine ear
And chastise with the valour of my tongue
All that impedes thee from the golden round
Which fate and metaphysical aid doth seem
To have thee crowned withal.[2]

*(Enter a Messenger. He runs up to Lady Macbeth and
throws himself at her feet.)*

MESSENGER

(he has been running)

The King comes here to-night.

LADY MACBETH

Thou'rt mad to say it!
Is not Macbeth with him?

MESSENGER

So please you, it is true. Macbeth is coming.
I have the speed of him.

LADY MACBETH

*(to the Porter at the gates who has
been awakened)*

Give him tending; he brings great news.

(Exit Porter and the Messenger.)

The raven himself is hoarse
That croaks the fatal entrance of Duncan
Under my battlements. Come, you spirits
That tend on mortal thoughts, unsex me here,
And fill me from the crown to the toe top-full
Or direst cruelty. Make thick my blood;
Stop up th' access and passage to remorse,
Shake my fell purpose nor keep peace between
The effect and it. Come to my woman's breasts
And take my milk for gall, you murd'ring ministers,
Wherever in your sightless substances,
And pall thee in the dunnest smoke of hell,
That my keen knife see not the wound it makes,
To cry 'Hold, hold!'

(Enter Macbeth)

Great Glamis! worthy Cawdor!
Greater than both, by the all-hail hereafter!

*(They embrace. Trumpet sounds. Malcolm with atten-
dants comes from within the palace and go to the gates.
Enter other members of the court.)*

MACBETH

My dearest love.

LADY MACBETH

Thy letters have transported me beyond
This ignorant present, and I feel now
The future is in the instant.

*(The gates open wide. Enter Duncan, Banquo, Fleance,
Ross and attendants. All kneel.)*

DUNCAN

Is execution done on Cawdor? Are not
Those in commission yet returned?[3]

MALCOLM

My liege, they are not yet come back.

(Duncan moves to the throne.)

But I have spoke
With one that saw him die; who did report
That very frankly he confessed his treasons,
Implored your Highness' pardon, and set forth
A deep repentance. Nothing in his life
Became him like the leaving it. He died
As one that had been studied in his death
To throw away the dearest thing he owed
As 'twere a careless trifle.

(Duncan sits. All rise from their knees.)

DUNCAN

There's no art
To find the mind's construction in the face.
He was a gentleman on whom I built
An absolute trust.

(Macbeth goes to the throne, kneels at Duncan's feet.)

Here's the Thane of Cawdor![4]

(Macbeth rises. Lady Macbeth goes to his side.)

We coursed him at the heels,
But his great love, sharp as his spur, hath holp
Him to his wife before us.[5]
O worthiest cousin!
Would thou hadst less deserved
That the proportion both of thanks and payment
Might have been mine! Only I have left to say,
More is thy due than more than all can pay.[6]

MACBETH

The service and loyalty I owe,
In doing it pays itself.

DUNCAN

I have begun to plant thee and will labour
To make thee full of growing.
                            (to Banquo, who drops to one knee)
Noble Banquo,
Thou hast no less to have done so, let me enfold thee
And hold thee to my heart.

BANQUO

There if I grow,
The harvest is your own.

(Banquo rises.)

DUNCAN

My plenteous joys,
Wanton to hide themselves
In drops of sorrow.
(rises from the throne)
Sons, kinsmen, thanes,
And you whose places are the nearest, know
We will establish our estate upon
Our eldest, Malcolm, whom we name hereafter
The Prince of Cumberland; which honour must
Not unaccompanied invest him only,
But signs of nobleness, like stars, shall shine
On all deservers. Give me your hand.

*(Duncan comes down from the throne. Court breaks up,
exits severally. With Banquo and some others, Duncan
makes his way up the wall to the tower. Murmured conversation.)*

LADY MACBETH
(to Macbeth)
The Prince of Cumberland—that is a step
On which you must fall down or else o'er-leap,
For in your way it lies.[7]

DUNCAN
*(to Banquo, as they make their way
over the ramparts)*
This castle hath a pleasant seat. The air
Nimbly and sweetly recommends itself
Unto our gentle senses.[8]
This guest of summer,
The temple-haunting martlet, does approve
By his loved mansionry that the heaven's breath
Smells wooingly here. No jutty, frieze,
Buttress, nor coign of vantage, but this bird
Hath made his pendant bed and procreant cradle.
Where they must breed and haunt, I have observed
The air is delicate.[9]

(Duncan exits with train into the tower.)

LADY MACBETH

And when goes hence?[10]

MACBETH

To-morrow, as he proposes.

LADY MACBETH

O, never, never,
Shall sun that morrow see!

> *(Macbeth and Lady Macbeth are left alone on the stage.*
> *A pause.)*

Your face, my Thane, is as a book where men
May read strange matters.
But be the serpent under't.
[Put] this night's business into my dispatch.

> *(The open gateway has begun to fill with a band of*
> *cripples. Macbeth sees them.)*

MACBETH

(in a hushed voice)

We will speak further.

LADY MACBETH

Leave all the rest to me.

> *(Exit Lady Macbeth. Left alone, Macbeth tries to avoid*
> *the gaze of the cripples in the gateway. He can't keep*
> *his eyes from the tower.)*

MACBETH

If it were done when 'tis done, then t'were well
It were done quickly. If th' assassination
Could trammel up the consequence and catch
With his surcease success, that but this blow
Might be the be-all and end-all—; here,
But here upon [t]his bank and shoal of time,
We'ld jump the life to come.[11]

> *(Enter Priest from palace. He goes to gateway. Cripples*
> *groan as he begins to shut the gates. Macbeth's question*
> *stops him.)*

MACBETH

Comes the King forth, I pray you?[12]

PRIEST

No, sir. There [are] a crew of wretched souls
That stay his cure. Their malady convinces
The great assay of art; but at his touch,
Such sanctity hath heaven given his hand,
They presently amend.[13]

MACBETH

What's the disease you mean?[14]

PRIEST

'Tis called the evil.
A most miraculous work in this good King:
How he solicits heaven
Himself best knows, but strangely-visited people,
All swol'n and ulcerous, pitiful to the eye,
The mere despair of surgery, he cures;
To the succeeding royalty he leaves
The healing benediction.[15]

> *(At these last words, the Priest shuts the gates, locking himself out with the cripples. From far away comes once the chant, "All hail, Macbeth, King of Scotland." And there is a tiny pulsing of drums.)*

MACBETH

I am his kinsman.

> *(A change comes over his face, a look of doubt. The drums stop.)*

He hath borne his faculties so meek, hath been
So clear in his great office, that his virtues
Will plead like angels, trumpet-tongued against
The deep damnation of his taking-off.[16]

> *(Enter Lady Macbeth.)*

MACBETH

How now! What news?

> *(Night has fallen, a still night, but there are occasional flashes of distant lightning.)*

LADY MACBETH

He has almost supped.

MACBETH

Hath he asked for me?

LADY MACBETH

Know you not he has?

MACBETH

We will proceed no further in this business.

LADY MACBETH

Was the hope drunk
Wherein you dressed yourself? Art thou afeared
To be the same in thine own act and valour
As thou art in desire?

MACBETH

I dare do all that may become a man;
Who dares do more is none.

LADY MACBETH

What beast was't then,
That made you break this enterprise to me?
I have given suck, and know
How tender 'tis to love the babe that milks me:
I would, while it was smiling in my face,
Have plucked my nipple from his boneless gums,
And dashed the brains outs, had I so sworn as you
Have done to this.

MACBETH

If we should fail?

LADY MACBETH

We fail?
But screw your courage to the sticking place
And we'll not fail. When Duncan is asleep
(Whereto the rather shall his day's hard journey
Soundly invite him), his two chamberlains
Will I with wine and wassail so convince
That memory, the warder of the brain,
Shall be [a] fume, and the receipt of reason
A limbeck only. When in swinish sleep
Their drench'd natures lie as in a death,
What cannot you and I perform upon
Th' unguarded Duncan? what not put upon
His spongy officers, who shall bear the guilt
Of our great quell?

MACBETH

Bring forth men-children only;
For thy undaunted mettle should compose
Nothing but males. Will it not be received,
When we have marked with blood those sleepy two
Of his own chamber and used their very daggers,
That they have done't?

LADY MACBETH

Who dares receive it other,
As we shall make our griefs and clamour roar
Upon his death?

MACBETH

I am settled and bend up
Each corporal agent to this terrible feat.

> *(Enter, from the tower, Banquo and Fleance. They start
> down the wall. Macbeth and Lady Macbeth hide in the
> shadows.)*

BANQUO
How goes the night, boy?

FLEANCE
The moon is down; I have not heard the clock.

BANQUO
(unbuckling his sword and belt)
Hold, take my sword. There's husbandry in heaven;
Their candles are all out.
> *(handing Fleance his big plumed hat)*

Take thee that too.
A heavy summons lies like lead upon me,
And yet I would not sleep.

> *(They have reached the courtyard and stand near where Macbeth and Lady Macbeth are hidden.)*

BANQUO
Merciful powers,
Restrain me in the curs'd thoughts that nature
Gives way to in repose.

MACBETH
(in a whisper to Lady Macbeth)
Away!¹⁷

> *(She steps behind Banquo and Fleance and starts up the wall. Banquo hears her without knowing where the sound comes from.)*

BANQUO
(to Fleance)
Give me my sword!
Who's there?

> *(Macbeth comes out of the shadow and approaches Banquo, taking his attention away from Lady Macbeth who gets up the wall and into the tower unnoticed.)*

MACBETH
A friend.

BANQUO
What, sir, not yet at rest? The King's abed.
He hath been in unusual pleasure and
Sent forth great largess to your offices.
This diamond he greets your wife withal.

> *(He gives a jewel to Macbeth, who takes it in silence. Pause.)*

BANQUO

I dreamt last night of the three weird sisters.
To you they have showed some truth.

MACBETH

I think not of them.
Yet when we can entreat an hour to serve,
We would spend it on some words upon that business,
If you would grant the time.

BANQUO
(starting away)

At your kind'st leisure.

MACBETH

If you shall cleave to my consent, when 'tis,
It shall make honour for you.

BANQUO
(stopping; a bit coldly, pointedly)

So I lose none
[In] seeking to augment it.

MACBETH

Good repose the while!

BANQUO

Thanks, sir. The like to you.

> *(Banquo and Fleance exit into the palace. Macbeth
> stands alone in the courtyard. Very faintly over the air
> comes the voodoo "Effect."[18] Macbeth starts back.)*

MACBETH

Is this a dagger which I see before me,
The handle toward my hand? Come, let me clutch thee!
I have thee not, and yet I see thee still.
Art thou not, fatal vision, sensible
To feeling as to sight? or art thou but
A dagger of the mind, a false creation
Proceeding from the heat-oppress'd brain?

> *(The "Effect" changes. Music higher.)*

I see thee still;
And on thy blade and dudgeon gouts of blood,
Which was not so before.

> *(The music and chanting rise, then Macbeth kills it with
> the shout.)*

There's no such thing.

("Effect" out. Silence.)

It is the bloody business which informs
Thus to mine eyes.

(Pause. Silence.)

Now o'er the one half-world
Nature seems dead, and wicked dreams abuse
The curtained sleep. Witchcraft celebrates
Dark Hecate's offerings.

*(Lady Macbeth appears above in the door of the tower
room. She leaves the doors open and comes down the
battlements to Macbeth.)*

LADY MACBETH

The doors are open, and the surfeited grooms
Do mock their charge with snores. I have drugged their possets,
That death and nature do contend about them
Whether they live or die.

*(Macbeth stands staring up at the tower. She speaks
sharply.)*

Had he not resembled
My father as he slept, I had done't.[19]

MACBETH
(with decision)

I go, and it is done.[20]

(He starts up to the tower.)

MACBETH

Thou sure and firm-set earth,
Hear not my steps which way they walk, for fear
The very stones prate of my whereabouts.[21]

*(He crosses to the tower and exits. Macbeth appears in
the door to the tower room for a moment.)*

Who's there? What, ho?

(He goes back in again.)

LADY MACBETH

Alack, I am afraid they have awaked,
And 'tis not done! Th' attempt, and not the deed,
Confounds us. Hark! I laid their daggers ready —
He could not miss 'em.

*(Macbeth comes out of the door again and down the
wall to Lady Macbeth. His hands are bloody, and he
carries two daggers.)*

My husband!

MACBETH

I have done the deed. Didst thou not hear a noise?

LADY MACBETH

I heard the owl scream and the crickets cry.

MACBETH

Did not you speak?[22]

LADY MACBETH

When? Now?[23]

MACBETH

As I descended.

LADY MACBETH

Ay.

MACBETH

Hark! Who lies i' th' second chamber?

LADY MACBETH

Malcolm.[24]

MACBETH

This is a sorry sight.

> (Macbeth stands dazed, staring down on his bloody
> hands.)

LADY MACBETH

A foolish thought, to say a sorry sight.

MACBETH

There's one did laugh in's sleep, and one cried 'Murder!'
That they did wake each other. I stood and heard them.
But they did say their prayers and addressed them
Again to sleep.

LADY MACBETH

There are two lodged together.

MACBETH

One cried 'God bless us!' 'Amen!' the other,
As they had seen me with these hangman's hands,
List'ning to their fear. I could not say, 'Amen!'
When they did say, 'God bless us!'

> (A gust of wind.)

LADY MACBETH

Consider it not so deeply.

MACBETH

But wherefore could I not pronounce 'Amen'?
I had most need of blessing, and 'Amen'
Stuck in my throat.

LADY MACBETH

These deeds must not be thought
After these ways; so, it will make us mad.

MACBETH

Methought I heard a voice cry, 'Sleep no more!
Macbeth does murder sleep'—the innocent sleep,
Sleep that knits up the ravelled sleeve of care,
The death of each day's life, sore labour's bath,
Balm of hurt minds, great nature's second course,
Chief nourisher in life's feast.

LADY MACBETH

What do you mean?

MACBETH

Still it cried. 'Sleep no more!' to all the house;
'Glamis hath murdered sleep, and therefore Cawdor
Shall sleep no more, Macbeth shall sleep no more!'

LADY MACBETH

Who was it that thus cried?

(A wind again. The distant flash of lightning.)

LADY MACBETH

Why, worthy Thane,
You do unbend your noble strength to think
So brainsickly of things. Go get some water
And wash this filthy witness from your hand.
Why did you bring these daggers from the place?
They must lie there: go carry them and smear
The sleepy grooms with blood.

MACBETH

I'll go no more.
I am afraid to think what I have done;
Look on't again and I dare not.

LADY MACBETH

Infirm of purpose! Give me the daggers.

(She snatches the daggers from his hands.)

The sleeping and the dead
Are but pictures. 'Tis the eye of childhood
That fears a painted devil.

(A gust of wind.)

If he do bleed,
I'll gild the faces of the grooms withal,
For it must seem their guilt.

*(She starts up the wall. From outside the gates comes a
double knock. Stopping.)*

I hear a knocking!

*(She listens for a moment, then turns quickly and runs
up the battlements and exits into the tower. Wind. The
knocking again, louder.)*

MACBETH

Whence is that knocking?
How is't with me when every noise appals me?

*(Lady Macbeth comes back out of the tower, runs down
the wall to Macbeth, who is staring at his hands again.)*

LADY MACBETH

My hands are of your colour.
Retire we to our chamber.
A little water clears us of this deed.
How easy it is when—

(Knocking, very loud.)

Hark! More knocking!

(Knocking.)

Get on your nightgown.

(Lady Macbeth hurries into the palace. Knocking.)

MACBETH
(as he goes after her)

Wake Duncan with thy knocking! I would thou couldst.

(Exit Macbeth. Enter, after a moment, the Porter.)

PORTER
*(as he crosses the courtyard to the
gates)*

Knock! Knock! Knock! Knock! Here's a knocking indeed! If a man were porter
of hell gate, he should grow old turning the key.

*(Knocking. He sets down his lantern and begins fum-
bling.)*

Knock! Knock! Knock!

*(The lantern, set down-stage, casts his shadow gro-
tesquely across the gates. Struck with an idea, the Porter
puts his fingers on his head so as to give his shadow
horns.)*

(assuming a false voice)

Who's there, i' th' name of Beelzebub?

(aside, in his own voice)

I'll let in some of all professions, that go the primrose way to th' everlasting
bonfire.

(More knocking.)

You'll sweat for't.

(Knocking.)

Who's there, i' th' other devil's name?

*(pretending to see through the key-
hole)*

Faith, here's an equivocator, who committed treason enough for God's sake, yet could not equivocate to heaven. O come in, equivocator.

(Knocking.)

PORTER
(in his own voice again)

Knock, knock, knock.

(More knocking.)

Knock, knock. What are you?

(A gust of wind and the lantern is out.)

This place is too cold for hell. I'll devil-porter it no further.

(Knocking.)

Anon, anon!

*(He opens the gates, admitting Macduff and Lennox.
There begins to creep into the scene, with the opening
of the door, the first weak light of early dawn.)*

MACDUFF

Was it so late, friend, ere you went to bed,
That you lie so late?

PORTER

Faith, sir, we were carousing till the second cock; and drink, sir, is a great provoker of three things.

MACDUFF

What three things does drink especially provoke?

PORTER

Marry, sir, nose-painting, sleep, and urine. Lechery, sir, it provokes and un-provokes; it provokes the desire, but takes away [the performance]. Much drink may be said to be an equivocator with lechery; it makes his stand to, and not stand to, [and] giving him the lie, leaves him.

MACDUFF

I believe drink gave thee [the] lie last night.

PORTER

That it did, sir, i' the very throat on me.

MACDUFF

Is thy master stirring?

(Enter Macbeth in his nightgown.)
Our knocking has awaked him; here he comes.

LENNOX

Good morrow, noble sir!

MACBETH

Good morrow, both!

MACDUFF

Is the King stirring, worthy Thane?

MACBETH

Not yet.

MACDUFF

He did command me to call timely on him;
I have almost slipped the hour.

MACBETH

There is his door.

MACDUFF

I'll make so bold to call.

> *(Macduff goes up the wall and exits into the tower room.*
> *A slight pause. Wind. Low thunder.)*

LENNOX

The night has been unruly. Where we lay,
Our chimneys were blown down; and, as they say,
Lamentings heard i' th' air,

> *(Wind.)*

Strange screams of death.
Some say the earth was feverous and did shake.

MACBETH

'Twas a rough night.

> *(Macduff's voice is heard shouting in the tower room.*
> *He enters, running down the battlements.)*

MACDUFF

Ring the alarum bell!
O horror, horror, horror![25]

> *(Porter hurries to ring the gong.)*

MACBETH/LENNOX

What's the matter?

MACDUFF

Tongue nor heart
Cannot conceive nor name thee!

MACBETH

What is't you say?

MACDUFF

See, and then speak yourselves.

> *(Macbeth and Lennox run up the wall and exit into the tower.)*

MACDUFF
> *(shouting)*

Awake, awake!
Murder and treason!

> *(Loud clanging of the bell. Murmurings.)*

Banquo and Malcolm!

> *(Enter, severally, in their nightgowns, ladies and gentlemen of the court, some bearing lights. Confusion.)*

Malcolm, awake!

> *(Enter Lady Macbeth.)*

LADY MACBETH

What's the business,
That such a hideous trumpet calls to parley
The sleepers of the house? Speak, speak!

MACDUFF

O gentle lady
'Tis not for you to hear what I can speak:

> *(Enter Banquo.)*

The repetition in a woman's ear
Would murder as it fell.

> *(Lennox re-enters from the tower room and comes down the wall to Malcolm, who is just entering.)*

MALCOLM

What is amiss?[26]

MACDUFF

You are, and do not know't.
The spring, the head, the fountain of your blood
Is stopped, the very source of it is stopped.[27]

> *(Silence of gong.)*

Your royal father's murdered.

> *(Sensation among the ladies and gentlemen of the court.)*

MALCOLM

O, by whom?

LENNOX

Those of his chamber, as it seemed, had done't.
Their hands and faces were all badged with blood;
So were their daggers which unwiped, we found
Upon their pillows. They stared and were distracted.
No man's life was to be trusted with them.

> *(A shot is fired from within the tower house, followed by another. Macbeth appears in the doorway carrying two smoking pistols.[28])*

MACBETH

O, yet I do repent me of my fury
That I did kill them.

MACDUFF

Did you so?

MACBETH

Here lay Duncan; there, the murderers,
Steeped in the colours of their trade, their daggers
Unmannerly breeched with gore! Who could refrain?

LADY MACBETH

Help me hence, ho!

> *(She collapses.)*

BANQUO

Look to the lady.[29]

> *(Lady Macbeth is carried out.)*

And when we have our naked frailties hid,
That suffer in exposure, let us meet
And question this most bloody piece of work,
To know it further. Fears and scruples shake us.
In the great hand of God I stand.

MACBETH

And so do I.[30]

ALL

So all.

BANQUO

Let's briefly put on manly readiness,
And meet i' th' hall together.[31]

MACBETH

Well contended.[32]

> *(General murmuring. All exit, except Malcolm, Macduff and Lady Macduff, who are at one corner of the stage under the wall, and Macbeth, who stands on the wall above, neither hearing nor seeing the others.)*

MACDUFF

Let's not consort with them.
To show an unfelt sorrow is an office
Which the false man does easy.[33]

MALCOLM

Let's away!

(Low thunder, and out.)

Our tears are not yet brewed.[34]

LADY MACDUFF

What will you do?[35]

MACDUFF

I'll to the coast.[36]

(Thunder.)

LADY MACDUFF

This flight is madness. When our actions do not,
Our fears do make us traitors.[37]

MALCOLM

Where we are,
There's daggers in men's smiles; the near in blood,
The nearer bloody.[38]
This murderous shaft that's shot
Hath not yet lighted, and our safest way
Is to avoid the aim. Therefore to horse,

(Lady Macduff starts to remonstrate further, but Macduff silences her.)

MALCOLM

And let us not be dainty of leave-taking
But shift away.

(Macduff hurries Malcolm off around the wall. Macbeth, standing on the battlements above, does not see them exit. Lady Macduff waits where they have left her for a moment, then turns, weeping, and runs into the palace. Macbeth comes down from the battlements, crosses to the throne, and slumps wretchedly into it.)

MACBETH

Had I but died an hour before this chance,
I had lived a bless'd time; for from this instant
There's nothing serious in mortality:
All is but toys. Renown and grace is dead,
The wine of life is drawn, and the mere lees
Is left this vault to brag of.[39]

*(There is more of the light of pale, early dawn. A figure
appears in the crack of light where the gate stands ajar,
with another behind him. They push the gates slowly,
almost furtively, open. They drag themselves into the
courtyard. A dozen or so follow. They are the cripples.
Macbeth watches them, fascinated as they limp over to
him, a grotesque, silent little army. Suddenly, they all
stop moving and fall to their knees at his feet. He stiffens
in the throne. From far off comes the chant, 'All hail,
Macbeth! Hail, King of Scotland!' Then, from above,
come the hoarse voices of the three Witches, chanting
quickly and sharply.)*

THREE WITCHES

Weary sev'nights, nine times nine.
Shall he dwindle, peak, and pine.[40]

*(The three Witches are seen huddled on the wall. Under
their chant has come a rapid throb of drums. This
reaches a crescendo under a new voice that is Hecate's,
loud and rasping. He is seen suddenly at the very top
of the tower, leaning over the throned Macbeth below.
The light of an angry dawn flames brighter behind him
as he speaks. The courtyard is in shadows. The cripples
are strange shapes in the gateway. Hecate and the three
Witches are birds of prey.)*

HECATE

I'll drain him dry as hay.
Sleep shall neither night nor day
Hang upon his penthouse lid.

(Drums stop.)

He shall live a man forbid.[41]

(A thump of the drum on the last syllable of 'forbid.')
END OF ACT ONE[42]

ACT TWO

Scene One

*The palace. Late afternoon. The curtain rises on a big
flourish.[1] Macbeth, in kingly robes and crowned, sits on
the throne. The lords and captains are drawn up before
him, for he is in council. But the entire court is present:
ladies, attendants and all. The scene is very gala.*

MACBETH

We hear Macduff and Malcolm are gone hence,
Stol'n to the coast in the secret,[2] not confessing

Their cruel parricide, filling their hearers
With strange invention.

(Enter Banquo.)

But of that to-morrow,
When therewithal we shall have cause of state
Craving us jointly.

(Banquo has advanced into the courtyard, and now stands center facing Macbeth.)

Here's our chief guest.[3]

BANQUO

(bows; formally)

Let your Highness command upon me.

MACBETH

(making an attempt at cheerful conversation)

Ride you this afternoon?

BANQUO

(coldly)

Ay, my good lord.

(Slight pause.)

MACBETH

We should have else desired your good advice
In this day's council; but we'll take to-morrow.

(to the court)

Let every man be master of his time
Till seven at night. To make society
The sweeter welcome, we will keep ourselves
Till supper time alone.

(rising)

While then, God be with you!

(The court—lords, ladies, captains and attendants—bow themselves out, the lords and military persons, with some of the attendants, through the gateway, the others into the palace. Only Banquo remains, motionless, looking at Macbeth, whose eyes have never left his. After they are alone, Macbeth sits again on the throne, still held in Banquo's gaze. Silence.)

BANQUO

(finally; menace and mockery in his tone)

Thou hast it now—King, Cawdor, Glamis, all,
As the weird women promised; and, I fear,
Thou played'st most foully for't.

> *(Macbeth starts but is stopped by a new sharpness in Banquo's voice.)*

Yet it was said
It should not stand in thy posterity,
But that myself should be the root and father of many kings.

> *(He goes slowly up to the throne as he speaks and stands grinning into Macbeth's face.)*

If there comes truth from them
(As upon thee, Macbeth, their speeches shine),
Why, by the verities on thee made good,
May they not be my oracles as well?[4]

> *(A look of decision comes into Macbeth's face.)*

MACBETH
(very quietly, very casually)

Is't far you ride?

BANQUO
(not understanding; bluffs his way with a slightly mocking bow)

As far, my lord, as will fill up the time
'Twixt this and supper.

MACBETH

Goes Fleance with you?

BANQUO

Ay, my good lord.

> *(Finishing his bow, he starts away. He is nearly at the gate when Macbeth speaks.)*

MACBETH
(quietly and dangerously)

Fail not our feast.[5]

BANQUO
(turning; meets his eye again; just as dangerously)

My lord, I will not.

> *(Exit Banquo. Macbeth is left alone in the courtyard, brooding on his throne. Pause. Then, through the air, queer and faint, comes the chant of the voodoos: 'All hail, Macbeth! Hail, King of Scotland!' Macbeth starts. The chant dies away. There is a moment's silence.)*

MACBETH

To be thus is nothing, but to be safely thus—

> *(The voodoo music begins again, very softly. Panicky, Macbeth rises, look about, then calls.)*

Seyton!

(He comes down from the throne and passes across the courtyard. The music has grown louder. Macbeth's call rises to a shriek. It stops the music.)

Seyton!

(Enter Seyton.)

Sirrah, a word with you. Attend those men our pleasure?

SEYTON

They are, my lord, without the palace gate.[6]

MACBETH

Bring them before us.

(Exit Seyton.)

Our fears in Banquo stick deep.

(The voodoo music is heard again, softer than ever, mostly drums. Macbeth looks up at the sound.)

He chid the sisters
When first they put the name of King upon me,
And bade them speak to him. Then, prophet-like,
They hailed him father to a line of kings.
Upon my head they placed a fruitless crown
And put a barren sceptre in my gripe,
Thence to be wrenched with an unlineal hand,
No son of mine succeeding. If 't be so,
For Banquo's issue have I filled my mind;
For them the gracious Duncan have I murdered:
Put rancours in the vessel of my peace
Only for them, and mine eternal jewel
Given to the common enemy of man
To make them kings—the seeds of Banquo kings!

(There is heard faintly the derisive, cackling laughter of the three Witches.)

Who's there?

(Macbeth wheels about at the sound, just as Seyton re-enters with the two Murderers. The Murderers fall on their faces. Macbeth looks down at them for a moment, then motions Seyton away.)

Now go to the door and stay there till we call.

(Exit Seyton.)

Was it not yesterday we spoke together?

FIRST MURDERER
(rising)

It was, so please your Highness.

MACBETH

Well then, now
Have you considered of my speeches?
(crossing to the throne)
Know that it was he, in the times past, which held you
So under fortune, which you thought had been
Our innocent self?

FIRST MURDERER

You made it known to us.

MACBETH

Do you find
Your patience so predominant in your nature
That you can let this go? Are you so gospelled
To pray for this good man and for his issue,
Whose heavy hand hath bowed you to the grave
And beggared yours forever?

FIRST MURDERER
(suppressing his anger)
We are men, my liege.

MACBETH
(sitting down)
Ay, in the catalogue ye go for men,
As hounds and greyhounds, mongrels, spaniels, curs,
Shoughs, water-rugs, and demi-wolves are clept
All by the name of dogs.

FIRST MURDERER
(wildly)
I am one, my liege,
Whom the vile blows and buffets of the world
Have so incensed that I am reckless what
I do to spite the world.[7]

SECOND MURDERER
(rising; eagerly)
And I another![8]

MACBETH
(leaning forward on his throne)
Both of you know Banquo was your enemy.

BOTH MURDERERS

True, my lord.

MACBETH

So is he mine, and in such bloody distance
That every minute of his being thrusts

Against my near'st of life; and though I could
With barefaced power sweep him from my sight
And bid my will avouch it, yet I must not,
For certain friends that are both his and mine,
Whose loves I may not drop. Thence it is
That I to your assistance do make love,
Masking the business from the common eye
For sundry weighty reasons.

SECOND MURDERER

We shall, my lord, perform what you command us.

FIRST MURDERER

Though our lives—

> *(Macbeth rises from his throne, joyfully interrupting him.)*

MACBETH

Your spirits shine through you.

> *(coming between them; conspiratorially)*

It must be done tonight, within this hour at most.
Fleance his son, that keeps him company,
Whose absence is no less material to me
Than is his father's, must embrace the fate
Of that dark hour.

FIRST MURDERER

We are resolved, my lord.

MACBETH

> *(clasping their shoulders, half pushing them off)*

It is concluded.

> *(He unbolts the gates, whispering jokingly into the Murderers' ears as they slip out.)*

Banquo, thy soul's flight,
If it find heaven, must find it out to-night.

> *(The Murderers' laughter is heard off-stage until Macbeth slams shut the gate. He leans on it wearily. The silence is broken by Lady Macbeth, who has entered.)*

LADY MACBETH

Is Banquo gone from court?

MACBETH

> *(breaking down, now that he is alone with his wife)*

O, full of scorpions is my mind, dear wife![9]

LADY MACBETH
(crossing to the throne; staring at it
bitterly)

Naught's had, all's spent,
Where our desire is got without content.
'Tis safer to be that which we destroy
Than by destruction dwell in doubtful joy.[10]

MACBETH

In the affliction of these terrible dreams
That shake us nightly, better be with the dead
Than on the torture of the mind to lie
In restless ecstasy.

(The two Murderers appear in the corner under the
tower. They crouch there, waiting, listening.)

MACBETH

Duncan is in his grave;
After life's fitful fever he sleeps well.
Treason has done his worst: nor steel nor poison,
Malice domestic, foreign levy, nothing,
Can touch him further.

LADY MACBETH
(meaningfully)

Thou know'st that Banquo, and his Fleance, lives.[11]

SECOND MURDERER
(in a hoarse undertone to the First
Murderer)

He needs not our mistrust.[12]

(First Murderer instantly silences him. Macbeth over-
hears the noise and starts up, joyfully.)

MACBETH

There's comfort yet; they are assailable.
Then be thou jocund. Ere the bat hath flown
His cloistered flight, ere to black Hecate's summons
The shard-borne beetle with his drowsy hums
Hath rung night's yawning peal, there shall be done
A deed of dreadful note.[13]

LADY MACBETH

What's to be done?

MACBETH
(putting his arm about her)

Be innocent of the knowledge, dearest chuck,
Till thou applaud the deed. Come, seeling night,

Scarf up the tender eye of pitiful day,
And with thy bloody and invisible hand
Cancel and tear to pieces that great bond
Which keeps me pale. Light thickens, and the crow
Makes wing to th' rooky wood.
Good things of day begin to droop and drowse,
Whiles night's black agents to their preys do rouse.

> *(He starts off with Lady Macbeth. Lights dim on the court. It remains in shadow during the following scene, which is played in the corner under the tower. A pause. The Murderers under the tower are distinct in the twilight.)*

FIRST MURDERER

The west yet glimmers with some streaks of day.
Now spurs the lated traveller apace
To gain the timely inn, and near approaches
The subject of our watch.

> *(They prepare to spring on the approaching figure. Hecate, muffled, steps into the lighted area.)*

FIRST MURDERER

> *(sees that it is not Banquo; suspiciously)*

But who did bid thee join with us?[14]

HECATE

Macbeth.

FIRST MURDERER

> *(slight pause)*

Then stand with us.

SECOND MURDERER

Hark, I hear horses.[15]

BANQUO

> *(off stage)*

Give us a light [t]here, ho!

FIRST MURDERER

Then 'tis he: the rest
That are within the note of expectation
Already are i' th' court.

SECOND MURDERER

His horses go about.[16]

HECATE

Almost a mile; but he does it usually,
So all men do, from hence to th' palace gate
Make it their walk.[17]

SECOND MURDERER

A light, a light!

(Enter Banquo and Fleance with a torch.)

HECATE

'Tis he.[18]

FIRST MURDERER

Stand to't.

BANQUO

It will be rain to-night.

HECATE

Let it come down![19]

(He and the Murderers set upon Banquo.)

BANQUO

O, treachery! Fly, good Fleance, fly, fly, fly!
Thou mayest revenge—O slave!

(Dies, Fleance escapes.)

HECATE

There's but one down: the son is fled.[20]

SECOND MURDERER

We have lost best half of our affair.

FIRST MURDERER

Well, let's away, and say how much is done.

(Exit First and Second Murderers. Hecate is left standing over the body of Banquo. The three Witches appear suddenly on top of the battlements. They cackle derisively at Hecate, who looks up, ferociously.)

HECATE

Beldams as you are![21] Get you gone!

(Laughter stops.)

And at the pit of Acheron
Meet me i' th' morning. Thither he
Will come to know his destiny.
Your vessels and your spells provide,
Your charms and everything beside.
I am for th' air.

(Chanting is heard: "Fair is foul, and foul is fair/Hover through the fog and filthy air." The three Witches exit. Slight pause, as the chanting grows dim.)

HECATE

This night I'll spend
Unto a dismal and a fatal end.

(Waltz music starts, very faint and weird. He picks up Banquo's arm.)

Upon the corner of the moon
There hangs a vap'rous drop profound;
I'll catch it ere it comes to ground:
And that, distilled by magic sleights,
Shall raise such artificial sprites
As by the strength of their illusion
Shall draw him on to his confusion.

(Lights dim on Hecate, as he start to drag out Banquo. Music up. Lights up on a stage filled with waltzing figures. Others—elderly dignitaries—walk in and are greeted by Macbeth and Lady Macbeth.)

MACBETH

A hearty welcome.[22]

LORDS

Thanks to your Majesty.

MACBETH

Ourself will mingle with society
And play the humble host.

(He bows, goes from one to the other of his guests. Waltz music high. The two Murderers appear at the door.)

See, they encounter thee with their hearts' thanks.

(Seeing the First Murderer, he half turns away from him.)

MACBETH
(under his breath)

There's blood upon thy face.

FIRST MURDERER

'Tis Banquo's then.

MACBETH

'Tis better thee without than he within.
Is he dispatched?

FIRST MURDERER

My lord, his throat is cut: that I did for him.

MACBETH

Thou are the best o' th' cut-throats.
(to Second Murderer)
Yet he's good that did the like for Fleance.

SECOND MURDERER

Most royal sir, Fleance is scaped.[23]

MACBETH

Then comes my fit again. I had else been perfect;
Whole as the marble, founded as the rock,
As broad and general as the casing air.
But now I am cabined, cribbed, confined, bound in
To saucy doubts and fears.

(The waltz stops.)

But Banquo's safe?

(Ripples of laughter among the guests.)

FIRST MURDERER

Ay, my good lord. Safe in a ditch he bides,
With twenty trench'd gashes on his head,
The least a death to nature.

MACBETH

Thanks for that.

(More laughter.)

There the grown serpent lies; the worm that's fled
Hath nature that in time will venom breed,
No teeth for th' present.

> *(A silence has fallen among the guests. Macbeth, realizing that he is overheard, raises his voice and addresses the whole company.)*

Here had we now our country's honour roofed,
Were the graced person of our Banquo present—
Who may I rather challenge for unkindness
Than pity for mischance!

ROSS

His absence, sir, lays blame upon his promise.

> *(General murmur of courtly agreement. The couples turn back to each other.)*

MACBETH
(under his breath, to the Murderers)

Get thee gone. To-morrow
We'll hear ourselves again.

> *(Exit the two Murderers. Music starts up again and the dance resumes. Lady Macbeth comes over to her husband, curtsies.)*

LADY MACBETH

My royal lord.

> *(Macbeth takes her in his arms and waltzes her out onto the floor.)*

MACBETH
Sweet remembrancer!

> *(They dance for a while. Suddenly, the ghost of Banquo appears from behind the tower.[24] Music business, dancing business, etc.)*

MACBETH
> *(trying wildly to make her see what he sees)*

Prithee see there!

LADY MACBETH
Gentle my lord, sleek o'er your rugged looks;
Be bright and jovial among your guests to-night.[25]

MACBETH
Behold!

LADY MACBETH
Things without all remedy
Should be without regard. What's done is done.[26]

MACBETH
Look! Lo!

> *(He staggers toward the ghost, reeling among the dancers.)*

Why, what care I? If thou canst nod, speak too.
If charnel-houses and our graves must send
Those that we bury back, our monuments
Shall be the maws of kites.[27]

> *(Ghost vanishes.)*

LADY MACBETH
Shame itself![28]

MACBETH
> *(to his guests; shouting wildly)*

Which of you have done this?[29]

LENNOX
What, my good lord?

MACBETH
Thou canst not say I did it.

ROSS
His Highness is not well.

LADY MACBETH
My worthy friends. My lord is often thus,
And hath been from his youth.
The fit is momentary; upon a thought

He will again be well. If much you note him,
You shall offend him, and extend his passion.
Dance, and regard him not.

> *(aside to Macbeth; angrily)*

Are you a man?

MACBETH

Ay, and a bold one, that dare look on that
Which might appal the devil.

LADY MACBETH

What, quite unmanned in folly?

MACBETH

If I stand here, I saw him.

LADY MACBETH

Fie, for shame!

> *(Several of the gentlemen do not return to the dance but
> attend Macbeth instead. Ross hands him a cup of wine.)*

ROSS

My worthy lord.[30]

MACBETH

I do forget.
Do not muse at me, my most worthy friends:
I have a strange infirmity, which is nothing
To those that know me. Come, love and health to all!

> *(A serving boy comes by with a tray full of drinks, which
> the gentlemen take from him.)*

MACBETH

I drink to our friend Banquo, whom we miss.
Would he were here!

> *(The cup is at his lips when the ghost "Effect" re-
> appears.[31] It fills the whole gateway. The cup drops from
> Macbeth's hand. He screams.)*

MACBETH

Avaunt, and quit my sight! Let the earth hide thee!

LADY MACBETH

> *(to the gentlemen; worried and apol-
> ogetic)*

Think of this, good peers,
But as a thing of custom. 'Tis no other.

MACBETH

What man dare, I dare.
Take any shape but that, and my firm nerves
Shall never tremble.

(The dancers have fallen back on either side, leaving Macbeth to stand alone under the great face.)

Hence, horrible shadow!
Unreal mock'ry, hence!

(Ghost vanishes. Macbeth makes a desperate effort to regain control of himself.)

Why, so; being gone, I am a man again.

LADY MACBETH
(crossing to him; quietly but furious)

You have displaced the mirth, broke the good meeting
With most admired disorder.

MACBETH

Can such things be,
And overcome us like a summer's cloud
Without our special wonder?

(He sinks to the steps of the throne. The court crowds around him. Ross is at his side.)

MACBETH
(to Ross; pathetically)

Can you behold such sights?

ROSS

What sights, my lord?

LADY MACBETH

I pray you speak not: he grows worse and worse;
Question enrages him. At once, good night!

(The court, buzzing sympathies, begins to disperse.)

Stand not upon the order of your going,
But go at once.

(The guests hurry out, very apologetically.)

LENNOX
(as he bows himself out)

Good-night and better health
Attend his Majesty!

(A chorus of murmurings echo this sentiment.)

LADY MACBETH

A kind good night to all.

(All exit except Macbeth and Lady Macbeth. Lights start to dim.)

MACBETH
(still slumped on the step)

It will have blood, they say: blood will have blood.
Stones have been known to move, and trees to speak;

Augures and understood relations have
By maggot-pies and choughs and rooks brought forth
The secret'st man of blood. What is the night?

LADY MACBETH

Almost at odds with morning, which is which.

MACBETH

Strange things I have in head, that will to hand—

>   *(Voodoo music begins, very faintly. He looks up.)*

More shall they speak, for now I am bent to know
By the worst means the worst.[32]

>   *(rising)*

I will to-night
(And betimes I will) to the weird sisters.

>   *(Lady Macbeth backs away, fearfully. Macbeth stands,*
>   *arms upraised, shouting his invocation. Music stops.*
>   *Silence.)*

MACBETH

How now, you secret, black, and midnight hags!

>   *(Lights start to dim. Distant thunder and lightning.)*

I conjure you by that which you profess,
Howe'er you come to know it, answer me.

>   *(Music of the voodoo steals in again, rising to a cres-*
>   *cendo with the invocation.)*

Though you untie the winds and let them fight
Against the churches, though the yesty waves
Confound and swallow navigation up,
Though bladed corn be lodged and trees blown down,
Though castles topple on their warders' heads,
Though palaces and pyramids do slope
Their heads to their foundations, though the treasure
Of nature's germens tumble all together
Even till destruction sicken—answer me![33]

>   *(Tremendous burst of thunder. The stage is pitch black.*
>   *Slowly, the gates swing open, letting in a strange light.*
>   *Hecate is in silhouette against it. He beckons to Mac-*
>   *beth.)*

Scene Two

The jungle. A cauldron is smoking over a blazing fire.
It is masked by a double half-circle of voodoo women,
who are squatting in front of it. The three Witches, raised

somewhat above the stage level, are already in a state of ecstasy from the fumes rising out of the cauldron.

SECOND WITCH

By the pricking of my thumbs,
Something wicked this way comes.

(The leaves part and Macbeth enters, followed by Hecate. All rise.)

HECATE

(to Macbeth)

Say, if th' hadst rather hear it from their mouths,
Or from their masters?[1]

MACBETH

Call 'em.

(Drums begin. Macbeth stands to one side.)

HECATE

Round about the cauldron go;[2]

(The half-circles become a full one, moving around the cauldron in time to the drums and the chanting.)

In the poisoned entrails throw.
Toad, that under the cold stone
Days and nights has thirty-one.

(Each of the following speeches is chanted by a different voodoo celebrant.)

FIRST VOICE

Fillet of fenny snake,
In the cauldron boil and bake.[3]

SECOND VOICE

Eye of newt, and toe of frog.[4]

THIRD VOICE

Wool of bat.[5]

FOURTH VOICE

And tongue of dog.[6]

FIFTH VOICE

Adder's fork.[7]

SIXTH VOICE

And blindworm's sting.[8]

SEVENTH VOICE

Lizard's leg.[9]

EIGHTH VOICE

And howlet's wing—[10]

ALL

Double, double, toil and trouble,
Fire burn, and cauldron bubble.

[The following speeches were unassigned in Welles's script.]

Scale of dragon.

Tooth of wolf.

Witch's mummy.

Maw and gulf of the ravined salt-sea shark.
Finger of birth-strangled babe
Ditch-delivered by a drab.[11]

ALL

Double, double, toil and trouble,
Fire burn, and cauldron bubble.
For a charm of powerful trouble,
Like a hell-broth boil and bubble.[12]

HECATE

Pour in sow's blood, that hath eaten
Her nine farrow; grease that's sweaten
From the murderer's gibbet throw
Into the flame.
Cool it with a baboon's blood,
Then the charm is firm and good.[13]

ALL

Double, double, toil and trouble;
Fire burn, and cauldron bubble.

MACBETH

What is't you do?

HECATE

A deed without a name?[14]

FIRST WITCH

(speaking through her teeth in the queer voice of her "control;" screams out his name)

Macbeth, Macbeth, Macbeth, beware Macduff!
Beware the Thane of Fife! Dismiss me.—Enough.[15]

SECOND WITCH

(also possessed)

Macbeth, Macbeth, Macbeth—
Be bloody, bold, and resolute! Laugh to scorn
The pow'r of man, for none of woman born
Shall harm Macbeth.[16]

MACBETH

Then live, Macduff,—what need I fear of thee?
But yet I'll make assurance double sure
And take a bond of fate. Thou shalt not live;
That I may tell pale-hearted fear it lies
And sleep in spite of thunder.

THIRD WITCH
*(as the other two; his name violently
screamed, the message pronounced)*

Macbeth, Macbeth, Macbeth—
Be lion-mettled, proud, and take no care
Who chafes, who frets, or who conspirers are!
Macbeth shall never vanquished be until
Great Birnam Wood to high Dunsinane Hill
Shall come against him.[17]

MACBETH
(partly to himself, partly to Hecate)

That will never be.
Who can impress the forest, bid the tree
Unfix his earth-bound root? Sweet bodements, good!
(to the Witches; raising his voice)
Yet my heart
Throbs to know one thing. Tell me, if your art
Can tell so much: Shall Banquo issue ever
Reign in this kingdom?

(The Witches are hysterical.)

HECATE

Seek to know no more.[18]

(General panic.)

MACBETH

I will be satisfied.

(Silence.)

Deny me this,
And an eternal curse fall on you!

(General derisive laughter.)

HECATE
(silencing the laughter)

Show his eyes, and grieve his heart!
Come like shadows, so depart![19]

(Drums begin. The first apparition rises.[20])

MACBETH
(terrified)
Thou are too like the spirit of Banquo. Down!
(Second apparition.)

Thy crown does sear mine eyeballs. And thy hair,
Thou other gold-bound brow, is like the first.
(Third apparition.)

A third is like the former. Filthy hags,
Why do you show me this?
(Fourth apparition.)

A fourth? Start, eyes!
(Fifth and sixth apparitions.)

What, will the line stretch out to th' crack of doom?
(Seventh apparition.)

A seventh? I'll see no more.
Horrible sight! Now I see 'tis true;
For the blood-boltered Banquo smiles upon me
And points at them for his.
(turning to Hecate)
What? Is this so?

HECATE
Ay, sir, all this is so.[21]

(Macbeth turns back, but the apparitions have vanished.)

MACBETH
Blood hath been shed ere now, i' th' olden time
Ere human statute purged the gentle weal;
Ay, and since too, murders have been performed
Too terrible for the ear. The time has been,
That, when the brains were out, the man would die,
And there an end. But now they rise again,
With twenty mortal murders on their crowns.[22]

HECATE
But why stands Macbeth thus amazedly?[23]

MACBETH
Let this pernicious hour
Stand aye accursed in the calendar!
(with determination)
From this moment
The very firstlings of my heart shall be
The firstlings of my hand.
(There is the first light of dawn.)

HECATE

No boasting like a fool!
Seize upon Macduff, give to th' edge o' th' sword
His wife, his babes, and all unfortunate souls
That trace him in his line.[24]

MACBETH

This deed I'll do before this purpose cool.
                    (suddenly fearful again)
But no more sights!

> *(He runs out. The celebrants laugh wildly. Hecate raises*
> *his arm in the gesture that he uses for cursing Macbeth.*
> *Sudden and absolute silence.)*

HECATE

He shall spurn fate, scorn death, and bear
His hopes 'bove wisdom, grace, and fear:
                    (to the celebrants)
And you all know security
Is mortals' chiefest enemy.[25]

> *END OF ACT TWO*

ACT THREE

Scene One

The palace.[1] Early morning.

Lady Macduff enters with her Son, and a Nurse[2] carrying
a baby.

LADY MACDUFF

What had he done to make him fly the land?

NURSE

You must have patience, madam.[3]

LADY MACDUFF

He had none.

NURSE

You know not
Whether it was his wisdom or his fear.[4]

LADY MACDUFF

Wisdom? To leave his wife, to leave his babes,
His mansion and his titles in a place
From whence himself does fly? He loves us not,
He wants the natural touch. For the poor wren

(The most diminutive of birds) will fight,
Her young ones in her nest, against the owl.

NURSE

O your husband,
He is noble, wise, judicious, and best knows
The fits o' th' season.[5]

LADY MACDUFF

(to her Son)

Sirrah, your father's dead;
And what will you do now? How will you live?

SON

As birds do, mother.

LADY MACDUFF

What, with worms and flies?

SON

With what I get.

LADY MACDUFF

Poor bird! thou'dst never fear the net nor lime,
The pitfall nor the gin.

SON

Why should I, mother? Poor birds they are not set for.
My father is not dead for all your saying.

LADY MACDUFF

Yes, he is dead. How wilt thou do for a father?

SON

Nay, how will you do for a husband?

LADY MACDUFF

Why, I can buy me twenty at any market.

SON

Then you'll buy 'em to sell again.

NURSE

Thou speak'st with all thy wit; and yet, i' faith,
With wit enough for thee.[6]

SON

Was my father a traitor, mother?

LADY MACDUFF

Ay, that he was!

SON

What is a traitor?

NURSE

Why, one that swears and lies.

SON

And be all traitors that do so?

LADY MACDUFF

Every one that does so is a traitor and must be hanged.

SON

And must they all be hanged that swear and lie?

LADY MACDUFF

Every one.

SON

Who must hang them?

LADY MACDUFF

Why, the honest men.

SON

Then the liars and swearers are fools, for there are liars and swearers enow to beat the honest men and hang [up] them.

NURSE

Now God help thee, poor monkey![7]

LADY MACDUFF

But how wilt thou do for a father?

SON

If he were dead, you'ld weep for him. If you would not, it were a good sign that I should quickly have a new father.

LADY MACDUFF

Poor prattler, how thou talk'st!

> *(Enter the Priest. He hurries over to Lady Macduff and speaks to her, half under his breath.)*

PRIEST

Bless you, fair dame!
I doubt some danger does approach you nearly.
Be not found here. Hence with your little ones!
Heaven preserve you!
I dare abide no longer.[8]

> *(He exits. The Nurse is hysterical.)*

LADY MACDUFF

Whither should I fly?
I have done no harm. But I remember now
I am in this earthly world, where to do harm
Is often laudable, to do good sometime

Accounted dangerous folly. Why then, alas,
Do I put up this womanly defense
To say I have done no harm?

(Enter the two Murderers.)

What are these faces?

FIRST MURDERER

Where is your husband?

LADY MACDUFF

I hope, in no place so unsanctified
Where such as thou mayst find him.

FIRST MURDERER

He's a traitor.

SON
(goes over and faces him)

Thou liest, thou shag-eared villain!

FIRST MURDERER

What, you egg!

(He shoots him.)

Young fry of treachery!

SON

He has killed me, mother.
Run away, I pray you!

*(He dies. Lady Macduff goes to her Son and is shot. The
Nurse, carrying the baby, runs out, shrieking 'Murder!',
the two Murderers in pursuit. Her cries echo through
the palace. There is an awful scream, gunshots, then
silence.)*

Scene Two

The coast.
*A fence of grass blades set against blackness, and
through which enter, as the light of a hot noon reveals
the scene, Macduff and Malcolm.*

MALCOLM

Let us seek out some desolate shade, and there
Weep our sad bosoms empty.

MACDUFF

Let us rather
Hold fast the mortal sword and, like good men,
Bestride our downfall'n birthdom.[1]

What you have spoke, it may be so perchance.
I think our country sinks beneath the yoke,
It weeps, it bleeds, and each new day a gash
Is added to her wounds. I think withal
There would be hands uplifted in my right;
And here from gracious England have I offer
Of goodly thousands. But, still, Macbeth
Was once thought honest; you have loved him well;
He hath not touched you yet.[2]
I am not treacherous.

MALCOLM

But Macbeth is.

MACDUFF

Bleed, bleed, poor country!
I have lost my hopes.[3]

MALCOLM

Perchance even there where I did find my doubts.
Why in that rawness left you wife and child,
Without leave-taking?

MACDUFF

Fare thee well, lord.
I would not be the villain that thou think'st
For the whole space that's in the tyrant's grasp.

MALCOLM
(stopping Macduff with his words)

When I shall tread upon the tyrant's head
Or wear it on my sword, yet my poor country
Shall have more vices than it had before,
More suffer, and more sundry ways than ever,
By him that shall succeed.

MACDUFF

What should he be?

MALCOLM

It is myself I mean.

MACDUFF

Not in the legions
Of horrid hell can come a devil more damned
In evils to top Macbeth.

MALCOLM

I grant him bloody,
Sudden, malicious, smacking of every sin
That has a name. But there's no bottom, none,

In my voluptuousness. Your wives, your daughters,
Your matrons, and your maids could not fill up
The cistern of my lust.
Better Macbeth than such a one to reign.

MACDUFF
(coming back to Malcolm)
Boundless intemperance in nature is a tyranny.
But fear not yet, we have willing dames enough.

MALCOLM
With this there grows
In my most ill-composed affection such
A staunchless avarice that I should forge
Quarrels unjust against the good and loyal,
Destroying them again.

MACDUFF
This avarice sticks deeper.

MALCOLM
Nay, had I pow'r, I should
Pour the sweet milk of concord into hell,
Uproar the universal peace, confound
All unity on earth.

MACDUFF
(turns away; wretchedly)
O Scotland, Scotland!

MALCOLM
If such a one be fit to govern, speak.

MACDUFF
Fit to govern?
No, not to live! O nation miserable,
When shalt thou see thy wholesome days again,
Since the truest issue of thy throne
Now does blaspheme his breed?
(turning back to him again)
Thy royal father
Was a most sainted king; the queen that bore thee,
Oft'ner upon her knees than on her feet,
Died every day she lived.
(starts to leave)
O my breast, thy hope ends here!

MALCOLM
Macduff!

(Macduff stops.)

This noble passion,
Wiped out all scruples, reconciled my thoughts
To thy good truth and honour. Devilish Macbeth
By many of these trains hath sought to win me
Into his power; but God above
Deal between thee and me. [Here abjure]
The taints and blames I laid upon myself
For strangers to my nature. I am yet
Unknown to woman. My first false speaking
Was this upon myself. What I am truly,
Is thine and my poor country's to command.

MACDUFF

Such welcome and unwelcome things at once
'Tis hard to reconcile.

(Enter Ross.)

My ever gentle cousin, welcome hither.

MALCOLM

Good God betimes remove
The means that makes us strangers!

ROSS

Sir, amen.

MACDUFF

Stands Scotland where it did?

ROSS

Alas, poor country,
Almost afraid to know itself. It cannot
Be called our mother but our grave.
The dead man's knell
Is there scarce asked for who, and good men's lives
Expire before the flowers in their caps,
Dying or ere they sicken.

MACDUFF

How does my wife?

ROSS

Why, well.

MACDUFF

And all my children?

ROSS

Well too.
Now is the time of help. Your eye in Scotland

Would create soldiers, make our women fight
To doff their dire distresses.

MALCOLM

Be't their comfort
We are coming thither. Gracious England hath
Lent us good Siward and ten thousand men.

ROSS

Would I could answer
This comfort with the like. But I have words
That would be howled out in the desert air,
Where hearing should not latch them.

MACDUFF

What concern they?
If it be mine,
Keep it not from me, quickly let me have it.

ROSS

Let not your ears despise my tongue for ever.
Your wife is dead, sir,
Killed.[4] Your wife and babes
Killed, savagely slaughtered.

MALCOLM

Merciful heaven!

        (A pause.)

MACDUFF

My children too?

ROSS

Wife, children, servants, all
That could be found.

MACDUFF

And I must be from thence?
My wife killed too?

ROSS

I have said.

MALCOLM

Be comforted.
Let's make us med'cines of our great revenge
To cure this deadly grief.

MACDUFF

He has no children. All my pretty ones?
Did you say all? O hell-kite! All?

What, all my pretty chickens and their dam
At one fell swoop?

MALCOLM

Dispute it like a man.

MACDUFF

I shall do so;
But I must also feel it as a man.
I cannot but remember such things were
That were most precious to me. Did heaven look on,
And would not take their part?

MALCOLM

Be this the whetstone of your sword. Let grief
Convert to anger; blunt not the heart, enrage it.

MACDUFF

O, I could play the woman with mine eyes
And braggart with my tongue. But, gentle heavens,
Cut short all intermission. Front to front
Bring thou this fiend of Scotland and myself.
Within my sword's length set him. If he scape,
Heaven forgive him too!

MALCOLM

This tune goes manly.
He's ripe for shaking, and the pow'rs above
Put on their instruments. Receive what cheer you may.
The night is long that never finds the day.

(Exit all.)

Scene Three[1]

Lady Macbeth enters.

THREE WITCHES

Her eyes are open.[2]
Their sense is shut.[3]

LADY MACBETH

Out, damn'd spot! Out, I say! One—two—why then 'tis time to do't. Hell is
murky. Fie, my lord, fie! a soldier, and afeard? What need we fear who knows
it, when none can call our pow'r to accompt? Yet who would have thought the
old man to have [had] so much blood in him? The Thane of Fife had a wife.
Where is she now? What, will these hands ne'er be clean? Mar all with this
starting. Here's the smell of the blood still. All the perfumes of Arabia will not
sweeten this little hand. Oh, oh, oh! Wash your hands, put on your nightgown!
I tell you yet again, Banquo's buried. He cannot come out on's grave. Even so?

To bed, to bed! There's knocking at the gate. Come, come, come, come, give
me your hand! What's done cannot be undone. To bed, to bed, to bed!

(Exit Lady Macbeth.)

THREE WITCHES

Unnatural deeds do breed unnatural troubles.
Infected minds keep eyes upon her.[4]

(Enter Macduff, Malcolm, Ross and their forces.)

MALCOLM

We learn no other but the confident tyrant
Keeps still in Dunsinane and will endure
Our setting down before't.[5]
Some say he's mad; others, that lesser hate him,
Do call it valiant fury.[6]

MACDUFF

Now does he feel
His secret murders sticking on his hands
Those he commands move only in command,
Nothing in love. Now does he feel his title
Hang loose about him, like a giant's robe
Upon a dwarfish thief.[7]

MALCOLM

What wood is this before us?[8]

HECATE

The Wood of Birnam.[9]
Let every soldier hew him down a bough,
And bear't before him. Thereby shall you shadow
The numbers of your host and make discovery
Err in report of you.[10]

MACDUFF

It shall be done.[11]

(Lights fade out completely.)

Scene Four

The palace.
Macbeth, wild-eyed and dressed only in his trousers and
shirt, is on the throne, with five or six runners on their
faces before him.

MACBETH

Bring me no more reports. Let them fly all,
Till Birnam Wood remove to Dunsinane.
What's the boy Malcolm?

Was he not born of woman? The spirits that know
All mortal consequences have pronounced me thus:
'Fear not, Macbeth. No man that's born of woman
Shall e'er have power upon thee.'[1]

> *(Enter Servant, who runs up to the throne and throws himself at Macbeth's feet.)*

Where got'st thou that goose look?

SERVANT
(breathlessly)

There is ten thousand—

MACBETH

Geese, villain?

SERVANT

Soldiers, sir.

MACBETH
(striking him violently across the face)

What soldiers, whey-face?

SERVANT
(covering his face with his hands; terrified)

The English force, so please you.

MACBETH

Take thy face hence.

> *(Exit Servant. The others remain on their knees.)*

Seyton!—I am sick at heart.
I have lived long enough. My way of life
Is fall'n into the sear, the yellow leaf,
And that which should accompany old age,
As honour, love, obedience, troops of friends,
I must not look to have. Seyton!

> *(Still no answer. He turns to one of the kneeling figures.)*

How does your patient, doctor?

DOCTOR
(looking up)

Not so sick, my lord,
As she is troubled with thick-coming fancies
That keep her from her rest.

MACBETH
(turning away)

Cure her of that!

DOCTOR

Therein the patient must minister to himself.

> *(Macbeth wheels on him. He bows his head to the ground again, quietly.)*

MACBETH

Throw physic to the dogs, I'll none of it!
Seyton! Seyton, I say!

> *(Enter Seyton, running.)*

SEYTON

What's your gracious pleasure?[2]

MACBETH

What news more?

SEYTON
(prostrating himself)

All is confirmed, my lord, which was reported.

MACBETH

Hang our banners on the outward walls.

> *(All but three of the messengers rise at this, and exit.)*[3]

The cry is still, 'They come!' Our castle's strength
Will laugh a siege to scorn. Here let them lie
Till famine and the plague eat them up.[4]

> *(Servants appear with Macbeth's coat, sword and plumed hat. They hurry over to him and help to dress him.)*

MACBETH

Hang those that talk of fear!
Come, put my belt on now! Give me my sword!
Come, sir, dispatch! Put on, I say!
Seyton, send out.[5]

> *(Macbeth stands up, fully dressed and brave in his shining regalia. The Doctor stands near the throne.)*[6]

MACBETH
(to him; proudly)

Doctor, the thanes fly from me.[7]

> *(From outside the palace comes a strange, high-pitched chorus of wails. It is heard very suddenly, and the effect should be startling. All jump to their feet, frightened, and stand waiting, listening. Silence.)*

MACBETH

What is that noise?[8]

> *(The sound is heard again. There is more reaction.)*

SEYTON

It is the cry of women, my good lord.

> *(General relaxation. But all are still mystified. The sound is heard again. It continues, growing louder.)*

MACBETH

I have almost forgot the taste of fears.
The time has been my sense would have cooled
To hear a night-shriek, and my fell of hair
Would at a dismal treatise rouse and stir
As life were in't. I have supped full with horrors.
Direness, familiar to my slaughterous thought,
Cannot once start me. Wherefore was that cry?

DOCTOR

The Queen, my lord, is dead.[9]

> *(Her body is brought in and set before Macbeth. He stares at it. The chanting stops.)*

MACBETH

She should have died hereafter:
There would have been a time for such a word.
To-morrow, and to-morrow, and to-morrow
Creeps in this petty pace from day to day
To the last syllable of recorded time,
And all our yesterdays have lighted fools
The way to dusty death. Out, out, brief candle!
Life's but a walking shadow, a poor player
That struts and frets his hour upon the stage
And then is heard no more. It is a tale
Told by an idiot, full of sound and fury,
Signifying nothing.

> *(The Porter runs down from his watch on the battlements.)*

MACBETH

Thou com'st to use thy tongue: thy story quickly!

PORTER

Gracious my lord,
I should report that which I say I saw,
But know not how to do't.[10]

MACBETH

Well, say, sir.

PORTER

As I did stand my watch upon the wall,
I looked toward Birnam, and anon methought
The wood began to move![11]

> *(Sensation. Screams. All exit in confusion except Porter
> and Macbeth, who has jumped on the Porter and holds
> him by the throat.)*

MACBETH

Liar and slave!

PORTER

Let me endure your wrath if't be not so.
I say, a moving grove.[12]

> *(The tops of palm trees begin slowly to rise over the
> battlements. The jungle creeps in the gates. Slowly.
> Slowly.)*

MACBETH

If thou speak'st false,
Upon the next tree shalt thou hang alive
Till famine cling thee.

> *(Suddenly, Macbeth sees the jungle growing. He lets the
> Porter drop and stares at it.)*

MACBETH

I care not if thou dost for me as much.

> *(The trees rise. The leaves move in. Voodoo drums. The
> Porter picks himself up and scrambles off. A pause.)*

'Fear not, till Birnam Wood
Do come to Dunsinane.' Arm, arm, and out!
There is no flying hence nor tarrying here.
I 'gin to be aweary of the sun,
And wish the estate o' th' world were now undone.

> *(Cries and shots from within the foliage.)*

Ring the alarum bell! Blow wind, come wrack,
At least we'll die with harness on our back.

> *(A bell begins to clang. Cries and shots up. Macbeth
> starts up the battlements.)*

What's he that was not born of woman? Such a one
Am I to fear, or none.[13]

> *(Enter Young Siward from the mass of still rising leaves,
> pistol in hand. He confronts Macbeth.)*

YOUNG SIWARD

What is thy name?

MACBETH

Thou'lt be afraid to hear it.

YOUNG SIWARD

No, though thou call'st thyself a hotter name
Than any is in hell.

> *(Macbeth shoots him.)*

MACBETH

My name's Macbeth.

> *(Siward falls.)*

Thou wast born of woman.

> *(He turns and continues up the wall. Enter Macduff through the gates.)*

But swords I smile at, weapons laugh to scorn,
Brandished by man that's of [a] woman born.

MACDUFF

Let me find him, Fortune! Tyrant, show thy face![14]

> *(Macbeth, on the wall above, hears his voice and stands frozen with horror. Macduff moves toward the wall, looking at him.)*

I cannot strike at wretched kerns, whose arms
Are hired to bear their staves.
My wife and children's ghosts will haunt me still.

> *(He has started up the battlements. Macbeth wheels and starts running madly over the bridge. Macduff sees him.)*

Turn, hellhound, turn![15]

> *(This stops Macbeth, who turns to face him.)*

MACBETH

Of all men else I have avoided thee.
But get thee back! My soul is too much charged
With blood of thine already.

MACDUFF

Then yield thee, coward,
And live to be the show and gaze o' th' time.
We'll have thee, as our rarer monsters are,
Painted upon a pole, and underwrit
'Here may you see the tyrant.'

MACBETH

I will not yield.
Though Birnam Wood be come to Dunsinane,
Yet I will try the last.

MACDUFF

I have no words.[16]

> *(He fires at Macbeth, who shoots back. He fires his other gun. All aims have missed. Macduff draws his sword and runs up to Macbeth. They fight. The stage below is filled with the leaves that the army is bearing. All sound way down here, even the drums.)*

MACBETH

Thou losest labour.
I bear a charm'd life, which must not yield
To one of woman born.

MACDUFF

Despair thy charm,

> *(On the word "charm," there is sudden and complete silence.)*

And let the angel whom thou still hast served
Tell thee, Macduff was from his mother's womb
Untimely ripped.

> *(Macbeth is off his guard, and Macduff runs him through. Macbeth stands, teetering and clutching his wound. The silence is broken by the weird chant of the Witches: 'All hail, Macbeth! Hail, King of Scotland!')*

MACBETH

Accurs'd the tongue that tells me so,
And be these juggling fiends no more believed.

> *(He falls dead, his body hidden behind the battlements at the top of the tower. The derisive cackle of the Witches is heard. Macduff kneels behind the battlements and rises to silence the laughter, holding in his hand Macbeth's bloody head. He throws the head into the mass of waving leaves below.)*

MACDUFF

Hail, King!

> *(At this, the army drops the branches and the jungle collapses, revealing a stage filled with people. Malcolm is on the throne, crowned. All but Hecate and the three Witches bow before him. They have caught Macbeth's head and stand above the body of Lady Macbeth.)*

MACDUFF

For so thou art. Behold where stands
The usurper's curs'd head.

(The Witches gleefully hold the head aloft.)

The time is free.
Hail, King of Scotland!

VOICES OF VOODOO WOMEN

All hail, Malcolm.

*They are interrupted by a thunderous chorus from the
army.)*

ARMY

Hail, King of Scotland.

VOICES OF VOODOO WOMEN

Thrice to thine, and thrice to mine,
And thrice again, to make up nine.[17]

HECATE

Peace!

*(The drums, army, music, voices of voodoo women—all
are instantly silent.)*

The charm's wound up.[18]

THE END

NOTES

I,i

1. The production's only permanent set piece was Macbeth's palace, inspired by San Souci, the capital of Henri Christophe, the tyrant who ruled Haiti from 1811 to 1820. All of the other scenes—in the jungle, along the coast, and so forth—were played downstage of the palace before painted backdrops. At rise, Hecate, the three Witches, and the circle of voodoo celebrants were positioned around a smoking cauldron. Upstage, and nearly hidden behind the cauldron, was a troupe of voodoo drummers, who began to play as the curtain went up.

2. Jack Carter was not Welles's original choice for Macbeth. Carter inherited the role from Juano Hernandez, who quit the production after only three rehearsals to accept the title role in the N.B.C. radio series, "John Henry." In time, Hernandez would find his way to Hollywood, where he appeared in such films as *Intruder in the Dust.*

3. I,iii,38.

4. a man in Welles's production.

5. Banquo, 39.

6. voodoo celebrants, of whom there were a dozen, and an equal number of men.

7. 48–50.

8. The voodoo women intone the Witches' speeches.

9. Third Witch, 68.

10. First Witch, 69.

11. Angus is eliminated from Welles's script, with his lines assigned to Ross.

12. Second Witch, 49.

13. Angus, 109–11.
14. 70.
15. 50.
16. 130–42.
17. 118–20.
18. III,v,1.
19. voodoo celebrants.
20. I,iii,34. From the Witches' speech, embellished by Welles.
21. First Witch, 22–23.
22. Ibid., 18–21.
23. All, 37.

I,ii

1. I,v,28.
2. 1–27.
3. I,iv,1.
4. I,vi,20.
5. 21–24.
6. I,iv,14–21.
7. Macbeth, 48–50.
8. I,vi,1–3.
9. Banquo, 4–10.
10. I,v,58, "And when goes hence?"
11. I,vii,1–7.
12. Malcolm, IV,iii,139.
13. Doctor, 140–44.
14. Macduff, 146, ". . . he means?"
15. Malcolm, 147–56.
16. I,vii,13–20.
17. Welles's line.
18. In this case the "effect" was aural. In II,i—the ghost's appearances from behind the tower and in the gateway—huge papier-mâché masks were seen under a strobe light to make a chilling impression.
19. II,ii,5–8/12–13.
20. II,i,62.
21. 56–58.
22. Lady Macbeth, II,ii,16.
23. His question and her answer are given by Welles to her as two questions. The punctuation of their next two lines is also changed.
24. 19, "Donalbain." Eliminated from Welles's script.
25. 70/60.
26. Donalbain, 92.
27. Macbeth, 93–95.
28. The handguns used in this scene, and again in III,i and III,iv, were flintlock blunderbuss pistols that belled out at the end. A rifle version was also designed for Macbeth's honor guard in II,i (the coronation scene).
29. Macduff, 114.
30. Ibid., 127.

31. Macbeth, 128–29.
32. All, 130.
33. Malcolm, 131–33.
34. Donalbain, 118–19.
35. Malcolm, 131.
36. Ibid., 133, "I'll to England."
37. IV,ii,3–4.
38. Donalbain, II,iii,135–37.
39. 87–92.
40. First Witch, I,iii,22–23.
41. Ibid., 18–21.
42. The production's only intermission occurred at this point. A musical interlude was provided, consisting of "River," arranged by Jordan, and "Adagio Aframerique" by Porter Grainger.

II,i

1. For this, the coronation scene, Virgin Thomson arranged a medley of waltzes, not by Strauss, as legend holds, but by his contemporary, Josef Lanner.
2. III,i,29–30, "We hear our bloody cousins are bestow'd / In England and in Ireland."
3. 11.
4. 1–9.
5. 27.
6. Servant, 46.
7. Second Murderer, 108–11.
8. First Murderer, 112.
9. III,ii,35.
10. 4–7.
11. Macbeth, 37.
12. III,iii,3.
13. III,ii,39–44.
14. III,iii,1.
15. Third Murderer, 9.
16. First Murderer, 12.
17. Third Murderer, 13–14.
18. Ibid., 15.
19. First Murderer, 17.
20. Third Murderer, 20.
21. III,v,2.
22. III,iv,2.
23. First Murderer, 20.
24. The first of two papier-mâché masks. See note I,i,18.
25. III,ii,26–28.
26. III,ii,11–12.
27. III,iv,69–73.
28. 67.
29. 48.
30. Lady Macbeth, 83.

31. The second mask.
32. 139/134–35.
33. IV,i,48–60.

II,ii

1. First Witch, IV,i,62–63.
2. Ibid., 4.
3. Second Witch, 12–13.
4. Ibid., 14.
5. Ibid., 15.
6. Ibid., 15.
7. Ibid., 16.
8. Ibid., 16.
9. Ibid., 17.
10. Ibid., 17.
11. Third Witch, 22–31.
12. Ibid., 35–36; Second Witch, 18–19.
13. First Witch, 64–67; Second Witch, 37–38.
14. All, 49.
15. First Apparition, 71–72.
16. Second Apparition, 77/79–81.
17. Second Apparition, 77; Third Apparition, 90–94.
18. All, 103.
19. All, 110–11.
20. a procession of Banquo's heirs, the Tudor kings, seen through strobe lighting.
21. First Witch, 125.
22. III,iv,75–81.
23. First Witch, IV,i,125–26.
24. Macbeth, 153/151–52.
25. III,v,30–34.

III,i

1. Dunsinane. Welles does not indicate if Lady Macduff and her children remain by choice, or if they are, in effect, under house arrest.
2. replaces Ross in this scene (IV,ii).
3. Ross, 2.
4. Ibid., 4–5.
5. Ibid., 15–17.
6. Lady Macduff, 43–44.
7. Ibid., 57.
8. Messenger, 64–72.

III,ii

1. IV,iii,2–4.
2. Malcolm, 11/39–44/12–14.
3. 32/24.
4. Welles's line.

III,iii

1. Welles describes this scene as "entirely incomplete." It can be assumed, however, that Lady Macbeth and the Witches are at Dunsinane, while Hecate attends Malcolm and Macduff in Birnam Wood.
2. Doctor, V,i,21.
3. Gentlewoman, 22.
4. Doctor, 66–67/72.
5. Siward, V,iv,7–9.
6. Caithness, V,ii,13–14.
7. Angus, V,ii,16–22.
8. Siward, V,iv,3.
9. Menteith, 3.
10. Malcolm, 4–7.
11. Soldiers, 8.

III,iv

1. V,iii,1–7.
2. 29.
3. Presumably, the Doctor is one of those who exits.
4. V,v,1–4.
5. V,iii,36/47–54.
6. He has returned to report the death of Lady Macbeth.
7. 49.
8. V,v,7.
9. Seyton, 16.
10. Messenger, 30–32.
11. Ibid., 33–35.
12. Ibid., 36–38.
13. V,vii,2–4.
14. 22/14.
15. V,viii,3.
16. 7.
17. All, I,iii,35–36.
18. All, 37.

Julius Caesar

PREFACE

Rather than merely reviving Shakespeare's account of a tyrant's downfall in ancient Rome, Welles, in this the inaugural production of the Mercury Theatre, set about to arouse the passions of his audience with a simulation of the chaos then overtaking Europe. In doing so, he exploited their inevitable superstitions about dictatorships—so successfully, in fact, that more than one critic would proclaim that, in Welles's hands, *Julius Caesar* had about it "the immediate ring of today's headlines."[1]

In the 1930s, the sight of fascist salutes and martial throngs, and the sound of demagogic ranting and angry mobs, had become a commonplace for anyone who listened to the radio or saw the newsreels or read such popular magazines as *Time* and *Newsweek*. Whatever else was not within their personal experience—such as stealth or conspiracy or gangsterism—had, in all probability, become familiar to the general public through their exposure to the movies. These were the sights and sounds that Welles employed as theatrical devices in *Julius Caesar*. For his audience, the production, which Welles subtitled "The Death of a Dictator," had the same immediacy as banner headlines that day after day proclaimed new and increasingly gruesome horrors being committed just across the Atlantic Ocean. "If the play ceases to be Shakespeare's tragedy," applauded one thunderstruck observer, "it does manage to become ours."[2]

For him to properly exploit such emotional reverberations, however, Welles had to go beyond merely overlaying the outward appearances of contemporary catastrophe on a production in which they were plainly anachronistic. Other updatings of Shakespeare, such as the W.P.A. production of *Coriolanus* the year before, had been received with disapprobation and ridicule. Welles needed a structure to carry his explosive symbols, and the one that best suited his purpose was melodrama.

His own working style quite naturally drew him to this genre, designed as it is for overdrawn characterizations, smashing climaxes, uncontrolled violence, and sentimental appeal. *Julius Caesar* included all of these. The frank theatricality that Welles used in fashioning his production as a political melodrama had both unity and coherence. Elements that otherwise would have seemed ridiculously overwrought were accepted as perfectly natural in the pervasive flamboyance of the melodramatic atmosphere from which they emerged.

Except for an occasional stage direction, none of the production's extreme theatricality was written into the text. Indeed, Welles's abridgement of *Julius Caesar* was little different in kind than his and Roger Hill's school-boy condensations of Shakespeare for the Todd Troupers. Those passages dealing with internecine rivalries were all but eliminated. By summarily cutting out most of the final two acts, Welles did away with the triumvirate and the ghost of Caesar.

Shakespeare begins his play with an encounter between two tribunes and members of the general public whose republican liberties it is the tribunes' duty to maintain. Rather than deal with the workings of the republic, Welles chose instead to open his production with Caesar's bravura entrance and the ominous warning from out of the darkness that accompanies it.

While shaping his text to emphasize the rapid flow of events, Welles did not wholly eliminate the complexities of Brutus as a man "with himself at war." Brutus voices his feelings about the necessity for stopping the ambitious Caesar and his repugnance against committing the slaughter. And while his lines were not reworked to give him proletarian sympathies, within the theatrical schema Brutus became identified with contemporary liberals. For more than one reviewer, this Roman aristocrat exemplified "the unhappy fate of the liberal in a world torn by strife between the extreme left and the extreme right."[3]

Likewise, many who attributed the play's contemporary quality to Welles's direction were equally convinced that it was merely a matter of highlighting what were, in fact, Shakespeare's own political sensibilities. This led them to expound on his liberalism and hatred of dictatorships. Curiously overlooked, even by the left, was Shakespeare's fealty to that long succession of absolute monarchs, the Tudor line. Nor was anything made about one of the primary objections that the conspirators had to Caesar—namely, that he (like Bolingbroke) was a usurper.

Theatrical effects devised to make *Julius Caesar* seem contemporary were thus misunderstood as methods for extracting the *real* Shakespeare. Welles, "in the sharp design of his production, has caught the play's meaning [and] lifted an Elizabethan voice into the modern world of dictators to make a lusty shout of protest."[4] Such judgments cannot be attributed simply to a particular critic's lack of historical grounding. In a majority of those reviewing this production, there appears to have been an overwhelming desire to believe that *Caesar*'s original meaning had, at long last, been revealed.

The production's foremost booster was John Mason Brown of the *New York Post*. Brown had been disappointed by the "Voodoo" *Macbeth*, and his exacting standards were notoriously hard to meet. When the Mercury company learned that Brown, after attending the final dress rehearsal, was enthralled and delighted by the production, they had good reason for optimism regarding its critical reception. In his review Brown was moved to hyperbole. "Orson Welles stages the tragedy magnificently in modern dress and makes it an unforgettable experience." His more serious judgment was that *Julius Caesar*, though ceasing to be Shakespeare's tragedy, became, instead, one which belonged to a modern audience. But even for Brown, the Mercury production best served to underscore Shakespeare's currency. "Mr. Welles proves in his production that Shakespeare was indeed not of an age but for all time."[5]

Richard Watts echoed this sentiment. Noting how lackluster the theatre season had been, Watts was relieved to find in this *Julius Caesar* "something to stand up and cheer about." A major reason for his approbation was that "never once does it seem to you that anything new has been written into Shakespeare's *intent* (italics mine)." The production also led Watts to a revelation that he described almost wistfully: "You cannot escape the feeling that, with the clairvoyance of genius, [Shakespeare] was predicting for us the cauldron of modern Europe."[6]

So enthralled were the Mercury audiences that even the most perceptive among them often lost sight of what was actually going on. Euphemia Van Rensseler Wyatt revealed a precise awareness of the liberties that Welles had taken with Shakespeare's text. But when it came to the mob's encounter with Cinna the Poet, she too was swept along by the virulence and brutality that Welles had built into this brief scene.

Not even the Group Theatre in all their frenzy against dictators ever divised a more thrilling scene than that in which the poet, Cinna, is swallowed up by an angry mob, and yet one comes home to find that Shakespeare wrote it just that way.[7]

Possibly Wyatt, annoyed by the Group's patently doctrinaire productions, was pleased to believe that a faithful adaptation of Shakespeare could serve the same purpose. As Stark Young pointed out, however, Welles reordered this scene from Shakespeare's play (III,iii) more radically than any other in his production. "The scene in Shakespeare is short, and is partly comic relief. This Mercury version makes a long scene of it, writes in lines [taken from I,i of *Coriolanus*], puts in much business and turns it all into gripping sarcasm and horror."[8]

Although it was clearly not Shakespeare's intention to make this short scene, which lacks any significant action and wherein none of the major characters of the play appears, the emotional high point of his play, that is what it became in Welles's hands.[9] Stark Young described the aftermath of this climactic moment.

We jump then to the quarrel scene of Brutus and Cassius. For the rest of the play is Brutus'—Brutus realizing his disaster, Brutus in a brief scene with his page, Brutus running on his sword, and over Brutus' body Antony's epilogue of praise.[10]

At its most vital point, *Julius Caesar* dealt with the fate of a single man. To Norman Lloyd, who played Cinna, his character "symbolized what was happening in the world, if your name was Greenburg—and even if you weren't

Jewish."[11] The Mercury audience made Cinna's experience their own, representing as it did their worst fears for themselves and for those dearest to them abroad.

Welles imposed upon himself strict limitations in adapting *Caesar*, *Macbeth*, and *Five Kings*; and audiences, while delighting in his handling of these materials, also found their abiding conservatism satisfied with the knowledge that every word of text was, in fact, written by Shakespeare. Welles's own devotion to his favorite author would not have allowed him to do otherwise. (Such limitations, it should be pointed out, did not extend to the texts of his other W.P.A. and Mercury productions, which he often rewrote at will.)

In his assimilation of the modernist spirit, Welles became imbued with many of its formal devices, which he used to give such productions as *Julius Caesar* intellectual and emotive qualities that surpassed anything previously seen on the American stage. Perhaps the closest analogy between his adaptation of *Caesar* and the use of classic drama to illuminate contemporary social and political concerns can be found in the work of Bertolt Brecht, whose adaptation of Marlowe's *Edward II* (written in collaboration with Leon Feuchtwanger) has to do with the feudal struggle for power. In Brecht's version this struggle is seen in Marxist terms, with his protagonist rejecting everything that is closest to him for the sake of principle. During the production, Brecht utilized silent movie titles projected on a screen to break the barrier of theatrical illusion in the interests of didacticism. Even his translation, with its intentionally rough and irregular language, served the same purpose—namely, "to show that human feelings are contradictory, fiercely fought and full of conflicts."[12] Despite such extreme deviations, it is plain to see that Brecht's *Edward II* is not only derived from Marlowe's tragedy but also shares a strong affinity to it.

Welles had neither the ideological nor theoretical commitment of a Bertolt Brecht. Nor did he enjoy the same kind of artistic and financial support. But, as his production of *Julius Caesar* would demonstrate, Welles was able to extend such resources as he had at his command to their utmost, and to stretch the imaginative and aesthetic possibilities available to his audience.

NOTES

1. John Mason Brown, *New York Post*, 12 November 1937.

2. Ibid.

3. Heywood Broun, *The New Republic*, 29 December 1937.

4. John Anderson, *New York Journal American*, 12 November 1937.

5. Brown, *The New Republic*.

6. *New York Herald-Tribune*, 12 November 1937.

7. *Catholic World*, December 1937.

8. *The New Republic*, 1 December 1937.

9. Originally, it had also been Welles's intention to follow the Cinna scene with an intermission; however, he soon thought better of this, and the play was presented without interruption.

10. Ibid.

11. Telephone interview, Los Angeles, 16 June 1972.

12. John Willett, *The Theatre of Bertolt Brecht* (New York: New Direction Books, 1968), p. 95.

JULIUS CAESAR

Adapted and directed by Orson Welles
Music by Marc Blitzstein
Sets and lighting by Samuel Leve

Mercury Theatre, New York, 11 November 1937

CAST

Julius Caesar	Joseph Holland
Marcus Antonius	George Coulouris
Publius	Joseph Cotten
Marcus Brutus	Orson Welles
Cassius	Martin Gabel
Casca	Hiram Sherman
Trebonius	John A. Willard
Ligarius	Grover Burgess
Decius Brutus	John Hoyt
Metellus Cimber	Stefan Schnabel
Cinna	Elliott Reid
Flavius	William Mowry
Marullus	William Alland
Artemidorus	George Duthrie
Cinna the Poet	Norman Lloyd
Lucius	Arthur Anderson
Calphurnia	Evelyn Allen
Portia	Muriel Brassler

Senators, Citizens, Soldiers, Attendants

*Darkness as overture begins.[1] Lights up[2] and music cuts
as Caesar speaks.[3]*

CAESAR

Bid every noise be still![4]

VOICE

Caesar![5]

CAESAR

Peace yet again![6]
Who is it in the throng[7] that calls on me?
Marc Antony!

ANTONY

Caesar, my lord?

CAESAR

I hear a tongue shriller than all the music
Cry 'Caesar!'

VOICE

Caesar!

CAESAR

Ha! Who calls?
Speak. Caesar is turn'd to hear.

VOICE

Beware the ides of March.

CAESAR

(to Antony)

What man is that?
What say'st thou to me? Speak once again.

ANTONY

A soothsayer bids you beware the ides of March.[8]

CAESAR

Set him before me; let me see his face.

ANTONY	PUBLIUS	METELLUS
Come from the throng.[9]	Look upon Caesar.[10]	Come forth.

(A long pause. Caesar studies the man.)

CAESAR

He is a dreamer. Let us leave him.

PUBLIUS

Pass![11]

(Exit Caesar and his party.)

ALL

Hail Caesar![12]

(The mob follows after Caesar. Flavius detains the Carpenter and brings him down to the apron. Marullus and the Cobbler follow.)

FLAVIUS

What trade art thou?[13]

CARPENTER

Why, sir, a carpenter.

FLAVIUS

What dost thou with thy best apparel on?[14]

MARULLUS

You, sir. What trade are you?

COBBLER

Truly, sir, I am a cobbler.

FLAVIUS

Thou art a cobbler, art thou?
Why dost thou lead these men about the streets?

COBBLER

Truly, sir, to wear out their shoes, to get myself into more work. But indeed,
   sir, we make holiday to see Caesar and rejoice in his triumph.

FLAVIUS

Wherefore rejoice?

MARULLUS

You blocks, you stones, you worse than senseless things!
Knew you not Pompey? Many a time and oft
Have you climbed up to walls and battlements,
Your infants in your arms, and there have sat
The live-long day, with patient expectation,
To see great Pompey pass the streets of Rome.
And do you now put on your best attire?
And do you now cull a holiday?
And do you now strew flowers in his way
That comes in triumph over Pompey's blood?

(Exit Carpenter and Cobbler.)

FLAVIUS

Go you down that way towards the Capitol;
This way will I. Disrobe the images.

MARULLUS

May we do so?

FLAVIUS

Let no images
Be hung with Caesar's trophies.
These growing feathers plucked from Caesar's wing
Will make him fly an ordinary pitch,
Who else would soar above the view of men
And keep us all in servile fearfulness.

(Exit Flavius and Marullus. Ad-lib low. Brutus enters.
Enter Cassius upstage ramp.)

CASSIUS

Will you go to see the order of the course?[15]

BRUTUS

Not I.

CASSIUS

I pray you do.

BRUTUS

I am not gamesome. I do lack some part
Of that quick spirit that is Antony.
Let me not hinder, Cassius, your desires.
I'll leave you.

CASSIUS

Brutus, I do observe you now of late;
I have not from your eyes that gentleness
And show of love as I was wont to have.
You bear too stubborn and too strange a hand
Over your friend that loves you.

BRUTUS
(turns to Cassius)

Cassius,
Be not deceived. If I veiled my look,
I turn the trouble of my countenance
Merely upon myself. Vex'd I am
Of late with passions of some difference,
Conceptions only proper to myself,
Which give, perhaps, some soil to my behaviour[s].

CASSIUS

Tell me, good Brutus, can you see your face?

BRUTUS

No, Cassius; for the eye sees not itself
But by reflection, by some other things.

CASSIUS

'Tis just.
(sits on front step)
And it is very much lamented, Brutus,
That you have no such mirrors as will turn
Your hidden worthiness into your eye,
That you might see your shadow. I have heard
Where many of the best respect in Rome
(Except immortal Caesar), speaking of Brutus
And groaning underneath this age's yoke,
Have wished that noble Brutus had his eyes.

BRUTUS
(sits)

Into what dangers, Cassius, would you lead me,
That you would have me seek into myself
For that which is not in me?

CASSIUS

Therefore, good Brutus, be prepared to hear;
And since you know you cannot see yourself
So well as by reflection, I, your glass,
Will modestly discover to yourself
That of yourself which you yet know not of.
And be not jealous on me, gentle Brutus,
Were I a common laughter, or did use
To stale with ordinary oaths my love
To every new protester; if you know
That I do fawn on men and hug them hard,
And after scandal them; or if you know
That I profess myself in banqueting
To all the rout, then hold me dangerous.

CROWD

(off-stage; shout)

Hail!

BRUTUS

What means this shouting? I do fear the people
Choose Caesar for their king.

CASSIUS

Ay, do you fear it?
Then must I think you would not have it so.

BRUTUS

I would not, Cassius; yet I love him well.
But wherefore do you hold me here so long?
What is it that you would impart to me?
If it be aught toward the general good,
Set honour in one eye and death i' th' other,
And I will look on both indifferently;
For let the gods so speed me as I love
The name of honour more than I fear death.

CASSIUS

I know that virtue to be in you, Brutus,
As well as I do know your outward favour.
Well, honour is the subject of my story.
I cannot tell what you and other men
Think of this life; but for my single self,
I had as lief not be as live to be
In awe of such a thing as I myself.
I was born as free as Caesar; so were you.
We both have fed as well, and we can both
Endure the winter's cold as well as he.

For once, upon a raw and gusty day,
The troubled Tiber chafing with her shores,
Caesar said to me, 'Dar'st thou, Cassius, now
Leap in with me into this angry flood
And swim to yonder point?' Upon the word,
Accoutred as I was, I plunged in
And bade him follow. So indeed he did.
The torrent roared, and we did buffet it
With lusty sinews, throwing it aside
And stemming it with hearts of controversy.
But ere we could arrive the point propos'd,
Caesar cried, 'Help me, Cassius, or I sink!'
I, as Aeneas, our great ancestor,
Did from the flames of Troy upon his shoulder
The old Anchises bear, so from the waves of Tiber
Did I the tired Caesar. And this man
Is now become a god, and Cassius is
A wretched creature and must bend his body
If Caesar carelessly nod on him.
He had a fever when he was in Spain,
And when the fit was on him, I did mark
How he did shake. 'Tis true, this god did shake.
His coward lips did from their colour fly,
And that same eye whose bend doth awe the world
Did lose his luster. I did hear him groan.
Ay, and that tongue of his that bade the Romans
Mark him and write his speeches in their books,
'Alas,' it cried, 'give me some drink, Titinius,'
As a sick girl! Ye gods, it doth amaze me
A man of such a feeble temper should
So get the start of the majestic world
And bear the palm alone.

CROWD
(off-stage)

Hail Caesar!

BRUTUS

Another general shout?
I do believe that these applause are
For some new honours that are heaped upon Caesar.

CASSIUS

Why, man, he doth bestride the narrow world
Like a Colossus, and we petty men
Walk under his huge legs and peep about

To find ourselves dishonourable graves.
Men at some time are masters of their fates.
The fault, dear Brutus, is not in our stars,
But in ourselves, that we are underlings.
'Brutus' and 'Caesar.' What should be in that 'Caesar'?
Why should that name be sounded more than yours?
Write them together: yours is as fair a name.
Sound them: it doth become the mouth as well.
Now in the names of all the gods at once,
Upon what meat doth this our Caesar feed
That he is grown so great? Age, that art shamed.
Rome, thou hast lost the breed of noble bloods.
When went there by an age since the great Flood
But it was fam'd with more than with one man?
When could they say (till now) that talked of Rome
That her wide walks encompass'd but one man?

BRUTUS

That you do love me, I am nothing jealous.
What you would work me to, I have some aim.
How I have thought of this, and of these times,
I shall recount hereafter. For this present,
I would not so (with love I must entreat you)
Be any further moved.

(Fanfare off-stage.)

The games are done, and Caesar is returning.

(Enter Casca upstage right.)

CASSIUS

Casca.

CASCA

Would you speak with me?

CASSIUS

Ay, Casca. Tell us what hath chanced to-day.[16]

CASCA

Why, there was a crown offered Caesar; and being offered him, he put it by with the back of his hand thus; and then the people fell a-shouting.

BRUTUS

What was the second cry for?

CASCA

Why, for that too.

CASSIUS

They shouted thrice. What was the last cry for?

BRUTUS

Was the crown offer'd him thrice?

CASCA

Ay; and he put it by thrice, every time gentler than the other; and at every putting-by mine honest neighbours shouted.

CASSIUS

Who offered him the crown?

CASCA
(to Brutus)

Why, Antony.

CASSIUS

Tell us the manner of it.

CASCA

I can as well be hanged as tell.

(Cassius grabs Casca.)

It was mere foolery; I did not mark it. I saw Marc Antony offer him a crown—yet 'twas not a crown neither, 'twas one of those coronets—and, as I told you, he put it by once; but for all that, to my thinking, he would fain have had it. Then he offered it to him again; and then he put it by again; but to my thinking, he was very loath to lay his fingers off it. And then he offered it the third time. He put it the third time by; and still as he refused it, the rabblement hooted, and clapped their chopt hands, and uttered such a deal of stinking breath because Caesar refused the crown that it had, almost, choked Caesar; for he swounded and fell down at it. And for mine own part, I durst not laugh, for fear of opening my lips and receiving the bad air.

CASSIUS

But soft, I pray you. What, did Caesar swound?

CASCA

He fell down in the market place and foamed at the mouth and was speechless.

BRUTUS

'Tis very like: he hath the falling sickness.

CASSIUS

No, Caesar hath it not; but you, and I
And honest Casca, we have the falling sickness.

BRUTUS

What said he when he came unto himself?

CASCA

Before he fell down, when he preceived the common herd was glad he refused the crown, he offered them his throat to cut. An I had been a man of any occupation, if I would not have taken him at a word. And so he fell. When he came to himself again, he said, if he had done or said anything amiss, he desired them to think it was his infirmity. Three or four wenches where I stood cried, 'Alas, good soul!' and forgave him with all their hearts. But there's no heed to be taken of them. If Caesar had stabbed their mothers, they would have done no less.

CASSIUS

Did Cicero say anything?

CASCA

Ay, he spoke Greek.

CASSIUS

To what effect?

CASCA

Those that understood him smiled at one another and shook their heads; but for mine own part, it was Greek to me. I could tell you more news too: Marullus and Flavius, for pulling scarfs off Caesar's images, are put to silence. There was more foolery yet, if I could remember it.

BRUTUS

And so it is. For this time I will leave you.[17]
(to Cassius)
What have you said
I will consider; what you have to say
I will with patience hear, and find a time
Both meet to hear and answer such high things.
Till then, my noble friend, chew upon this:
Brutus had rather be a villager
Than to repute himself a son of Rome
Under these hard conditions as this time
Is like to lay upon us.[18]
Farewell both.[19]

(Exit Brutus.)

CASSIUS

Well, Brutus, thou art noble; yet I see
Thy honourable mettle may be wrought
From that it is disposed.

CASCA

Therefore it is meet
That noble minds keep ever with their likes;
For who so firm cannot be seduced?[20]

CASSIUS

If I were Brutus now and he were Cassius,
He should not humour me. I will this night,
In several hands, in at his windows throw,

As if they came from several citizens,
Writings, all tending to the great opinion
That Rome holds of his name; wherein obscurely
Caesar's ambition shall be glanc'd at . . .

(Enter Caesar, followed by Publius and Marc Antony.)

And after this let Caesar seat him sure.

*(Caesar stops his companions and slowly crosses down
to Cassius.)*

CAESAR

(looking directly at Cassius)

Marc Antony.[21]

ANTONY

(joining him)

Caesar?

CAESAR

Let me have men about me that are fat,
Sleek-headed men, and such as sleep a-nights.
Yond Cassius has a lean and hungry look.
He thinks too much; such men are dangerous.
He is a great observer, and he looks
Quite through the deeds of men. He loves no plays
As thou dost, Antony; he hears no music.
Seldom he smiles, and smiles in such a sort
As if he mocked himself and scorned his spirit
That could be moved to smile at anything.
Such men as he be never at heart's ease
Whiles they behold a greater than themselves,
And therefore are they very dangerous.

ANTONY

(laughing)

Fear him not, Caesar; he's not dangerous.

CAESAR

I had rather tell thee what is to be feared
Than what I fear; for always . . . I am Caesar.

*(Thunder. The lights wash out on a burst of lightning.
Thunder and darkness. Rain. A second burst of lightning
shows the stage to be empty.[22] Enter Cassius left in
darkness. Enter Cinna[23] down right with an electric
torch, which he shines upon Cassius as they speak. The
lights come up slightly on the apron.)*

CINNA

Who's there?[24]

CASSIUS

A Roman.

CINNA

Cassius by your voice.[25]

CASSIUS

Your ear is good.[26]
Good even, Cinna. Brought you Caesar home?[27]

CINNA

What night is this?[28]

CASSIUS

A very pleasing night to honest men.

CINNA

Are you not moved when all the sway of earth
Shakes like a thing unfirm? O Cassius,
I have seen tempests when the scolding winds
Have riv'd the knotty oaks, and I have seen
Th' ambitious ocean swell and rage and foam
To be exalted with the threat'ning clouds;
But never till to-night, never till now,
Did I go through a tempest dropping fire.[29]

CASSIUS

Why, saw you any thing more wonderful?[30]

CINNA

O there were drawn
Upon a heap a hundred ghastly women,
Transformed with their fear, who swore they saw
Men, all in fire, walk up and down the streets.
And yesterday the bird of night did sit
Even at noonday upon the market place,
Hooting and shrieking. When these prodigies
Do so conjointly meet, let not men say
'These are their reasons—they are natural.'[31]

CASSIUS

Indeed it is a strange-dispos'd time.[32]

CINNA

Who ever knew the heavens menace so?[33]

CASSIUS

Those that have known the earth so full of faults.
Now could I, Cinna, name to thee a man
Most like this dreadful night,
A man no mightier than thyself or me.

CINNA

'Tis Caesar that you mean. It is not, Cassius?[34]

CASSIUS

Those that with haste will make a mighty fire
Begin it with weak straws. What trash is Rome,
For the base matter to illuminate
So vile a thing as Caesar!

CINNA

They say the senators to-morrow
Mean to establish Caesar as a king,
And he shall wear his crown by sea and land
In every place save here in Italy.[35]

CASSIUS

I know where I will wear this dagger then.

CINNA

Hold my hand,
And I will set this foot of mine as far
As who goes farthest.[36]

CASSIUS

There's a bargain made.
Now know you, Cinna, I have moved already
Some certain of the noblest-minded Romans
To undergo with me an enterprise
Of honourable dangerous consequence.

(Enter Casca upstage through the darkness, running.[37])

CINNA

Stand close a while.[38]

CASSIUS

He is a friend.
(running after him)
Casca, where haste you so?

CASCA

To find you out. Who's that? Metellus Cimber?

CASSIUS

No, it is Cinna, one incorporate
To our attempts. Am I not stayed for, Casca?

CASCA
*(crossing down to Cinna and shaking
his hand)*
I am glad on't. What a fearful night is this!
There's two or three of us have seen strange sights.

CASSIUS

Am I not stay'd for? Tell me.

CASCA

Yes, you are.
O Cassius, if you could
But win the noble Brutus to our party—

CASSIUS

Be you content. Good Casca, take this paper
Where Brutus may but find it; and throw this
In at his window. Set this up with wax
Upon old Brutus' statue. All this done,
Repair to Pompey's Porch, where you shall find us.
Is Decius Brutus and Trebonius there?

CASCA

All but Metellus Cimber, and he's gone
To seek you at your house. Well, I will hie
And so bestow these papers as you bade me.

(Exit Casca.)

CASSIUS

Come, Cinna, you and I will yet ere day
See Brutus at his house. Three parts of him
Is ours already, and the man entire
Upon the next encounter yields him ours.

(Exit Cassius and Cinna into the darkness with the electric torch. The storm continues for a moment, then subsides. The lights come up to reveal Brutus alone on stage, reading letters.)

BRUTUS

  'Brutus, thou sleep'st. Awake, and see thyself!
  Shall Rome, &c. Speak, strike, redress!'[39]
'Brutus, thou sleep'st. Awake!'
Such investigations have been often dropp'd
Where I have took them up.
'Shall Rome, &c.' Thus must I piece it out:
Shall Rome stand under one man's awe? What, Rome?
My ancestors did from the streets of Rome
The Tarquin drive when he was called a king.[40]
It must be by his death; and for my part,
I know no personal cause to spurn at him,
But for the general. He would be crowned.
How that might change his nature, there's the question.
It is the bright day that brings forth the adder,
And craves wary walking. Crown him that,

And then I grant we put a sting in him
That at his will he may do danger with.
Th' abuse of greatness is, when it disjoins
Remorse from power. And to speak truth of Caesar,
I have not known when his affections swayed
More than his reason. But 'tis a common proof
That lowliness is young ambition's ladder,
Whereto the climber upward turns his face;
But when he once attains the upmost round,
He then unto the ladder turns his back,
Looks into the clouds, scorning the base degrees
By which he did ascend. So Caesar may.
Then lest he may, prevent.[41]

(Enter Portia.)

PORTIA

Brutus, my lord.

BRUTUS

Portia! What mean you? Wherefore rise you now?
It is not for your health thus to commit
Your weak condition to the raw morning.

PORTIA

Nor for yours neither. Y' have ungently, Brutus,
Stole from my bed. And yesternight at supper
You suddenly arose and walked about,
Musing and sighing with your arms across;
And when I asked you what the matter was,
You stared upon me with ungentle looks,
And with an angry wafter of your hand,
Gave sign for me to leave you. So I did,
Hoping it was but an effect of humour,
Which sometimes hath its hour with every man.
It will not let you eat nor talk nor sleep,
And could it work so much upon your condition,
I should not know you Brutus. Dear my lord,
Make me acquainted with your cause of grief.

BRUTUS

I am not well in health, and that is all.

PORTIA

Brutus is wise and, were he not in health,
He would embrace the means to come by it.

BRUTUS

Why so I do.

PORTIA

Is Brutus sick?
And will he steal out of his wholesome bed
To dare the vile contagion of the night,
And tempt the rheumy and unpurg'd air,
To add to his sickness? No, my Brutus.
You have some sick offense within your mind,
Which by the right and virtue of my place
I ought to know of.

BRUTUS

Gentle Portia.

PORTIA

Is it expected I should know no secrets
That appertain to you? Am I your self
But, as it were, in sort or limitation?
To keep with you at meals, comfort your bed,
And talk to you sometimes? If it be no more,
Portia is Brutus' harlot, not his wife.

BRUTUS

You are my true and honourable wife,
As dear to me as are the ruddy drops
That visit my sad heart.

PORTIA

If this were true, then should I know this secret.
I grant I am a woman; but withal
A woman that Lord Brutus took to wife,
A woman well-reputed, Cato's daughter.
Think you I am no stronger than my sex,
Being so fathered and so husbanded?
Tell me your counsels; I will not disclose 'em.

(The sound of knocking.)

BRUTUS

Hark! One knocks. Portia, go in awhile,
And by and by thy bosom shall partake
The secrets of my heart.
All my engagements I will construe to thee,
All the charactery of my sad brows.
Leave me with haste.

(Exit Portia. More knocking. Enter Lucius.)

BRUTUS

Go to the gate. Somebody knocks.[42]

LUCIUS

Sir, 'tis your brother Cassius.

BRUTUS

Is he alone?

LUCIUS

No, sir, there are moe with him.

BRUTUS

Do you know them?

LUCIUS

No, sir. Their hats are plucked about their ears,
That by no means I may discover them
By any mark of favour.

BRUTUS

Let 'em enter.

(Exit Lucius.)

Between the acting of a dreadful thing
And the first motion, all the interim is
Like a phantasma or a hideous dream.
The genius and the mortal instruments
Are then in council, and the state of a man,
Like to a little kingdom, suffers then
The nature of an insurrection.

(Enter Lucius with the conspirators: Cassius, Casca, Decius, Cinna, Metellus Cimber, and Trebonius.)

BRUTUS

(to Lucius)

Get you to bed again; it is not yet day.[43]

(Exit Lucius.)

CASSIUS

I think we are too bold upon your rest.
Good morrow, Brutus. Do we trouble you?

BRUTUS

I have been up this hour, awake all night.
Know I these men that come along with you?

CASSIUS

Yes, every man of them; and no man here
But honours you; and every one doth wish
You had but that opinion of yourself
Which every noble Roman bears of you.

(pauses)

This is Trebonius.

BRUTUS

He is welcome hither.

CASSIUS

This, Metellus Cimber.

BRUTUS

He is welcome too.

CASSIUS

This, Casca; this, Cinna; and this is Decius Brutus.

BRUTUS

They are all welcome.

CASSIUS

(to Brutus)

Shall I entreat a word?

(A long pause as they stand to one side whispering.)

DECIUS

Here lies the east. Doth not the day break here?

CASCA

(watching Brutus and Cassius)

No.

CINNA

O, pardon, sir, it doth; and yon grey lines
That fret the clouds are messengers of day.

BRUTUS

(crossing to them)

Give me your hands all over, one by one.

CASSIUS

And let us swear our resolution.

BRUTUS

No, not an oath. If not the face of men,
The sufference of our souls, the time's abuse—
If these be motives weak, break off betimes,
And every man hence to his idle bed.
So let high-sighted tyranny range on
Till each man drop by lottery. But if these
(As I am sure they do) bear fire enough
To kindle cowards and to steel with valour
The melting spirits of women, then, countrymen,
What need we any spur but our own cause
To prick us to redress? what other bond
Than secret Romans that have spoke the word
And will not palter? and what other oath
Than honesty to honesty engaged
That this shall be, or we will fall for it?
Swear priests and cowards and men cautelous,

Old feeble carrions and such suffering souls
That welcome wrongs; unto bad causes swear
Such creatures as men doubt; but do not strain
The even virtue of our enterprise,
Nor th' insuppressive mettle of our spirits,
To think that or our cause or our performance
Did need an oath; when every drop of blood
That every Roman bears, and nobly bears,
Is guilty of a several bastardy
If he do break the smallest particle
Of any promise that hath passed from him.

CASSIUS

But what of Cicero? Shall we sound him?
I think he will stand very strong with us.

TREBONIUS

Let us not leave him out.[44]

METELLUS

No, by no means.[45]

CASCA

O, let us have him, for his silver hairs
Will purchase us a good opinion
And buy men's voices to commend our deeds.[46]

BRUTUS

O, name him not.
For he will never follow anything
That other men begin.

CASSIUS

Then leave him out.

CASCA

Indeed he is not fit.

DECIUS

Shall no man else be touched but only Caesar?

CASSIUS

Decius, well urged. I think it is not meet
Marc Antony, so well beloved of Caesar,
Should outlive Caesar. We shall find of him
A shrewd contriver; and you know, his means,
If he improve them, may well stretch so far
As to annoy us all; which to prevent,
Let Antony and Caesar fall together.

BRUTUS

Our course will seem too bloody, Caius Cassius,

To cut the head off and then hack the limbs;
For Antony is but a limb of Caesar.
Let us be sacrificers, but not butchers, Caius.
We all stand up against the spirit of Caesar,
And in the spirit of men there is no blood.
O that we then could come by Caesar's spirit
And not dismember Caesar! But, alas,
Caesar must bleed for it. And, gentle friends,
Let's kill him boldly, but not wrathfully;
Let's carve him as a dish fit for the gods,
Not hew him as a carcass fit for hounds.
And for Marc Antony, think not of him;
For he can do no more than Caesar's arm
When Caesar's head is off.

CASSIUS

Yet I fear him;
For in the ingrated love he bears to Caesar—

BRUTUS

Alas, good Cassius, do not think of him!
If he love Caesar, all that he can do
Is to himself—take thought, and die for Caesar.
And that were much he should; for he is given
To sports, to wildness, and much company.

TREBONIUS

There is no fear in him. Let him not die;
For he will live, and laugh at this hereafter.

(Clock strikes.)

DECIUS

Peace![47]

CINNA

Count the clock.[48]

CASCA

The clock hath stricken three.[49]

DECIUS

'Tis time to part.[50]

CASSIUS

But it is doubtful yet
Whether Caesar will come forth to-day or no;
For he is superstitious grown of late.
It may be these apparent prodigies
May hold him from the Capitol to-day.

DECIUS

Never fear that. If he be so resolved,
Let me work;
For I can give his humour the true bent,
And I will bring him to the Capitol.

CASSIUS

Nay, we will all of us be there to fetch him.

BRUTUS

By the eight hour. Is that the uttermost?

DECIUS

Be that the uttermost, and fail not then.[51]

*(He starts to exit left but stops upon seeing Ligarius
enter, followed by Lucius.)*

LUCIUS

Here is a sick man that would speak with you.

*(Brutus crosses to Ligarius to shake his hand. Lucius
exits. Metellus whispers to Cassius.)*

CINNA

Caius Ligarius.

LIGARIUS

I am not sick if Brutus have in hand
Any exploit worthy the name of honour.

BRUTUS

Such an exploit have I in hand, Ligarius,
Had you a healthful ear to hear of it.

LIGARIUS

By all the gods that Romans bow before,
I here discard my sickness; now bid me run,
And I will strive with things impossible;
Yea, get the better of them. What's to do?

CASSIUS

A piece of work that will make sick men whole.[52]

LIGARIUS

But are not some whole that we must make sick?

BRUTUS

That must we also.

LIGARIUS

Set on your foot,
And with a heart new-fired I follow you,
To do I know not what; but it sufficeth
That Brutus leads me on.

BRUTUS

Follow me then.

> *(Exit Brutus followed by the others. The lights wash out.
> A clock strikes eight in the darkness. The lights come
> up to reveal Caesar alone on stage.)*

CAESAR

Nor heaven nor earth have been at peace to-night.
Thrice hath Calphurnia in her sleep cried out
'Help, ho! They murder Caesar!'

> *(Enter Calphurnia.)*

Who's within?

CALPHURNIA

What means you, Caesar? Think you to walk forth?
You shall not stir out of your house to-day.

CAESAR

Caesar shall forth. The things that threatened me
Ne'er looked but on my back. When they shall see
The face of Caesar, they are vanish'd.

CALPHURNIA

Caesar, I never stood on ceremonies,
Yet now they fright me. There is one within
Recounts most horrid sights seen by the watch.
A lioness hath whelp'd in the streets,
And graves have yawned and yielded up their dead.
Fierce fiery warriors fought upon the clouds
In ranks and squadrons and right form of war,
Which drizzled blood upon the Capitol.
The noise of battle hurtled in the air,
Horses did neigh, and dying men did groan,
And ghosts did shriek and squeal about the streets.
O Caesar, these things are beyond all use,
And I do fear them.

CAESAR

What can be avoided
Whose end is purposed by the mighty gods?
Yet Caesar shall go forth; for these predictions
Are to the world in general as to Caesar.

CALPHURNIA

When beggars die there are no comets seen;
The heavens themselves blaze forth the death of princes.

CAESAR

Cowards die many times before their deaths;
The valiant never taste of death but once.

Of all the wonders that I yet have heard,
It seems to me most strange that men should fear,
Seeing that death, a necessary end,
Will come when it will come.

CALPHURNIA

Do not go forth to-day! Call it my fear
That keeps you in the house and not your own.
We'll send Marc Antony to the Senate House,
And he shall say that you are not well to-day.

CAESAR

Marc Antony shall say I am not well,
And for thy humour I will stay at home.
(Enter Decius.)
Here's Decius Brutus; he shall tell them so.

DECIUS

Caesar, all hail! Good morrow, worthy Caesar;
I come to fetch you to the Senate House.

CAESAR

And you come in very happy time
To bear my greetings to the senators
And tell them that I will not come to-day.
Cannot is false; and that I dare not, falser:
I will not come to-day. Tell them so, Decius.

CALPHURNIA

Say he is sick.

CAESAR

Shall Caesar send a lie?
Have I in conquest stretched mine arm so far
To be afeared to tell greybeards the truth?
Decius, go tell them Caesar will not come.

DECIUS

Most mighty Caesar, let me know some cause,
Lest I be laughed at when I tell them so.

CAESAR

The cause is my will: I will not come.
That is enough to satisfy the Senate;
But for your private satisfaction,
Because I love you, I will let you know.
Calphurnia here, my wife, stays me at home.
She dreamt to-night she saw my statue,
Which, like a fountain with a hundred spouts,
Did run pure blood; and many lusty Romans
Came smiling and did bathe their hands in it.

And these does she apply for warnings and portents
And evil imminent, and on her knee
Hath begged that I will stay at home to-day.

DECIUS

This dream is all amiss interpreted;
It was a vision fair and fortunate.
Your statue spouting blood in many pipes,
In which so many smiling Romans bathed,
Signifies that from you great Rome shall suck
Reviving blood, and that great men shall press
For tinctures, stains, relics and cognizance.
This is by Calphurnia's dream is signified.

CAESAR

And this way have you well expounded it.

DECIUS

I have, when you have heard what I can say;
And know it now. The Senate has concluded
To give this day a crown to mighty Caesar.
If you shall send them word you will not come,
Their minds may change. Besides, if it were a mock
Apt to be rendered, for some one to say
'Break up the Senate till another time,
When Caesar's wife shall meet with better dreams.'
If Caesar hide himself, shall they not whisper
'Lo, Caesar is afraid'?
Pardon me, Caesar; for my dear dear love
To your proceedings bids me tell you this,
And reason to my love is liable.

CAESAR

How foolish do your fears seem now, Calphurnia!
I am ashamed I did yield to them.

(Exit Calphurnia. Enter Brutus.)

What, Brutus, are you stirred so early too?

(Enter Casca.)

Good morrow, Casca.

(Enter Trebonius.)

What, Trebonius?

(Enter Cinna and Metellus.)

Now, Cinna! Now, Metellus!
What is't o'clock?

(Enter Ligarius.)

LIGARIUS

Caesar, 'tis strucken eight.[53]

CAESAR

Caius Ligarius!
Caesar was ne'er so much your enemy
As that same ague.

(Enter Antony.)

See, Antony, that revels long a-nights,
Is notwithstanding up. Good morrow, Antony.

ANTONY

So to most noble Caesar.

CAESAR
(turning back to Ligarius)

I have an hour's talk in store for you;
Remember that you call on me to-day;
Be near me, that I may remember you.

(Caesar starts off with Antony and the others.)

LIGARIUS
(lingering behind)

Caesar, I will.
(to Trebonius; aside)
And so near will I be
That your best friends shall wish I had been further.

(The stage is left empty. Then enter Artemidorus, reading a paper.)

ARTEMIDORUS

'Caesar, beware of Brutus; take heed of Cassius; come not near Casca; have an eye to Cinna; trust not Trebonius; mark well Metellus Cimber; Decius Brutus loves thee not; thou hast wronged Caius Ligarius. There is but one mind in all these men, and it is bent against Caesar. Look about you.

'Thy lover,

'Artemidorus.'

If thou read this, O Caesar, thou mayest live.

(Fanfare. Enter mob; then Caesar, Brutus, Cassius, Casca, Decius, Ligarius, Publius,[54] Antony, Cinna, Trebonius, and Metellus Cimber.)

ALL

Hail, Caesar![55]

VOICE

Caesar![56]

(Silence.)

CAESAR

The ides of March are come.[57]

VOICE

Ay, Caesar, but not gone.

ARTEMIDORUS

Caesar! Read this schedule.

DECIUS

Trebonius doth desire you to o'er-read
(At your best leisure) this his humble suit.

PUBLIUS	CAESAR
(to Cassius)	*(low)*
I wish your enterprise to-day may thrive.[58]	What touches us ourselves shall be last served.[59]

ARTEMIDORUS

O Caesar, read mine first; for mine's a suit
That touches Caesar nearer. Delay not, Caesar!

CASSIUS	DECIUS
What enterprise?	*(low)*
	Trebonius sues for an immediate repeal.[60]

ARTEMIDORUS

Read it instantly!

DECIUS

What, is the fellow mad?[61]

METELLUS

Sirrah![62]

DECIUS

Give place!

(Artemidorus is rushed off left by Cinna and Metellus.)

CASSIUS

Publius!

PUBLIUS
(crossing to Caesar)

Fare you well.

Cinna re-enters and crosses to Cassius.)

CINNA

What said Publius?[63]

CASSIUS

He wished our enterprise might thrive.
I fear our purpose is discover'd.

DECIUS

Look how he makes to Caesar.[64]

CASCA

Mark him.

CASSIUS

Casca, be sudden, for we fear prevention.
Brutus, what shall be done? If this be known,
Cassius or Caesar never shall turn back,
For I will slay myself.

BRUTUS

Cassius, be constant.
For look, he smiles, and Caesar doth not change.

CASSIUS

Trebonius knows his time; for look you, Brutus,
He draws Marc Antony out of the way.

(Exit Antony and Trebonius.)

DECIUS

Young Cinna! Let him go
And presently prefer his suit to Caesar.

CINNA

Most high, most mighty, most puissant Caesar![65]

BRUTUS

(to Cassius)

He is addressed.

CINNA

Thy servant Cinna throws before thy seat
An humble heart—[66]

CAESAR

Be not fond
To think that Caesar bears such rebel blood
That will be thawed from the true quality
With that which melteth fools.

BRUTUS

(to Cassius)

Press near and second him.

CAESAR

I mean, sweet words,
Low-crook'd curtsies, and base spaniel fawning.
Thy brother by decree is banish'd.
If thou dost bend and pray and fawn for him,
I spurn thee like a cur out of my way.

Know, Caesar doth not wrong, nor without cause
Will he be satisfied.

CINNA

Is there no voice more worthy than my own,
To sound more sweetly in great Caesar's ear
For the repealing of my banished brother?[67]

CASSIUS

(moving toward Caesar)

Pardon, Caesar! Caesar, pardon!

CAESAR

I could be well moved, if I were as you;
If I could pray to move, prayers would move me:
But I am constant as the Northern Star,
Of whose true-fixed and resting quality
There is no fellow in the firmament.
The skies are painted with unnumb'red sparks,
They are all fire, and every one doth shine;
But there's but one in all doth hold his place.
So in the world: 'tis furnished well with men,
And men are flesh and blood, and apprehensive;
Yet in the number I do not know but one
That unassailable holds on his rank,
Unshaked of motion; and that I am he.

CINNA

O Caesar.

CAESAR

Hence! Wilt thou lift up Olympus?

DECIUS

Great Caesar!

CASCA

Speak hands for me!

(One by one, they stab Caesar, who falls into Brutus' arms.)[68]

CAESAR

Et tu, Brute? Then fall Caesar.

(He dies.)

BRUTUS

Liberty!

DECIUS

Freedom!

(Enter Metellus.)

CINNA

Tyranny is dead!

CASSIUS

Run hence, proclaim, cry it about the streets![69]

LIGARIUS

(starting off)

Peace! Freedom! Liberty!

DECIUS

Some to the common pulpits and cry out
'Liberty, freedom, and enfranchisement!'[70]

LIGARIUS

(off-stage)

Peace! Freedom! Liberty!

METELLUS

Stand fast together, lest some friend of Caesar's
Should chance—

CASSIUS

Talk not of standing! Publius, good cheer.
There is no harm intended to your person
Nor to no Roman else. So tell them, Publius.[71]

(Exit Publius.)

DECIUS

Go to the pulpit, Brutus.

CINNA

And Cassius too.

PUBLIUS

(off-stage)

Be not affrighted! Tyranny is dead![72]

DECIUS

Where's Publius?

(Enter Trebonius.)

TREBONIUS

Men, wives, and children stare, cry out, and run,
As it were doomsday.

PUBLIUS

(off-stage)

Tyranny is dead!

LIGARIUS

(far off-stage)

Peace, freedom, liberty! Freedom . . . liberty . . .

ALLAND[73]

(off-stage)

Freedom!

BRUTUS

How many ages hence
Shall this our lofty scene be acted over
In states unborn and accents yet unknown![74]
How many times shall Caesar bleed in sport,
That now on Pompey's basis lies along
No worthier than the dust!

CASSIUS

So oft as that shall be,
So often shall the knot of us be called
The men that gave their country liberty.

CINNA

What, shall we forth?[75]

CASSIUS

Ay, every man away.
Brutus shall lead.

(Enter Antony.)

DECIUS

Here comes Marc Antony.[76]

CASSIUS

Welcome, Marc Antony.[77]

ANTONY

I know not, gentlemen, what you intend,
Who else must be let blood, who else is rank.
If I myself, there is no hour so fit.
I do beseech ye, if you bear me hard,
Now, while your purpled hands do reek and smoke,
Fulfil your pleasure. Live a thousand years,
I shall not find myself so apt to die
As here by Caesar, and by you cut off,
The choice and master spirits of this age.

BRUTUS

O Antony, beg not your death of us!

CASSIUS

Your voice shall be as strong as any man's
In the disposing of new dignities.

BRUTUS

Only be patient till we have appeased
The multitude, beside themselves with fear,

And then, reasons will be given you[78]
Why I, that did love Caesar when I struck him,
Have thus proceeded.

ANTONY

I doubt not of your wisdom.
Let each man render me his bloody hand.
First, Marcus Brutus, will I shake with you;
Next, Caius Cassius, do I take your hand;
Now, Decius, yours; now yours, Metellus;
Yours, Cinna; and, my valiant Casca, yours;
Though last, not least in love, yours, good Trebonius.

CASSIUS

But what compact mean you to have with us?
Will you be pricked in number of our friends?

ANTONY

Friends am I with you all, and love you all,
Upon this hope, that you shall give me reasons
Why and wherein Caesar was dangerous.

TREBONIUS

Our reasons are so full of good regard
That were you, Antony, the son of Caesar,
You should be satisfied.[79]

ANTONY

That's all I seek;
And am moreover suitor that I may
Produce his body to the market-place
And in the pulpit, as becomes a friend,
Speak in the order of his funeral.

BRUTUS

You shall, Marc Antony.

CASSIUS

Brutus, a word with you.

(Aside; to Brutus)

You know not what you do. Do not consent
That Antony speak in his funeral.

CASCA

Know you how much the people may be moved
By that which he will utter?[80]

BRUTUS

By your pardon—
I will myself into the pulpit first.
Marc Antony, here, take you Caesar's body.

You shall not in your funeral speech blame us,
But speak all good you can devise of Caesar;
And say you do't by our permission.
Else shall you not have any hand at all
About his funeral. And you shall speak
In the same pulpit whereto I am going,
After my speech is ended.

ANTONY

Be it so; I do desire no more.

BRUTUS

Prepare the body then, and follow us.

(Exit Brutus and the other. Antony is alone.)

ANTONY

O mighty Caesar! dost thou lie so low?
Are all thy conquests, glories, triumphs, spoils,
Shrunk to this little measure?[81]
That I did love thee, Caesar, O, 'tis true!
If then thy spirit look upon us now,
Shall it not grieve thee dearer than thy death
To see thy Antony making his peace,
Shaking the bloody hands of thy foes,
Most noble! in the presence of thy corse?
Had I as many eyes as thou hast wounds,
Weeping as fast as they stream forth thy blood,
It would become me better than to close
In terms of friendship with thine enemies.
O, pardon me, thou bleeding piece of earth,
That I am meek and gentle with these butchers!
Thou art the ruins of the noblest man
That ever liv'd in the tide of times.
Woe to the hand that shed this costly blood!
Over thy wounds now do I prophesy
(Which, like dumb shows, do ope their ruby lips
To beg the voice and utterance of my tongue),
A curse shall light upon the limbs of men;
Domestic fury and fierce civil strife
Shall cumber all the parts of Italy;
Blood and destruction shall be so in use,
And dreadful objects so familiar,
That mothers shall but smile when they behold
Their infants quarter'd with the hands of war;
And Caesar's spirit, ranging for revenge,
With Atè by his side come hot from hell,

Shall in these confines with a monarch's voice
Cry 'Havoc!' and let slip the dogs of war.

> *(Black out. Antony off with Caesar's body. Brutus, Cassius, and the mob[82] enter in the darkness. The lights come up to reveal them, and a high, wooden pulpit positioned upstage center.)*

WILLARD	MOWRY	SHERMAN
We will be satisfied!	Let us be satisfied!	We will be satisfied!

CASSIUS

Then follow me and give me audience, friends.
And public reasons shall be render'd
Of Caesar's death.[83]

BRUTUS

Those that will hear me speak, let 'em stay here;
Those that will follow Cassius, go with him.

> *(Exit Cassius. Brutus ascends to the pulpit.)*

MOWRY

I will hear Brutus speak.

REID	COTTEN
I will hear Cassius, and compare their reasons.	I will hear Cassius!

CASSIUS

(off-stage)

People and senators, be not affrighted.
Fly not; stand still. Ambition's debt is paid.[84]

SCHNABEL

The noble Brutus is ascended.[85]

DUTHRIE

Silence!

BRUTUS[86]

Be patient till the last.

Romans, countrymen, and lovers, hear me for my cause, and be silent, that you may hear. Believe me for mine honour, and have respect to mine honour, that you may believe. Censure me in your wisdom, and awake your senses, that you may the better judge. If there be any in this assembly, any dear friend of Caesar's, to him I say that Brutus' love to Caesar was no less than his. If then that friend demand why Brutus arose against Caesar, this is my answer: not that I loved Caesar less, but that I loved Rome more. Had you rather Caesar were living, and die all slaves, than that Caesar were dead, to live all freemen? As Caesar loved me, I weep for him; as he was fortunate, I rejoice at it; as he was valiant, I honour him; but—as he was ambitious, I slew him. There is tears for his love; joy for his fortune; honour for his valour; and death for his ambition. Who is here so base that would be a bondman? If any, speak; for him have I offended. Who is here so vile that will not love his country? If any, speak; for him have I offended. I pause for a reply.

WILLARD

None, Brutus!

SHERMAN
None!

MOWRY
None!

DUTHIE
None!

COTTEN
None!

REID
None!

BRUTUS

Then none have I offended.

(Enter Antony with an escort of storm troupers carrying Caesar's body.)

Here comes his body, mourned by Marc Antony, who, though he had no hand in his death, shall receive the benefit of his dying, a place in the commonwealth, as which of you shall not? Good countrymen, let me depart alone, And, for my sake, stay here with Antony. Do grace to Caesar's corpse, and grace his speech. Tending to Caesar's glories which Marc Antony, By our permission, is allowed to make. With this I depart, that, as I slew my best lover for the good of Rome, I have the same dagger for myself when it shall please my country to need my death.

(Exit Brutus. The mob shifts uneasily.)

ANTONY

For Brutus' sake I am beholding to you.

SHERMAN
(low)

What does he say of Brutus?

BURGESS

He says for Brutus' sake
He finds himself beholding to us all.

MOWRY

For Brutus' sake.

WILLARD

'Twere best he speak no harm of Brutus here!

REID

This Caesar was a tyrant.

(Murmurings and low ad-libs.)

SCHNABEL

We are blest that Rome is rid of him!

MOWRY

Nay, that's certain.

DUTHIE

Caesar was a tyrant!

COTTEN

A tyrant.

SHERMAN

Peace!

REID

Peace!

ANTONY

You gentle Romans—

SHERMAN

Peace! Let us hear what Antony can say.

ALLAND

'Twere best he speak no harm of Brutus!

COTTEN

Caesar!

BURGESS

Gentle Romans!

MOWRY

Caesar was a tyrant!

SCHNABEL

Antony!

ANTONY

Friends—

REID

Friends?

WILLARD

Ay, 'twere best he speak—

ANTONY

(stopping them)

Romans, countrymen . . .

(Murmurs from the mob.)

. . . lend me your ears.

SHERMAN

Let us hear what Antony can say.

ANTONY

I come to bury Caesar, not to praise him.
The evil that men do lives after them;
The good is often interr'd with their bones.
So let it be with Caesar. The noble Brutus
Hath told you Caesar was ambitious.
If it were so, it was a grievous fault,

And grievously hath Caesar answered it.
Here under leave of Brutus and the rest
(For Brutus is an honourable man;
So are they all, all honourable men),
Come I to speak in Caesar's funeral.
He was my friend, faithful and just to me;
But Brutus says he was ambitious,
And Brutus is an honourable man.
He hath brought many captives home to Rome,
Whose ransoms did the general coffers fill.
Did this in Caesar seem ambitious?
When that the poor have cried, Caesar hath wept;
Ambition should be made of sterner stuff.
Yet Brutus says he was ambitious;
And Brutus is an honourable man.
You all did see that on the Lupercal
I thrice presented him a kingly crown,
Which he did thrice refuse.

(Loud murmuring.)

Was this ambition?
Yet Brutus says he was ambitious;

(Murmurs stop.)

And sure he is an honourable man.

(Low murmuring.)

I speak not to disprove what Brutus spoke,
But here I am to speak what I do know.

(Murmurs stop.)

You all did love him once, not without cause.
What cause withholds you then to mourn for him?
O judgment, thou art fled to brutish beasts,
And men have lost their reason! Bear with me.
My heart is in the coffin there with Caesar,
And I must pause till it come back to me.

SCHNABEL

Methinks there is much reason in his sayings.

(Background.)

LLOYD

If thou consider rightly of the matter,
   Caesar has had great wrong.

CARPENTER[87]

Methinks there's much reason.

WILLARD

I fear there will be a worse come in
   his place.

SCHNABEL

There's not a nobler man than
   Brutus.

ALLAND

There's much truth indeed.

SHERMAN
Mark'd ye his words?

BURGESS
He would not take the
crown.

MOWRY
Indeed, we must
consider rightly.

ALLAND
He would not take the crown!

REID
There's much in what he says.

COTTEN
We must consider rightly of what he
says.[88]

SCHNABEL
Therefore 'tis certain he was not ambitious.

WILLARD
If it be found so, some
will dear abide it.

LLOYD
He would not take the
crown; therefore, it
is certain he was not
ambitious.

REID
Poor Antony!

COTTEN
Look—Marc Antony is weeping.

DUTHIE
(big)
There's not a nobler man in Rome
than Antony.

ALLAND
Ay, if it be found so.

BURGESS
Some will dear abide it, if it be
found so.

(Andante.)

SHERMAN
Poor soul! his eyes are red as fire with weeping.

SCHNABEL
Marc Antony would
speak again

COTTEN
He's weeping.

ALLAND
Marc Antony
is weeping.

CARPENTER
See Marc Anthony!

MOWRY
Mark him!

LLOYD
He begins again to
speak.

REID
Peace.

COTTEN
Sssssh.

SHERMAN
Silence!

WILLARD
(low)
Antony.

DUTHRIE &
ALLAND
(low)
Peace.

MOWRY/COTTEN
Ssssssh.

REID
Sssssh.

SCHNABEL
Ssssh!

REID
(in a whisper)
Mark him.

ANTONY
But yesterday, the word of Caesar might
Have stood against the world. Now lies he there,
And none so poor do him reverence.
O masters, if I were disposed to stir
Your hearts and minds to mutiny and rage,
I should do Brutus wrong, and Cassius wrong,
Who (you all know) are honourable men.
I will not do them wrong. I rather choose
To wrong the dead, to wrong myself and you,
Than I should wrong such honourable men.
(Pause.)
But here's a parchment, with the seal of Caesar,
I found it in his closet, 'tis his will.
Let but the commons hear this testament
Which (pardon me) I do not mean to read,
And they would go and kiss dead Caesar's wounds
And dip their napkins in his sacred blood;
Yea, beg a hair of him for memory,
And dying, mention it in their wills,
Bequeathing it as a rich legacy   SHERMAN
Unto their issue.   Legacy?

LLOYD
Let's hear this testament of Caesar's.[89]

WILLARD
Read us the will, Marc Antony.

DUTHIE
Caesar's will?

SCHNABEL
Let's hear this will of Caesar's!

ALLAND
Read it, Marc Antony.
SHERMAN
(loud)
The testament!
COTTEN   BURGESS/MOWRY
(loud and slow)   The testament! The testament!
Read us the will.   REID
Yes, the testament!

ANTONY
(stopping them)
Have patience, gentle friends, I must not read it.
It is not meet you know how Caesar loved you.
You are not wood, you are not stones, but men;
And being men, hearing the will of Caesar,
It will inflame you, it will make you mad.

SCHNABEL
Yes, Antony!

(Murmurs.)

'Tis good you know not that you are his heirs.

(Murmuring stops.)

SHERMAN	LLOYD & ALLAND	SCHNABEL
(in low whisper)	*(low whisper)*	*(low whisper)*
We, Caesar's heirs?[90]	Caesar's heirs?	What does he mean?[91]

ANTONY
For if you should know, O what would come of it?

ALLAND
(low but intense)
Let's hear the will.

REID
The will!

CARPENTER
Yes, let's hear the will.

WILLARD
The will.

SHERMAN	COTTEN
(loud)	We'll hear the will.
Yes, we are men.[92]	

LLOYD
Read us the will, Marc Antony.

DUTHIE
We'll hear the will.

BURGESS
(loud; not too fast)
The will! The will!

MOWRY
The will!

SCHNABEL
Read us the will!

REID
(a loud call)
We will hear Caesar's will.

(Loud murmurs from the mob.)

ANTONY

Will you be patient?

(A long pause.)

SCHNABEL

(a loud call)

Read it, Marc Antony!

MOWRY

The will.

LLOYD

Read us the will. We'll hear the will.

WILLARD	BURGESS
(loud)	*(loud)*
Read us the will!	Testament!

SHERMAN

Read it!

ANTONY

Will you stay awhile?
I have o'ershot myself to tell you of it.
I fear I wrong the honourable men,
Whose daggers have stabbed Caesar; I do fear it.

SHERMAN	WILLARD	REID
Honourable men!	Murderers!	Honourable men.

MOWRY	SCHNABEL
Traitors!	Villains!

COTTEN

The testament, read us the testament.

LLOYD

Read us the will!

(A chant starts.)

ALLAND

The will!

MOWRY	REID & SHERMAN
The will.	*(at a faster tempo)*
	The will, the will, the will.

COTTEN

The will.

DUTHRIE

The will.

(They chant together, in unison, stomping their feet.)

ALL

The will! The will! The will!

SCHNABEL   ALLAND/LLOYD/CARPENTER
(big; stopping the chant)   *(slower and louder)*
Read us the will.   Read us the will!

MOWRY

Let's hear the will!

WILLARD

Marc Antony.

ANTONY
(stopping them with a gesture)
You will compel me then to read the will?

BIRD[93]

Yes, Antony.
ALLAND

The testament.
WILLARD/DUTHRIE

The will.
SHERMAN

Yes, read it.
REID

Yes, Antony.

ANTONY

Then make a ring around the corpse of Caesar,
And let me show you him that made the will.
Shall I descend? And will you give me leave?

SCHNABEL

Come down.

WILLARD

Descend.

SHERMAN

You shall have leave.

(Antony descends from the pulpit.)

SCHNABEL

Room for Antony. Room.

LLOYD   SHERMAN
(soft)   *(loud)*
Peace.   Most noble Antony.

BIRD   WILLARD/REID/CARPENTER
(low)   Ssssssss.
Silence.

ALLAND

A ring, stand round.

DUTHRIE
(low)

Stand from the hearse.

LLOYD

Room for Antony.

BURGESS   WILLARD

Room.   Stand from the body.

CARPENTER

Make room.

SHERMAN

Bear back.

REID   SCHNABEL

Room for Antony.   Stand back.

ANTONY

If you have tears, prepare to shed them now.
You all do know this mantle, I remember
The first time ever Caesar put it on;
'Twas on a summer's evening in his tent,
That day he overcame the Nervii.
Look, in this place ran Cassius' dagger through.
See what a rent the envious Casca made.
Through this, the well-beloved Brutus stabbed.
And as he plucked his cursed steel away,
Mark how the blood of Caesar followed it,
As rushing out of doors, to be resolved
If Brutus so unkindly knocked, or no;
For Brutus, as you know, was Caesar's angel.
Judge, O you gods, how dearly Caesar loved him.
This was the most unkindest cut of all;
For when the noble Caesar saw him stab,
Ingratitude, more strong than traitors' arms,
Quite vanquished him. Then burst his mighty heart,
And in his mantle muffling up his face,
Even at the base of Pompey's statue,
(Which all the while ran blood), great Caesar fell.
O what a fall was there, my countrymen!
Then I, and you, and all of us fell down,
Whilst bloody treason flourished over us.
O now you weep, and I perceive you feel
The dint of pity. These are gracious drops.
Kind souls, what weep you, when you but behold
Our Caesar's vesture wounded? Look you here,
Here is himself, married as you see with traitors.

(He pulls the coat from the corpse.)

REID	MOWRY	ALLAND
(high scream)	Caesar!	Caesar!

BIRD
O woeful day!

SHERMAN
Noble Caesar! Bloody, bloody, bloody!

DUTHRIE	CARPENTER
(slowly)	*(slowly)*
O piteous spectacle!	Bloody!

LLOYD	WILLARD
O most bloody, bloody!	Blood!

ALLAND
(accelerating)
O villains!

BIRD	SCHNABEL
They were all traitors.	O traitors!

DUTHRIE/MOWRY/REID
O traitors!

(Antony falls to his knees beside the body. A long pause.)

SHERMAN
(whisper)
Revenge!

REID
(whisper)
Revenge!

ALLAND
(short and quick)
Revenge!

SCHNABEL
(whisper)
Revenge!

WILLARD
We will be revenged.

LLOYD
(low but very intense)
Vengeance!

MOWRY
Vengeance!

COTTEN	DUTHRIE
Revenge, revenge, revenge!	Vengeance!

WILLARD	SHERMAN
Revenge! Revenge!	*(loud)*
	Vengeance!

REID
(loud)

We will be revenged.

(Antony rises and all are silent.)

ANTONY

Stay, countrymen.

(The storm troupers remove the body. Low revengeful murmurs from the mob.)

SCHNABEL

Peace there, hear the noble Antony.

(Murmuring stops.)

SHERMAN

We'll hear him.

WILLARD

We'll follow him.

MOWRY

We'll die with him.

ANTONY

Good friends, sweet friends, let me not stir you up
To such a sudden flood of mutiny.
They that have done this deed are honourable.
What private griefs they have, alas I know not,
That made them do it. They are wise, and honourable,
And will no doubt with reasons answer you.

(Low murmurings.)

I come not, friends, to steal away your hearts,

(Murmuring stops.)

I am no orator as Brutus is;
But as you know me all, a plain blunt man,
That love my friend, and that they know full well,
That gave me public leave to speak of him.
For I have neither wit, nor words, nor worth,
Action, nor utterance, nor the power of speech,
To stir men's blood. I only speak right on.
I tell you that which you yourselves do know,
Show you sweet Caesar's wounds, poor poor dumb mouths,
And bid them speak for me. But were I Brutus,
And Brutus Antony, there were an Antony
Would ruffle up your spirits, and put a tongue

In every wound of Caesar, that should move
The stones of Rome to rise and mutiny.

MOWRY

We'll mutiny.

SHERMAN

We'll burn the house of Brutus.

WILLARD

(low)

About.

REID

Seek.

BURGESS

Burn!

LLOYD

Fire!

SHERMAN

Kill!

COTTEN

Slay!

SCHNABEL

Go fetch fire.

DUTHIE

Pluck down benches.

LLOYD

(whisper)

Pluck down forms.

COTTEN

Windows.

SHERMAN

Anything.

ANTONY

Why friends, you go to do you know not what.
Wherein hath Caesar thus deserved your loves?
Alas you know not, I must tell you then.
You have forgot the will I told you of.

LLOYD

The will!

SHERMAN

Caesar's will?

(The mob murmurs, "Caesar's will.")

ANTONY

Here is the will, and under Caesar's seal.
To every Roman citizen he gives,
To every several man, seventy-five drachmas.

ALLAND

Caesar!

MOWRY

For all of us?

SHERMAN

Seventy-five?

DUTHIE

Drachmas.

COTTEN

Seventy-five.

WILLARD

Seventy-five.

REID

Caesar's seal?

CARPENTER

Seventy-five.

SCHNABEL

To every Roman.

LLOYD

For every Roman.

BURGESS

Caesar.

ANTONY
(going right on)

Moreover, he hath left you all his walks,
His private arbours, and new-planted orchards,

(Crowd murmurs.)

On this side Tiber; he hath left them you,

(Murmuring stops.)

And to your heirs for ever—common pleasures,
To walk abroad and recreate yourselves.
Here was a Caesar! When comes such another?

> *(Silence. The lights dim as the mob turns slowly upstage
> and moves to exit with an increasing tempo and cres-
> cendo of footsteps.)*

Now let it work. Mischief, thou art afoot,
Take thou what course thou wilt.

(Exit Antony. Enter Cinna the Poet.)

CINNA

I dreamt to-night that I did feast with Caesar,
And things unluckily change my fantasy.
I have no will to wander forth of doors,
Yet something leads me forth.

(He hears footsteps off-stage and turns to look. Individually or in pairs, the mob enters from every direction, surrounding Cinna.)

MOWRY

What is your name?

COTTEN

Whither are you going?

ALLAND

Where do you dwell?

ASH

Are you a married man, or a bachelor?

DUTHIE

Answer every man directly.

MOWRY

Ay, and briefly.

COTTEN   ALLAND

Ay, and truly.   And wisely.

CINNA

What is my name? Whither am I going? Where do I dwell?

MOWRY

Ay, sir.

CINNA

Am I a married man, or a bachelor?

(The others move in slightly.)

To answer every man, directly and briefly, wisely and truly: wisely
I say, I am a bachelor. Directly, I am going to Caesar's funeral.

DUTHIE

As a friend, or an enemy?

CINNA

As a friend.

(They move down around Cinna.)

COTTEN

Where do you dwell?

CINNA

By the Capitol.

MOWRY

Your name, sir.

CINNA

(business)[94]

Truly, my name is Cinna. I am Cinna the poet.

> *(Sherman, off-left, cries out wildly. Schnabel cries off-right.)*

CINNA

What shouts are these?[95]

> *(Schnabel enters up-stage right.)*

SCHNABEL

The other side o' th' city is risen.[96]

ALLAND

Why stay we here?[97]

MOWRY

To the Capitol![98]

> *(Off-stage shouts: "Come!" "To the Capitol!" "Come!")*

CINNA

One word, good citizens.[99]

COTTEN

His name's Cinna.

CINNA

The poet!

MOWRY

(tears up a poem and throws it at Cinna)

Tear him for his bad verses!

CINNA

(backing away)

I'm Cinna the poet. I am not Cinna the conspirator.

> *(He turns away, slowly.)*

SCHNABEL

No more talking on't.[100]

CINNA

(cringing)

I'm Cinna the poet! The poet! Not the conspirator!

> *(The mob engulfs Cinna and rushes him off-stage right. Silence.)*

CINNA
(off-stage; a frenzied cry)

I'm Cinna the poet!!!

> *(The lights dim. There is a series of drum and organ roars.[101] On the third, a column of helmeted soldiers can be seen in the half-light, entering from stage right, climbing the steps to the top platform, descending the ramp, and exiting stage left. The beating of a snare drum is heard. It grows in intensity, accompanied by the plaintive sound of a bugle and a french horn. The lights come up to reveal Brutus in uniform. Trebonius enters stage right as the music fades out.)*

BRUTUS

Is Cassius near?[102]

TREBONIUS

He is at hand.[103]

BRUTUS

A word, Trebonius, how did he receive you?

TREBONIUS

With courtesy, and with respect enough,
But not with such familiar instances,
Nor with such free and friendly conference
As he hath used of old.[104]

BRUTUS

Thou hast described
A hot friend cooling. Ever note, Trebonius,
When love begins to sicken and decay
It useth an enforced ceremony.
There are no tricks in plain and simple faith.

> *(Enter Decius from right.)*

BRUTUS

Decius, your master,
In his own change, or by ill officers,
Hath given me some worthy cause to wish
Things done, undone. But if he be at hand
I shall be satisfied.

DECIUS

I do not doubt
But that my noble master will appear

Such as he is, full of regard and honour.[105]

BRUTUS

He is not doubted. Comes his army on?

DECIUS

They mean this night in Sardis to be quartered.
The greater part, the horse in general,
Are come with Cassius.[106]

ASH[107]

Stand ho!

ALLAND

> *(Off-stage.)*

Stand!

> *(Enter Cassius quickly.)*

CASSIUS

Most noble brother, you have done me wrong.

BRUTUS

Wrong I mine enemies?
And if not so, how should I wrong a brother?

> *(Decius and Trebonius move off slightly.)*

CASSIUS

Brutus, this sober form of yours hides wrongs.

BRUTUS

Cassius, be content.
Speak your griefs softly, I do know you well.

CASSIUS
> *(to Decius)*

Bid our commanders lead their charges off a little.

BRUTUS

Trebonius, do the like.[108]

CASSIUS

That you have wronged me doth appear in this:
You have condemned and noted Lucius Pella
For taking bribes here of the Sardians;
Wherein my letters, praying on his side,
Because I knew the man, was slighted off.

BRUTUS

You wronged yourself to write in such a case.

CASSIUS

In such a time as this it is not meet
That every nice offence should bear his comment.

BRUTUS

Let me tell you, Cassius, you yourself
Are much condemned to have an itching palm
To sell and mart your offices for gold
To undeservers.

CASSIUS

I, an itching palm?
You know that you are Brutus that speaks this,
Or by the gods, this speech were else your last.

BRUTUS

The name of Cassius honours this corruption,
And chastisement doth therefore hide his head.

CASSIUS

Chastisement?

BRUTUS

Remember March; the ides of March remember.
Did not great Julius bleed for justice sake?
What villain touched his body that did strike,
And not for justice? What, shall one of us
That struck the foremost man of all this world
But for supporting robbers, shall we now
Contaminate our fingers with base bribes,
And sell the mighty space of our large honours
For so much trash as may be grasped thus?
I had rather be a dog, and bay the moon,
Than such a Roman.

CASSIUS

Brutus, bait me not,
I'll not endure it. You forget yourself,
To hedge me in. I am a soldier, I,
Older in practice, abler than yourself
To make conditions.

BRUTUS

Go to! You are not Cassius.

CASSIUS

I am.

BRUTUS

I say you are not.

CASSIUS

Urge me no more! I shall forget myself.
Tempt me no farther.

BRUTUS

Away, slight man!

CASSIUS

Is't possible? Must I endure all this?

BRUTUS

All this? Ay, more. Fret till your proud heart break.
Must I observe you? Must I stand and crouch
Under your testy humour? By the gods,
You shall digest the venom of your spleen,
Though it do split you. For from this day forth,
I'll use you for my mirth, yea, for my laughter,
When you are waspish.

CASSIUS

Is it come to this?

BRUTUS

You say you are a better soldier.
Let it appear so; make your vaunting true,
And it shall please me well. For mine own part,
I shall be glad to learn of noble men.

CASSIUS

You wrong me every way! You wrong me, Brutus!
I said, an elder soldier, not a better.
Did I say 'better'?

BRUTUS

If you did, I care not.

CASSIUS

When Caesar lived, he durst not have moved me.

BRUTUS

Peace, peace, you durst not so have tempted him.

CASSIUS

I durst not?

BRUTUS

No.

CASSIUS

What, durst not tempt him?

BRUTUS

For your life you durst not.

CASSIUS

Do not presume too much upon my love;
I may do that I shall be sorry for.

BRUTUS

You have done that you should be sorry for.
There is no terror, Cassius, in your threats;
For I am armed so strong in honesty,
That they pass me as the idle wind,
Which I respect not. I did send to you
For certain sums of gold, which you denied me;
For I can raise no money by vile means.
By heaven, I had rather coin my heart
And drop my blood for drachmas than to wring
From the hard hands of peasants their vile trash
By any indirection. I did send
To you for gold to pay my legions,
Which you denied me. Was that done like Cassius?

CASSIUS

I denied you not.

BRUTUS

You did.

CASSIUS

I did not.

(Pause.)

He was but a fool that brought
My answer back. Brutus hath rived my heart.
A friend should bear his friend's infirmities;
But Brutus makes mine greater than they are.

BRUTUS

I do not, till you practise them on me.

CASSIUS

You love me not.

BRUTUS

I do not like your faults.

CASSIUS

A friendly eye could never see such faults.

BRUTUS

A flatterer's would not, though they do appear
As huge as high Olympus.

CASSIUS

Come Antony, and young Octavius, come!
Revenge yourselves alone on Cassius.
For Cassius is aweary of the world:
Hated by one he loves; braved by his brother;

Checked like a bondman; all his faults observed,
Set in a note-book, learned and conned by rote
To cast into my teeth. O, I could weep
My spirit from mine eyes! There is my dagger;
I, that denied thee gold, will give my heart.
Strike as thou didst at Caesar. For I know,
When thou didst hate him worst, thou lovedst him better
Than thou ever lovedst Cassius.

                    BRUTUS

Sheathe your dagger.
Be angry when you will; it shall have scope.
Do what you will; dishonor shall be humour.

                    CASSIUS

Hath Cassius lived
To be but mirth and laughter to his Brutus,
When grief and blood ill-tempered vexeth him?

                    BRUTUS

When I spoke that, I was ill-tempered too.

                    CASSIUS

Do you confess so much? Give me your hand.

                    BRUTUS

And my heart too.

                    CASSIUS

I did not think you could have been so angry.

                    BRUTUS

O Cassius, I am sick of many griefs. Portia is dead.

                    CASSIUS

Ha! Portia?

                    BRUTUS

She is dead.

                    CASSIUS

How 'scaped I killing when I crossed you so?
From what sickness?

                    BRUTUS

Impatient of my absence,
And grief that young Octavius with Marc Antony
Have made themselves so strong. For with her death
That tidings came. With this she fell distract.

                    CASSIUS

And died so?

BRUTUS

Even so. Trebonius!

TREBONIUS

(off-stage)

My lord!

BRUTUS

Decius! Metellus! Let's call in question our necessities.

CASSIUS

Portia, art thou gone?

BRUTUS

No more I pray you.

(Enter the boys.)[109]

Metellus, I have here received letters,
That young Octavius and Marc Antony
Come down upon us with a mighty power,
Bending their expedition toward Philippi.

DECIUS

Myself have letters of the selfsame tenure.[110]

BRUTUS

With what addition?

DECIUS

Mine speak of seventy senators that died
By their proscriptions.[111]

BRUTUS

Well, to our work alive. What do you think
Of marching toward Philippi presently?

CASSIUS

I do not think it good.

BRUTUS

Your reason?

CASSIUS

This is it:
'Twere better that the enemy seek us;
So shall he waste his means, weary his soldiers,
Doing himself offence, whilst we, lying still,
Are full of rest, defense, and nimbleness.

BRUTUS

Good reasons must of force give place to better.
The people 'twixt Philippi and this ground
Do stand but in a forced affection;

For they have grudged us contribution.
The enemy, marching along by them,
By them shall make a fuller number up.
You must note beside,
That we have tried the utmost of our friends;
Our cause is ripe.
The enemy increaseth every day;
We, at the height, are ready to decline.
There is a tide in the affairs of men,
Which taken at the flood leads on to fortune;
Omitted, all the voyage of their life
Is bound in shallows and in miseries.
On such a full sea are we now afloat,
And we must take the current when it serves,
Or lose our ventures.

CASSIUS

Then with your will go on.
We'll along ourselves, and meet them at Philippi.

BRUTUS

The deep of night is crept upon our talk,
And nature must obey necessity,
Which we will niggard with a little rest.
There is no more to say.

CASSIUS

No more. Good night:
Early to-morrow will we rise, and hence.

BRUTUS

Farewell, Trebonius. Metellus. Decius.

TREBONIUS/METELLUS/DECIUS

Good night, my lord. Good night, Lord Brutus. Good night.

(They exit right.)

BRUTUS

Noble, noble Cassius,
Good night, and good repose.

CASSIUS

If we do lose this battle, then this is
The very last time we shall speak together.
Are you contented to be led in triumph
Through the streets of Rome?[112]

BRUTUS

No Cassius, no. Think not, thou noble Roman,
That ever Brutus will go bound to Rome.

CASSIUS

O my dear brother!
This was an ill beginning of the night!
Never come such division 'tween our souls;
Let it not, Brutus.[113]

BRUTUS

Everything is well.

CASSIUS

Good night, my lord.

BRUTUS

Good night, good brother.

(Exit Cassius upstage right, slowly.)

Lucius!

(Enter Lucius with his instrument.)

LUCIUS

Here my good lord.

BRUTUS

What, thou speak'st drowsily?
Poor knave, I blame thee not; thou art o'er-watched.
Look Lucius, here's the book I sought for so.

LUCIUS

I was sure your lordship did not give it to me.

BRUTUS

Bear with me good boy, I am much forgetful.
Canst thou hold up thy heavy eyes a while,
And touch thy instrument a strain or two?

LUCIUS

Ay my lord, an't please you.

BRUTUS

It does, my boy.
I trouble thee too much, but thou art willing.

LUCIUS

It is my duty sir.

BRUTUS

I should not urge thy duty past thy might,
I know young bloods look for a time of rest.

LUCIUS

I have slept my lord already.

BRUTUS

It was well done, and thou shalt sleep again;

I will not hold thee long. If I do live,
I will be good to thee.

> *(As Lucius sings, the lights begin to dim, so that by the*
> *end of his song, the stage is in darkness.)*

LUCIUS

Orpheus with his lute made trees,
And the mountain-tops that freeze,
Bow themselves, when he did sing.
Da dum de de dum.
To his music plants and flowers
Ever sprung; as sun and showers
There had made a lasting spring.
Da dum de de dum.
Every thing that heard him play,
Even the billows of the sea,
Hung their heads and then lay by.
In sweet music is such art:
Killing care and grief of heart
Fall asleep or, hearing, die.
Da dum de de dum.[114]

> *(The bugle, snare drum and french horn take over,*
> *reaching a crescendo as the lights come up to reveal the*
> *body of Cassius surrounded by his men. Brutus enters,*
> *sword in hand, and stands over Cassius. The snare drum*
> *continues to be heard underneath the following scene.)*

CINNA

Marc Antony is in your tents, my lord.[115]

BRUTUS

Are those my tents where I perceive the fire?

CINNA

They are, my lord.[116]

TREBONIUS

Statilius showed the torch-light, but
Came not back: he is or ta'en or slain.[117]

BRUTUS

Slaying is the word.
It is a deed in fashion.[118]

> *(looking at Cassius)*

Friends, I owe moe tears
To this dead man than you shall see me pay.
I shall find time, Cassius; I shall find time.[119]
O Julius Caesar, thou art mighty yet!
Thy spirit walks abroad and turns our swords
In our own entrails.[120] Trebonius!

TREBONIUS

What says my lord?[121]

BRUTUS

Why this, Trebonius.
Thou seest the world, how it goes,
Our enemies have beat us to the pit.
It is more worthy to leap in ourselves,
Than tarry till they push us.

(handing the sword to Trebonius)

I shall have glory by this losing day,
More than Octavius and Marc Antony
By this vile conquest shall attain unto.

METELLUS

Fly, my lord![122]

BRUTUS

Hence! I will follow.

(The lights and music wash out, leaving the stage in darkness. Then, shafts of light shoot up from the floor to reveal Marc Antony standing over the body of Brutus. He is accompanied by storm troupers carrying huge black banners.)

ANTONY

This was the noblest Roman of them all.
All the conspirators save only he
Did that they did, in envy of great Caesar;
He only, in a general honest thought,
And common good to all, made one of them.
His life was gentle, and the elements
So mixed in him, that Nature might stand up,
And say to all the world, this was a man.

THE END

NOTES

1. Identified in Blitzstein's score as "The Fascist March."
2. The Mercury Theatre had no stage curtain. Audiences for this production were confronted throughout with the brick stage wall, which was painted the color of dried blood. All of the various scene changes were handled with lighting.
3. Only Antony is with Caesar's party in this scene.
4. Casca, I,ii,14.
5. Soothsayer, 12 (offstage).
6. Casca, 14.
7. 15, "... the press ..."
8. Brutus, 19.
9. Cassius, 21.

10. Ibid.
11. Caesar, 24.
12. Arms raised in the fascist salute.
13. I,i,5.
14. Marullus, 8.
15. I,ii,25.
16. Brutus, 216.
17. 300.
18. 168–75.
19. Casca, 291.
20. Cassius, 308–10.
21. 190.
22. A thunder drum continued to rumble throughout the following scene (I,iii in Shakespeare).
23. Cicero was eliminated from Welles's script.
24. Cassius, I,iii,41.
25. Ibid., 42.
26. Casca, 43.
27. Cicero, 1.
28. Casca, 43.
29. Cicero, 3–10.
30. Ibid., 14.
31. Casca, 22–30.
32. Cicero, 33.
33. Casca, 44.
34. Ibid., 79.
35. Ibid., 85–89.
36. Casca, 117–20.
37. All of Casca's lines for this scene are taken from Cinna, 134–52.
38. Casca, 131.
39. II,i,46.
40. 49–54.
41. 11–28.
42. 60.
43. 39.
44. Casca, 142.
45. Cinna, 143.
46. Metellus, 144–46.
47. Brutus, 192.
48. Ibid.
49. Cassius, 193.
50. Trebonius, 194.
51. Cinna, 214.
52. Brutus, 327.
53. Brutus, II,ii,114.
54. Publius reads Popilius Lena's lines.
55. Artemidorus, III,i,3.
56. Soothsayer, 2 (offstage).

57. 1.
58. Popilius, 13.
59. 8.
60. Welles's line, probably from Brutus, 53–54.
61. Caesar, 9; Publius, 10.
62. Publius, 10.
63. Brutus, 15.
64. Ibid., 18.
65. Metellus, 32.
66. Ibid., 33–34.
67. Ibid., 48–51.
68. The conspirators were positioned in a diagonal line, from Casca upstage left to Brutus downstage right, with Caesar stumbling from one to the other and being stabbed.
69. Cinna, 78.
70. Cassius, 80–81.
71. Brutus, 89–91.
72. Brutus, 82; Cinna, 77.
73. Marullus in this scene.
74. Cassius, 111–13.
75. Decius, 118.
76. Brutus, 147.
77. Ibid.
78. 181, ''And then, we will deliver you the cause . . . ''
79. Brutus, 224–26.
80. Cassius, 234–35.
81. 148–50.
82. Throughout this scene (III,ii in Shakespeare), and the murder of Cinna the Poet (III,iii), the actors identified by their actual names are doubling as citizens of Rome. Welles scored their responses to Brutus and Antony along precise choral levels, thus the line fragments and innumerable repetitions. I saw no reason to annotate each and every one of them.
83. Brutus, III,ii,2/6–7.
84. III,i,82–83.
85. Welles's line.
86. For his speech, Brutus was framed in a cross of light, while, for Antony, the so-called Nuremberg effect was used.
87. Francis Carpenter, a Mercury extra used only in crowd scenes.
88. Second Citizen, 114, ''If thou consider rightly of the matter . . . ''
89. Welles's line.
90. Ibid.
91. Ibid.
92. Ibid., in response to Antony's ''Have patience, gentle friends'' speech.
93. Howard Bird, another Mercury extra.
94. He reaches into his pockets for copies of his poems and distributes them to the mob.
95. *Coriolanius*, I,i,43.
96. Ibid.
97. Ibid., 44.

98. Ibid.

99. Ibid., 11.

100. Ibid., 10.

101. A Hammond organ was struck full volume on all its bass keys for forty-five seconds.

102. *Caesar*, IV,ii,3.

103. Lucilius, 4.

104. Ibid., 15–18.

105. Pindarus, 10–12.

106. Lucilius, 28–30.

107. Walter Ash, the Mercury stage manager, offstage.

108. While not indicated in Welles's script, Decius and Trebonius undoubtedly exited at this point.

109. Decius, Metellus, and Trebonius.

110. Messala, 171.

111. Brutus, 177–78.

112. V,i,98–99/108–10.

113. IV,iii,233–36.

114. Shakespeare's stage direction merely calls for "Music, and a song." It is clear from the text, however, that Brutus wants a lute-song. For the lyric, Welles turned to III,i of *Henry VIII*, adding the refrain, "Da dum de de dum."

115. Pindarus, V,iii,10.

116. Titinius, 14.

117. Clitus, V,v,2–3.

118. 4–5.

119. V,iii,101–3.

120. 94–96.

121. Volumnius, V,v,16.

122. Clitus, 43.

Welles, at age 15, as Richard III in *Winter of Our Discontent*, his 1930 schoolboy antecedent for *Five Kings*. From the private collection of Richard Wilson.

MACBETH (Still slumped on the step)

It will have blood: they say, blood will have blood;
Stones have been known to move and trees to speak
Augurs and understood relations have
By magot-pies and choughs and rooks brought forth
The secret'st man of blood. What is the night?

LADY MACBETH

Almost at odds with morning, which is which. *CHOIR* *ASTRAL*

MACBETH *Come in*

Strange things I have in head that will to hand *SAW*
(The Voodoo music begins very faintly. He looks up)
More shall they speak, for now I am bent to know
By the worst means, the worst. *VOODOO DRUMS*
(Rising)
I will to-night,
And betimes I will *CUT DRUMS*
To the weird sisters;
(Lady Macbeth backs fearfully away. Macbeth stands.
Arms upraised, shouting his invocation)
(Music stops: Silence)
How now, you secret, black and midnight hags;
(Lights start to dim. Distant thunder and lightning)
I conjure you, by that which you profess, *DRUMS*
Howe'er you come to know it, answers me: *low Thunder drums*
(The music of the Voodoo steals in again, rising to a
crescendo with the invocation).
Though you untie the winds and let them fight
Against the churches; though the yesty waves *Thundy*
Confound and swallow navigation up; *wind up*
Though blades corn be lodged and trees blown down; *builds answer*
Though castles topple on their warder's heads; *me*
Though palaces and pyramids do slope *low gong*
Their heads to their foundations; though the treasure *vibrations on way up.*
of nature's germens tumble all together. *Crash 2 lightning*
Even till destruction sicken; answer me; *Blackout*
(Tremendous burst of thunder. Stage Pitch black. *Rain drums*
Slowly the great gates swing open letting in a *Cellophane*
strange light. Hecate is in silhouette against *Rain*
it. He beckons to Macbeth. *all Voodoo Drums (very loud)*

END OF SCENE

all choir playing wind whistles

Abdul comes center stage playing flute

[left margin handwritten:] *low Wind Starts building* / *Tympani* / *Build tympani Thunder drum + sheet + wind build up and up* / *Answer Me* / *Crash Thunder drums Tympani Thunder sheet* / *gong 2 flashes of lightning* / *Rain - Black out Curtain fast* / *during scene change Cellophane Rain (Big) Rain drum*

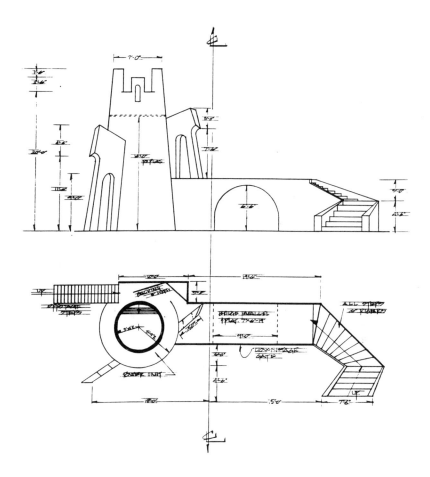

Nat Karson's ground plan (below) and elevation (above) for the 'Voodoo' *Macbeth*, drawn in one-quarter inch scale. Retraced by Nick Pagliante.

II,i, the coronation scene, with Edna Thomas as Lady Macbeth (above) and Jack Carter as Macbeth (far right). Note the jungle backdrop. Courtesy of the Federal Theatre Project Collection at George Mason University.

II,ii, in the jungle, with Carter (far right), the Three Witches (above), and Abdul the drummer (center). Courtesy of the Federal Theatre Project Collection at George Mason University.

Costume parade for II,i of the 'Voodoo' *Macbeth*. Note the weapons. These are rifle versions of the handguns used throughout the production. Courtesy of the Federal Theatre Project Collection at George Mason University.

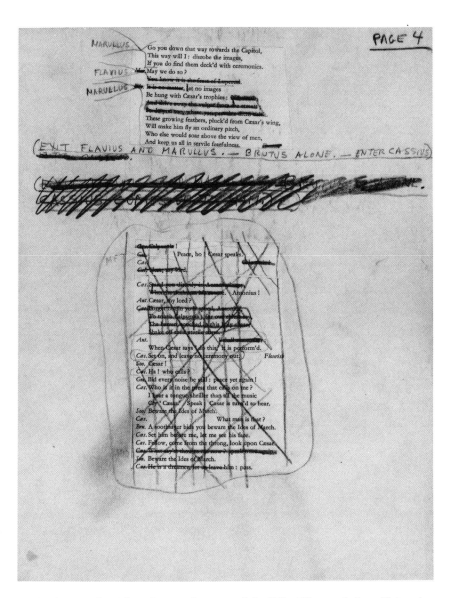

MARULLUS
Go you down that way towards the Capitol,
This way will I : disrobe the images,
If you do find them deck'd with ceremonies.

FLAVIUS
May we do so ?
You know it is the feast of Lupercal.

MARULLUS
It is no matter, let no images
Be hung with Cæsar's trophies :
And there away the vulgar from the streets :
So do you too, where you perceive them thick.
These growing feathers, pluck'd from Cæsar's wing,
Will make him fly an ordinary pitch,
Who else would soar above the view of men,
And keep us all in servile fearfulness.

(EXIT FLAVIUS AND MARULLUS. — BRUTUS ALONE. — ENTER CASSIUS)

Peace, ho ! Cæsar speaks.
Cas.
Cæs. Speak, speak : is Antonius near.
When to the chase is will sweat.   Antonius !
Ant. Cæsar, my lord ?
Cæs. Forget not, in your speed, Antonius,
To touch Calpurnia ; for our elders say,
The barren, touched in this holy chase,
Shake off their sterile curse.
Ant.
When Cæsar says 'do this,' it is perform'd.
Cas. Set on, and leave no ceremony out.   Flourish
Soo. Cæsar !
Cæs. Ha ! who calls ?
Cas. Bid every noise be still : peace yet again !
Cæs. Who is it in the press that calls on me ?
I hear a tongue, shriller than all the music
Cry 'Cæsar.' Speak ; Cæsar is turn'd to hear.
Soo. Beware the Ides of March.
Cæs.   What man is that ?
Bru. A soothsayer bids you beware the Ides of March.
Cæs. Set him before me, let me see his face.
Cas. Follow, come from the throng, look upon Cæsar.
Cæs. What say'st thou to me now ? speak once again.
Soo. Beware the Ides of March.
Cæs. He is a dreamer, let us leave him : pass.

Facsimile page for *Julius Caesar.* Courtesy of the Lilly Library, Indiana University, Bloomington, Indiana.

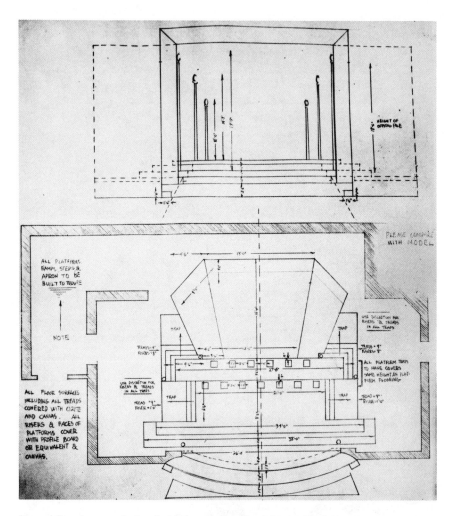

Samuel Leve's ground plan (below) and elevation (above) for *Julius Caesar,* drawn in one-quarter inch scale. The two rows of squares in the stage floor represent holes into which were placed 500-watt up-lights, thus creating the so-called Nuremburg effect. Courtesy of Samuel Leve.

"I am constant as the Northern Star," Caesar declares to the conspirators. Welles as Brutus is at the far left. Third from the right is Martin Gabel as Cassius. Between Gabel and Joseph Holland as Caesar is John Hoyt as Decius Brutus. Courtesy of Samuel Leve.

Welles as Brutus standing over the Nuremburg Lights. Courtesy of Samuel Leve.

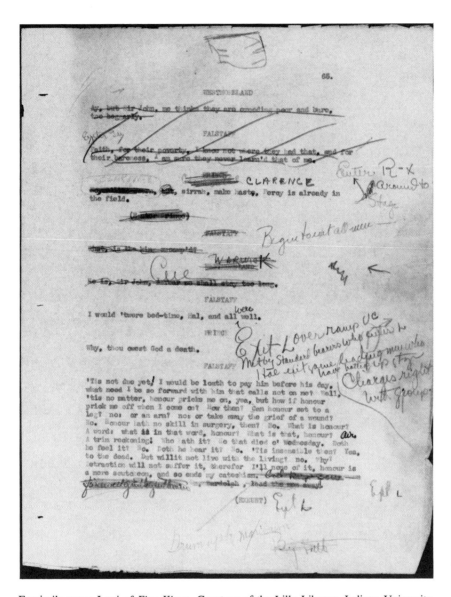

Facsimile page: I,xxi of *Five Kings.* Courtesy of the Lilly Library, Indiana University, Bloomington, Indiana.

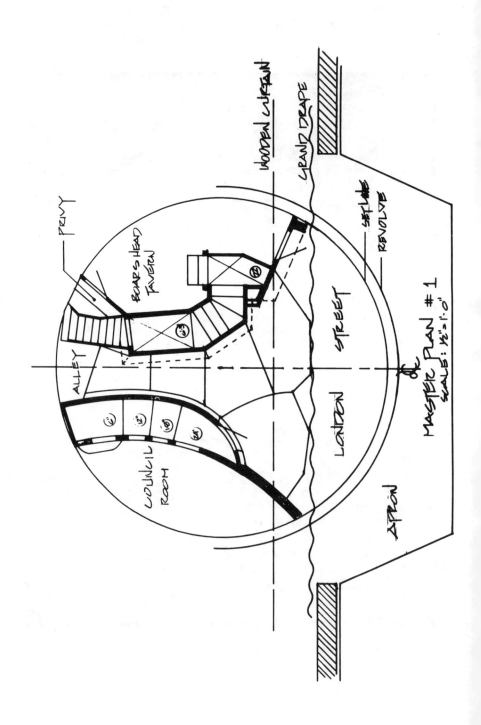

PRIVY

BOARS HEAD TAVERN

ALLEY

COUNCIL ROOM

WOODEN CURTAIN

GRAND DRAPE

SET LINE

REVOLVE

STREET

LONDON

APRON

MASTER PLAN # 1

SCALE: 1/2" = 1'-0"

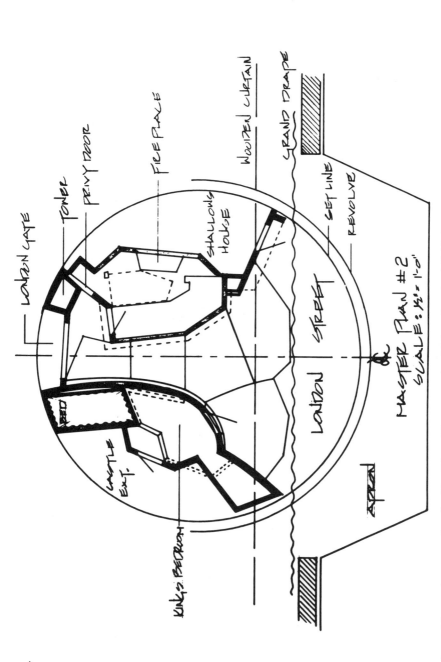

James Morcom's master plans for *Five Kings*. There were, in addition, three battlefield plans. Retraced by Nick Pagliante. Courtesy of John Keck.

The revolve in its first position: James Morcom's rendering of his London Street Plan #1, with the palace exterior (left) and Boar's Head Tavern (right). Courtesy of John Keck.

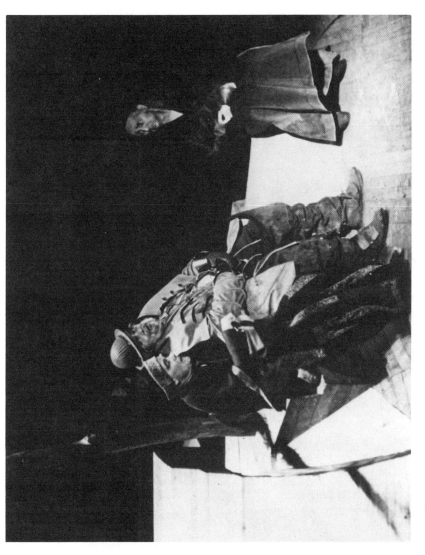

I,xix of *Five Kings*: "We have heard the chimes at midnight." Welles as Falstaff, with Edgar Kent as Shallow (left) and Fred Stewart as Silence (right). From the private collection of Richard Wilson.

I,iv of *Five Kings*: interior of the Boar's Head Tavern. Left to right: William Alland as Peto, Gus Schilling as Bardolph, Edgerton Paul as the Page, Sanford Siegal as Gadshill, Burgess Meredith as Prince Hal, Welles as Falstaff, and John Berry as Points. The door to the privy is behind Berry. Courtesy of the Lilly Library, Indiana University, Bloomington, Indiana.

I,x of *Five Kings:* a street outside the King's council room. Left to right: John Emery as Hotspur, MacGregor Gibb as Worcester, and Eustace Wyatt as Northumberland. Courtesy of the Lilly Library, Indiana University, Bloomington, Indiana.

III,xv of *Five Kings*: the French court. Left to right: Rosemary Carver as Alice, Margaret Curtis as Katherine, and Burgess Meredith as Henry V. Courtesy of the Lilly Library, Indiana University, Bloomington, Indiana.

Five Kings

PREFACE

Falstaff: We have heard the chimes at midnight, Master Shallow.

Shallow: That we have, that we have, that we have, in faith, Sir John, we have. Our
watchword was 'Hem, boys!' Come, let's to dinner . . . Jesus, the days that we
have seen! (II Henry IV, III,ii, 202–7)

Trudging through the snow, the bloated figure of Falstaff and his wizened companion pass across the opening frames of Welles's 1964 film *Chimes at Midnight*
(also known by the title *Falstaff*). Its final frames show an outsized coffin on
the way to the grave that Falstaff's erstwhile protégé, now Henry V, once
predicted ''doth gape/For thee thrice wider than for other men.''[1]

Looming over this vast chronicle of civil rebellion and royal succession was
that lump of a man, Falstaff, mocking both the heroic and the base. ''Banish
plump Jack,'' he once protested, ''and banish all the world.''[2] In Welles's film
version of *Five Kings*, Falstaff has indeed become all the world.

A quarter of a century earlier, while rehearsing *Five Kings* for its theatrical
opening, Welles revealed his intentions for the role of Falstaff.

I will play him as a tragic figure. I hope, of course, he will be funny to the audience,
just as he was funny to those around him. But his humor and his wit were aroused merely
by the fact that he wanted to please the prince. Falstaff, however, had the potential of
greatness in him.[3]

A more recent interview demonstrates that his tragic vision of Falstaff remained
unchanged. To *Chimes at Midnight*, however, something crucial had been added:

Welles's realization that this character had it in him to become the protagonist of Shakespeare's chronicles. "The relationship between Falstaff and the prince is no longer the simple one that one finds in Shakespeare. It is a foretelling, a preparation for the tragic ending."[4] The friendship between Falstaff and Prince Hal, and its eventual betrayal, provided Welles with the sort of narrative line (and ironic counterpoint) that had eluded him in *Five Kings*.

The concepts upon which Welles had based his unique and startling productions were plainly evident. Not only had *Macbeth* been transported to Haiti, its protagonist had become an instrument in the witches' plan for world domination. *Julius Caesar*, on the other hand, was recast as the story of a modern dictatorship, one that seemed to speak of terror as though it were stalking the very street on which the Mercury stood. The high marks given Welles for aesthetic achievement and political relevancy notwithstanding, he had, in effect, made each of his W.P.A. and Mercury productions no less thrilling and immediate than the most popular cinematic events of the day.

In the face of such expectations, his approach to *Five Kings* both surprised and disappointed. John K. Hutchens of the *Boston Evening Transcript* was among the most unkind of the production's many critics. He also seems to have been exceptionally candid in saying that

It seems a ponderous marathon without style or particular point of view and utterly lacking in the magic with which this same Mercury Theatre once honored the Bard in the matter of *Julius Caesar*.[5]

And it did, indeed, appear as if Welles had decided to stage this sprawling compilation of Shakespeare and Holinshed as little more than a worthwhile challenge to his own redoubtable skills, to be judged on how well he managed to acquit himself in the performance of so Herculean a labor. It would have seemed utterly presumptuous for a lesser figure merely to tackle so massive an amount of material. However, *Five Kings* was the brainchild of none other than Orson Welles, known far and wide as the "Boy Wonder" of the American theatre.

Supposedly, the plan was to divide *Five Kings* into two parts, with the first following snippets of *Richard II*, proceeding through both parts of *Henry IV*, and ending with the triumphant reign of *Henry V*. Apart from its 1930 antecedent, *Winter of Our Discontent*, there is no evidence that so much as a script existed for the second part of *Five Kings*. It can be assumed, however, that Welles would have proceeded through all three parts of *Henry VI* and ended with the reign of that ever-popular miscreant, *Richard III*. Whether or not the role of the Chorus, reciting passages from Holinshed, would have continued through part two is less certain.

During the production's final agony, even the bare fact of the years spanned in *Five Kings* was ridiculed. "The program notes that the action of the night's proceedings starts in 1399 and ends in 1420," quipped the *Philadelphia Pictorial*, "which was one thing that was quickly accepted without question by the audience. It seemed even longer to me."[6]

Five Kings also suffered by comparison with Margaret Webster's 1937 production of *Henry IV*.

To compare Orson Welles' Falstaff to Mr. Evans' Falstaff, John Emery's Hotspur to Wesley Addy's Hotspur, Burgess Meredith's Prince Hal to Winston O'Keefe's Prince of Wales or Mr. Welles' coarsely-keyed direction to the electrifying direction of Margaret Webster would be as unconscionable as it would be unkind.[7]

It is not surprising that Welles's avowedly "experimental" production should be weighed against such seasoned interpreters of Shakespeare. He was, in effect, set up for a fall, with his own unwillingness (or inability) to explain his intentions being partly responsible. Equally culpable was John Houseman, who chose to speak for Welles and delineated a production scheme so grandiose and impossible to fulfill as to be immediately self-defeating. To "J.D.B." of the *Christian Science Monitor*, Houseman confided that

the aim will be to combine the immediate quality of the Elizabethan stage with all the devices and techniques possible in the modern theatre. . . . We're using more light than it takes for a musical comedy, and that revolving stage is the biggest thing of its kind you ever saw.[8]

There was no further mention of a particular concept for *Five Kings*, and the difficult and distracting conditions surrounding its production undermined Welles's considerable efforts to develop one.

This, the most complete text of *Five Kings* extant, shows that Welles had already reduced by more than half the plays of Shakespeare on which it is based. As he shortened and rearranged these chronicles, Welles shifted the emphasis away from historical events and onto life in the streets of London and in the infamous Boar's Head Tavern.

His task was, of course, made easier by the fact that Shakespeare himself, in dramatizing this period of English history (as popular with his contemporaries as the Civil War years is with ours), had begun his undertaking with a certain paucity of suitable material. In chronicling the span of years between the reigns of Richard II and the royal Henrys, Shakespeare did not rely solely on historical events or personages. Rather, the plays are dominated by characters and situations invented by their author, thus providing them with the sort of dramatic element that a more faithful account of the period would have lacked.

In *I Henry IV*, Shakespeare devotes 1,501 lines to the historical plot, while 1,539 lines are given over to Falstaff and his cohorts—an almost equal balance. In *II Henry IV*, however, the weight has shifted, with 1,370 lines being concerned with history and 1,990 lines having to do with the antics of his legendary fat knight—a balance of approximately 3.5 to 5.

Welles made even greater use of this character in *Five Kings*. Because Falstaff appears with greater frequency in *II Henry IV*, Welles transposed lines from that play throughout his text. As a result, only one-third of its ninety-six-page first act, and two-fifths of its forty-three-page second act, concern themselves with the stuff of history. Even in death, after Mistress Pistol's account of how Sir John "went to Arthur's bosom," his presence continues to loom over the sixty-one pages of the third act.

His London cronies, Pistol, Nym, and Bardolph, follow Henry V to France; however, they can no longer count on his friendship, and, by III,vi of *Five Kings* (coincidentally, the same scene in *Henry V*), he is upholding the death sentence imposed upon Bardolph for robbing a church. As the young king walks among his army, new rustics emerge—more somber types than in times of old, in keeping with Henry's own metamorphosis.

Whatever its emphasis, clearly Welles had planned a full, albeit truncated and highly stylized, version of Shakespeare's chronicles.

Welles has placed the turbulent reign of the two Henrys on a revolving stage which swings the action realistically from street to pub to courtyard to palace, into lonely byways and onto battlefields. Unique in productions of this sort, only two scenes are played before backdrops and those two are so decorated as to create an illusion of palace rooms. The battlefields are typically Welles' creations of groups of steps over and around which the troops of Henry IV and of the Percys engage in graphic warfare. Perhaps the most gripping of these is the combat between Prince Hal and Hotspur, waged while the stage revolve gives a vivid semblance of action impossible to attain on a static stage.[9]

In the course of the evening, a number of scenes were, by all accounts, masterfully directed. The problem was that these individual scenes were not perceived as parts of a unified production but rather as a series of random stage pictures.

The people are great people or friendly or interesting and you are glad to renew your acquaintance with them. But between you and a really stirring reunion is this insistence on a political-military chronicle.[10]

No one was more insistent than Welles on presenting *Five Kings* in all its fulsomeness, and he did so in spite of the Theatre Guild's continuing demands that, if only in the interests of a conventional running time, the production be cut. His stage manager, Walter Ash, still blames the Guild for the demise of *Five Kings*: "Welles was right in his constant claim that, when it wasn't cut, it made sense, it worked. The more he cut, the more of a pageant it became."[11]

Throughout the tour of *Five Kings* (from Boston to Washington, D.C., to Philadelphia), Welles grappled with this seemingly impenetrable mountain of material. In his dispatch to the *New York Herald-Tribune*, columnist Herbert Drake suggests that, had Welles been given the extra week of uninterrupted rehearsal time that he had requested of the Guild, *Five Kings* might today be recognized as Welles's theatrical masterpiece.

It shapes up as the others did a week before they opened. It has all the marks of directorial genius. The Boy Wonder can still pull the rabbit-hearted Falstaff out of a hat, if the theatre will accommodate itself to his unusual working methods.[12]

For nearly two decades after its closing in Philadelphia, the sets and costumes for *Five Kings* remained in storage in a Bronx, New York, warehouse, with Welles insisting that somewhere, somehow it would be reborn. In 1960, for Dublin Gate Productions, and again, in 1964, with the film version, Welles mounted productions of something similar to *Five Kings*. However, both of these subsequent efforts lacked the scope, the ambitions, and the sheer magnificence of his original intentions.

NOTES

1. *II Henry IV*, V,v,54–55.
2. *I Henry IV*, II,iv,456.
3. *Christian Science Monitor*, 17 February 1939.
4. *Cahiers du Cinema*, December 1967.
5. 28 February 1939.
6. 21 March 1939.
7. *Philadelphia Enquirer*, 21 March 1939.
8. *Christian Science Monitor*, 17 February 1939.
9. Helen Eagen, *Boston Traveler*, 28 February 1939.
10. Hutchens, *Boston Evening Transcript*, 28 February 1939.
11. Personal interview, New York City, 9 June 1972.
12. 26 March 1939.

FIVE KINGS

Adapted and directed by Orson Welles
Music by Aaron Copland
Sets by James Morcom
Costumes by Millia Davenport
Lighting by Jean Rosenthal

Colonial Theater, Boston, 27 February 1939

CAST

Chorus	Robert Speaight
Henry IV	Morris Ankrum
Prince Hal, later Henry V	Burgess Meredith
Clarence	Richard Baer
Gloucester	Guy Kingsley
Henry Percy, called Hotspur	John Emery
Northumberland	Eustace Wyatt
Worcester	Macgregor Gibb
Westmoreland	John Adair
Warwick	Lawrence Fletcher
Vernon	John Straub
A Certain Lord	William Mowry
Archbishop of Canterbury	Edgar Barrier
Bishop of Ely	George Duthrie
Lord Chief Justice	Erskine Sanford
Falstaff	Orson Welles
Bardolph	Gus Schilling
Poins	John Berry
Peto	William Alland
Gadshill	Sanford Siegel
Page	Edgerton Paul
Pistol	Eustace Wyatt
Shallow	Edgar Kent
Silence	Fred Stewart
Bullcalf	Stephen Roberts
Mouldy	William Herz
Feeble	John A. Willard
Shadow	James Morcom

Davy	Francis Carpenter
Salisbury	Stephen Roberts
Bracy	John A. Willard
Court	Fred Stewart
Bates	John A. Willard
Williams	Richard Wilson
Gower	John Straub
Fluellen	Edgar Kent
Messengers	William Bishop
	Seymour Milbert
	Robert Earle
Servants to Hotspur	Francis Carpenter
	Stanley Poss
Lady Percy	Lora Baxter
Mistress Quickly	Alice John
Doll Tearsheet	Grace Coppin
King of France	William Mowry
Queen of France	Ellen Andrews
Montjoy, Ambassador of France	Gerold Kean
Burgundy	Edgerton Paul
French Soldier	Ross Elliott
French Lady	Ann Saks
Katherine, Princess of France	Margaret Curtis
Alice, her servant	Rosemary Carver

Lords, Soldiers, Servants

ACT ONE

Scene One

Enter Chorus.

CHORUS

O for a muse of fire, that would ascend
The brightest heaven of invention:
A kingdom for a stage, princes to act,
And monarchs to behold the swelling scene!
Then should the warlike Harry, like himself,
Assume the port of Mars, and at his heels
(Leashed in, like hounds) should famine, sword and fire
Crouch for employment. But pardon, gentles all,
The flat unrais'd spirits that hath dared

On this unworthy scaffold to bring forth
So great an object. Can this cockpit hold
The vasty fields of France? Or may we cram
Within this wooden O the very casques
That did affright the air at Agincourt?
O, pardon! since a crooked figure may
Attest in little place a million,
And let us, ciphers to this great accompt,
On your imaginary forces work.
Suppose within the girdle of these walls
Are now confined two mighty monarchies,
Whose high up-rear'd and abutting fronts
The perilous narrow ocean parts asunder.
Piece out our imperfections with your thoughts:
Into a thousand parts divide one man
And make imaginary puissance.
Think, when we talk of horses, that you see them
Printing their proud hoofs i' th' receiving earth:
For 'tis your thoughts that now must deck our kings,
Carry them here and there, jumping o'er times,
Turning th' accomplishment of many years
Into an hourglass; for the which supply,
Admit me Chorus to this history,
Who, Prologue-like, your humble patience pray,
Gently to hear, kindly to judge our play.[1]

                    (Exit Chorus.)

Scene Two

                    Enter Bolingbroke and lords.

                    BOLINGBROKE

So shaken as we are, so wan with care,
Find we a time for frighted peace to pant
And breathe short-winded accents of new broils.
No more the thirsty entrance of this soil
Shall daub her lips with her own children's blood:
No more shall trenching war channel her fields,
Nor bruise her flow'rets with the arm'd hoofs
Of hostile paces. Those opposed eyes
Which, like the meteors of a troubled heaven,
All of one nature, of one substance bred,
Did lately meet in the intestine shock
And furious close of civil butchery,
Shall now in mutual well-beseeming ranks

March all one way and be no more opposed
Against acquaintance, kindred, and allies.[1]

(Enter Exton, with Attendants bearing a coffin.)

EXTON

Great king, within this coffin I present
Thy buried fear. Herein all breathless lies
The mightiest of thy greatest enemies,
Richard of Bordeaux, by me hither brought.[2]

BOLINGBROKE

Exton, I thank thee not; for thou hast wrought
A deed of slander, with thy fatal hand,
Upon my head and all this famous land.

EXTON

From your own mouth, my lord, did I this deed.

BOLINGBROKE

They love not poison that do poison need,
Nor do I thee, though I did wish him dead.
Lords, I protest my soul is full of woe
That blood should sprinkle me to make me grow.

*(Exit Exton and Attendants with coffin. Enter Clergy.
Enter Chorus in the pit.)*

CHORUS

And the duke of Lancaster was led by the archbishop to the seat royall, who
there standing, made a signe of the crosse on his forehead and [on] his
brest, and said these words following.

KING HENRY

In the name of God, Amen. I Henrie of Lancaster claime the realme of
England and the crowne, with all the appurtenances, as I that am descended
by right line of the blood coming from that good lord king Henrie the third,
and through the right that God of his grace hath sent me, with the helpe of
my kin, and of my freends, to recover the same, which was in point to be
undone for default of good goveranace and due justice.[3]

(Revolve.)

Scene Three

Alley.
Enter the Prince, Poins and Bardolph.

PRINCE

Bardolph!

BARDOLPH

God save your grace!

PRINCE

And yours, most noble Bardolph! And how doth thy master, Falstaff? Doth
the old boar feed in the old frank?

BARDOLPH

Yea, my lord. Yea, my lord.[1]

Scene Four

Boar's Head Tavern.

PRINCE

Shall we steal upon them, Ned, at supper?[1]

POINS

I am your shadow, my lord; I'll follow you.

PRINCE

How might we see Falstaff bestow himself in his true colours, and not ourselves
be seen?

POINS

Put on leathern jerkins and aprons, and wait upon him at his table as drawers.

BARDOLPH

Jerkins!

(Enter Mistress Quickly.)

MISTRESS QUICKLY

O, the Prince of Wales! The Lord preserve thy good grace! The Lord bless that
sweet face of thine![2]

PETO

Hal! Welcome to London.[3]

DRAWER

The prince.

GADSHILL

My lord.

PRINCE

Shh! Where's Falstaff?

(The sound of someone passing wind inside the privy.)

MISTRESS QUICKLY

O, Jesu!

*(Falstaff throws open the top half of the door to the
privy.)*

FALSTAFF

(sings)

"When Arthur first in court"—Empty the jordan.

(Enter Page.)
Sirrah, you giant, what says my doctor to my water?[4]

PAGE

He said, sir, the water itself was good healthy water; but, for the party that owned it, he might have more diseases than he knew for.

FALSTAFF

Men of all sorts take a pride to gird at me. The brain of this foolish compounded clay-man is not able to invent anything that intends to laughter more than I invent or is invented on me. I am not only witty in myself, but the cause that wit is in other men.

PAGE

Sir John, what humour's the prince of?[5]

FALSTAFF

A good shallow young fellow. I have forsworn his company hourly any time this two-and-twenty years. Give me a cup of sack. And yet I am bewitched with the rogue's company. If the rascal have not given me medicines to make me love him, I'll be hanged.[6]

PAGE

They say Poins has a good wit.[7]

FALSTAFF

Hang him, baboon! Some sack! His wit's as thick as Tewksbury mustard.

PAGE

Why does the prince love him so, then?

FALSTAFF

Because their legs are both of a bigness, and 'a plays at quoits well, and eats conger and fennel, and rides the wild-mare with the boys, and swears with a good grace, and wears his boots very smooth; and such other gambol faculties 'a has, that show a weak mind and an able body, for the which the prince admits him. For the prince himself is such another; the weight of a hair will turn the scales between their avoirdupois.

(entering from the privy)
Give me some sack! How now, Hal!

PRINCE

Why, thou globe of sinful continents! How vilely did you speak of me even now before this honest, virtuous, civil serving boy!

FALSTAFF

No abuse, Hal. By this light flesh and corrupt blood, thou art welcome. Thou art indeed the most comparative, rascalliest, sweet young prince.[8]

(A pause.)
No abuse. No abuse, Hal.[9]

PRINCE

No abuse?

FALSTAFF

No, faith, boys, none. I dispraised thee before the wicked, that the wicked might not fall in love with thee. In which doing, I have done the part of a careful friend and a true subject, and thy father is to give me thanks for it. Give me some sack.

PRINCE

See now, whether pure fear and entire cowardice doth not make thee wrong this virtuous boy to close with us.

FALSTAFF

No abuse, Hal.

PRINCE

Is he of the wicked?

FALSTAFF

No, Hal, none.

PRINCE

Is thine hostess here of the wicked?

FALSTAFF

No, faith, boys, none.

PRINCE

Or honest Bardolph, whose zeal burns in his nose, of the wicked?

POINS

Answer, thou dead elm, answer.

FALSTAFF

The fiend hath pricked down Bardolph irrecoverable, and his face is Lucifer's privy-kitchen, where he doth nothing but roast malt-worms. For the boy, there is a good angel about him, but the devil blinds him too. And for the other.

MISTRESS QUICKLY

That's me, I warrant you.

FALSTAFF

I owe her money, and whether she be damned for that, I know not.

MISTRESS QUICKLY

No, I warrant you.

FALSTAFF

Go, you thing, go![10]

MISTRESS QUICKLY

Say, what thing? what thing?

POINS

What thing?

FALSTAFF

Why, a thing to thank God on.

MISTRESS QUICKLY

I am no thing to thank God on. I am an honest man's wife, and, setting thy knighthood aside, thou art a knave to call me so.

FALSTAFF

Setting thy womanhood aside, thou art a beast to say otherwise.

MISTRESS QUICKLY

Say, what beast, thou knave, thou?

FALSTAFF

What beast? Why, an otter.

BARDOLPH

An otter?[11]

MISTRESS QUICKLY

An otter?

PRINCE

Sir John, why an otter?

POINS

Why an otter?

FALSTAFF

Why, she's neither fish nor flesh; a man knows not where to have her.

MISTRESS QUICKLY

Thou art an unjust man in saying so. Thou or any man knows where to have me, thou knave, thou.

PRINCE

Bardolph!

(Exit Bardolph, Page, Drawer, Gadshill and Mistress Quickly.)

FALSTAFF

Now, Hal, what time of day is it, lad?

PRINCE

Thou art so fat-witted with drinking of old sack, and unbuttoning thee after supper, and sleeping upon benches after noon, that thou hast forgotten to demand that truly which thou wouldest truly know. What a devil hast thou to do with the time of day? Unless hours were cups of sack, and minutes capons, and clocks the tongues of bawds, and dials the signs of leaping houses, and the blessed sun himself a fair hot wench in flame-coloured taffeta, I see no reason why thou shouldst be so superfluous to demand the time of day.[12]

FALSTAFF

Indeed you come near me now, Hal.

(sings)

Empty the jordan.

(as before)
'Sblood, I am as melancholy as a gib-cat or a lugged bear.

PRINCE
Or an old lion, or a lover's lute.

FALSTAFF
Yea, or the drone of a Lincolnshire bagpipe.

PRINCE
What sayest thou to a hare, or the melancholy of a Moor Ditch?

FALSTAFF
Thou hast the most unsavory similes. But, Hal, thou hast done much harm upon me—God forgive thee for it! Before I knew thee, Hal, I knew nothing; and now am I, if a man should speak truly, little better than one of the wicked. I must give over this life. By the Lord, I will give it over!

PRINCE
Where shall we take a purse to-morrow, Jack?

FALSTAFF
Zounds, where thou wilt, lad! I'll make one.

PRINCE
I see a good amendment of life in thee—from praying to purse-taking.

FALSTAFF
Why, Hal, 'tis my vocation, Hal. 'Tis no sin for a man to labour in his vocation.

POINS
But, my lads, my lads, to-morrow morning, by four o'clock early, at Gad's Hill! There are pilgrims going to Canterbury with rich offerings, and traders riding to London with fat purses. If you will go, I will stuff your purses full of crowns.

FALSTAFF
Hal, wilt thou make one?

PRINCE
Who, I rob? I a thief? Not I, by my faith.

FALSTAFF
There's neither honesty, manhood, nor good fellowship in thee, nor thou cam'st not of the blood royal if thou darest not stand for ten shillings.

PRINCE
I care not.

PETO
Sir John, I prithee, leave the prince and me alone.[13]

POINS
We will lay him down such reasons for this adventure that he shall go.

FALSTAFF

Well, God give thee the spirit of persuasion and him the ears of profiting, that
what thou speakest may be believed, that the true prince may (for recreation
sake) prove a false thief.

POINS

(aside; to the Prince)

I have a jest to execute that I cannot manage alone.

FALSTAFF

For the poor abuses of time want countenance. Farewell.

PRINCE

Farewell, thou latter spring!

FALSTAFF

You shall find me in Eastcheap.

PRINCE

Farewell, All-hallown summer!

(Exit Falstaff.)

POINS

Falstaff, Bardolph and Gadshill shall rob those men that we have already waylaid;
yourself and I will not be there; and when they have the booty, if you and I do
not rob them, cut this head off from my shoulders.

PRINCE

How shall we part with them in setting forth?

PETO

Why, you will set forth before or after them.[14]

POINS

And appoint them a place of meeting, wherein it is at our pleasure to fail.

PETO

And then will they adventure upon the exploit themselves.[15]

POINS

Which they shall have no sooner achieved, but we'll set upon them.

PRINCE

Yea, but 'tis like that they will know us by our horses.

PETO

Tut!

POINS

I'll tie them in the wood.

PRINCE

By our habits, and by every other appointment, to be ourselves.

PETO

Your vizards you will change after you leave them; and, sirrah, I have cases of buckram for the nonce, to immask your noted outer garments.[16]

POINS

The virtue of this jest will be the incomprehensible lies that this same fat rogue will tell us when we meet at supper: how thirty, at least, he fought with; what wards, what blows, what extremities he endured.

PETO

Now, my good sweet honey lord, ride with us to-morrow.[17]

POINS

And in reproof of this lies the jest.

PRINCE

Well, I'll go with thee. Provide all things necessary and meet me to-night. Farewell.

POINS

Farewell, my lord.

(Exit Poins and Peto.)

PRINCE

I know you all, and will awhile uphold
The unyoked humour of your idleness.
Yet herein will I imitate the sun,
Who doth permit the base contagious clouds
To smother up his beauty from the world,
That, when he please again to be himself,
Being wanted, he may be more wond'red at
By breaking through the foul and ugly mists
Of vapours that did seem to strangle him.
If all the year were playing holidays,
To sport would be as tedious as to work;
But when they seldom come, they wished-for come,
And nothing pleaseth but rare accidents.
So, when this loose behaviour I throw off
And pay the debt I never promis'd,
By how much better than my word I am,
By so much shall I falsify men's hopes;
And, like bright metal on a sullen ground,
My reformation, glitt'ring o'er my fault,
Shall show more goodly and attract more eyes
Than that which hath no foil to set it off.
I'll so offend to make offense a skill,
Redeeming time when men think least I will.

(Revolve.)

Scene Five

Council room. Unfurnished.
Various lords discovered. Enter King Henry.

KING HENRY

Can no man tell me of my unthrifty son?
'Tis full three months since I did see him last.
If any plague hang over us, 'tis he.
I would to God, my lords, he might be found.
Inquire at London, 'mongst the taverns there,
For there, they say, he daily doth frequent,
with unrestrain'd loose companions,
Even such, they say, as stand in narrow lanes
And beat our watch and rob our passengers,
Which he, young wanton and effeminate boy,
Takes on the point of honour to support
So dissolute a crew.[1]

(Revolve.)

Scene Six

London street.
Enter Prince and Poins.

FALSTAFF

(off-stage)
Hal! Poins, and be hanged![1]

POINS

Come, I have removed Falstaff's horse.

PRINCE

Stand close.

(Exit Poins. Enter Falstaff.)

FALSTAFF

Poins!

PRINCE

Peace, ye fat-kidneyed rascal! What a brawling dost thou keep!

FALSTAFF

Where's Poins, Hal?

PRINCE

He is walked up to the top of the hill.

FALSTAFF

The rascal hath removed my horse and tied him I know not where. Poins!

PRINCE

I'll go seek him.

(Exit Prince.)

FALSTAFF

Hal! A plague upon you both! Bardolph! Peto! I'll starve ere I'll rob a foot further. An 'twere not as good a deed as drink to turn true man and to leave these rogues, I am the veriest varlet that ever chewed with a tooth.

(He whistles.)

Whew! Give me my horse, you rogues!

PRINCE

(off-stage)

Peace, ye fat-guts!

FALSTAFF

Give me my horse and be hanged!

(Enter Poins.)

POINS

Lie down, lay thine ear close to the ground, and list if thou canst hear the tread of travellers.[2]

FALSTAFF

Have you any levers to lift me up again, being down?

(Enter Prince.)

'Sblood, I'll not bear mine own flesh so far afoot again for all the coin in thy father's exchequer. I prithee, good Prince Hal, help me to my horse, good king's son.

PRINCE

Out, ye rogue! Shall I be your ostler?

FALSTAFF

Go hang thyself in thine own heir-apparent garters! If I be ta'en, an I have not ballads made on you all, and sung to filthy tunes, let a cup of sack be my poison.

(Enter Page, Bardolph and Gadshill.)

PRINCE

Go with your vizards![3]

(aside to Poins)

Ned, where are our disguises?

POINS

(aside to Prince)

Here.

PAGE

There's money of the king's coming down the hill.[4]

PRINCE

Sirs, you four shall front them in the narrow lane; Ned Poins and I will walk lower. If they scape from your encounter, then they light on us.

BARDOLPH

How many be there of them?[5]

PAGE

Some eight or ten.[6]

FALSTAFF

Zounds, will they not rob us?

POINS

Stand close.

(Exit Prince and Poins. Enter the Travellers.)

FALSTAFF

Stand!

TRAVELLER

Jesus bless us! We are undone!

FALSTAFF

Strike! down with them! cut the villains' throats! Hang ye, fat chuffs! You whoreson caterpillars! bacon-fed knaves!

(Exit the Thieves and Travellers. Enter Prince and Poins disguised. Enter the Thieves again.)

FALSTAFF

Come, my masters, let us share, and then merrily to horse. An the Prince and Poins be not two arrant cowards, there's no equity stirring. There's no more valour in that Poins than in a wild duck.

(The Prince screams like a wolf. He and Poins set upon the others, who run away, leaving the booty behind them.)

POINS

Villains!

(Curtain and revolve.)

Scene Seven

CHORUS

Now the earle of Northumberland, with his brother Thomas earle of Worcester, and his sonne the lord Henrie Persie, surnamed Hotspur, which were to aid king Henrie in the beginning of his reigne, both faithful friends, and earnest aiders, began now to envie his wealth and felicitie; and especiallie they were greeved, because the king demanded of the earle and his sonne such Scottish prisoners as were taken at Homeldon and Nesbit. Wherewith the Persies being sore offended, for that they claimed them as their owne proper prisoners, by the counsell of the lord Thomas Persie earle of Worcester, whose studie was ever (as some write) to procure malice, and set things in a broile, came to the king unto Windsore.[1]

(Raise curtain.)

Scene Eight

London street.
Enter the Percys. Business only.[1]

Scene Nine

Council room. Furnished.
King Henry and his lords and Archbishop of Canterbury
discovered.

KING HENRY

What think you, coz,
Of this young Percy's pride? The prisoners
Which he in this adventure hath surprised
To his own use he keeps, and sends me word
I shall have none but Mordake Earl of Fife.[1]

CANTERBURY

This is his uncle's teaching.[2]

WESTMORELAND

This is Worcester.

(Enter Hotspur, Worcester, Northumberland and Atten-
dants.)

KING HENRY

My blood hath been too cold and temperate,
Unapt to stir at these indignities,
And you have found me, for accordingly
You tread upon my patience; but be sure
I will from henceforth rather be myself,
Mighty and to be feared.[3]

WORCESTER

Our house, my sovereign liege, little deserves
The scourge of greatness to be used on it.

NORTHUMBERLAND

My lord—

WORCESTER

And that same greatness too which our own hands
Have holp to make so portly.

KING HENRY

Worcester!

NORTHUMBERLAND

Those prisoners in your highness' name demanded
Which Harry Percy here at Holmedon took—

KING HENRY

Get thee gone, for I do see
Danger and disobedience in thine eye.
You have good leave to leave us: when we need
Your use and counsel, we shall send for you.

(Exit Worcester.)

KING HENRY
(to Northumberland)

You were about to speak.

HOTSPUR

My liege, I did deny no prisoners.
But I remember, when the fight was done,
When I was dry with rage and extreme toil,
Breathless and faint, leaning upon my sword,
Came there a certain lord, neat and trimly dressed,
Fresh as a bridegroom, and his chin new reaped
Showed like a stubble land at harvest home.
He was perfum'd like a milliner,
And 'twixt his finger and his thumb he held
A pouncet box, which ever and anon
He gave his nose, and took't away again;
Who therewith angry, when it next came there,
Took it in snuff; and still he smiled and talked;
And as the soldiers bore dead bodies by,
He called them untaught knaves, unmannerly,
To bring a slovenly unhandsome corse
Bewixt the wind and his nobility.
With many holiday and lady terms
He questioned me, amongst the rest demanded
My prisoners in your majesty's behalf.
I then, all smarting with my wounds being cold,
To be so pestered with a popingay,
Out of my grief and my impatience
Answered neglectingly, I know not what—

He should, or he should not; for he made me mad
To see him shine so brisk, and smell so sweet,
And talk so like a waiting gentlewoman
Of guns and drums and wounds—God save the mark!—
And telling me the sovereignest thing on earth
Was parmacity for an inward bruise,
And that it was great pity, so it was,
This villainous saltpetre should be digged
Out of the bowels of the harmless earth,
Which many a good tall fellow had destroyed
So cowardly, and but for these vile guns,
He would himself have been a soldier.
This bald unjointed chat of his, my lord,
I answered indirectly, as I said,
And I beseech you, let not his report
Come current for an accusation
Betwixt my love and your high majesty.

KING HENRY
Why, yet he doth deny his prisoners.

WESTMORELAND
But with proviso and exception.[4]

CANTERBURY
That we at our own charge shall ransom straight
His brother-in-law.[5]

WARWICK
The foolish Mortimer.[6]

KING HENRY
I shall never hold that man my friend
Whose tongue shall ask me for one penny cost
To ransom home revolted Mortimer.

HOTSPUR
Revolted Mortimer?

NORTHUMBERLAND
He never did fall off, my sovereign liege,
But by the chance of war.[7]

HOTSPUR
To prove that true
Needs no more but one tongue for all those wounds,
Those mouth'd wounds, which valiantly he took
When on the gentle Severn's sedgy bank,
In single opposition hand to hand,

He did confound the best part of an hour
In changing hardiment with the great Glendower.

KING HENRY

Thou dost belie him, Percy, thou dost belie him!

CANTERBURY

He never did encounter with Glendower.[8]

WARWICK

He durst as well have met the devil alone
As Owen Glendower for an enemy.[9]

ELY

Art thou not ashamed?[10]

KING HENRY

Sirrah, henceforth
Let me not hear you speak of Mortimer.
Send me your prisoners with the speediest means,
Or you shall hear in such a kind from me
As will displease you. My Lord Northumberland,
We license your departure with your son—
Send us your prisoners, or you will hear of it.

(Exit the Percys. Revolve.)

Scene Ten

London street.
Enter the Percys.

HOTSPUR

As if the devil come and roar for them,
I will not send them. I will after straight
And tell him so.
'Sirrah, let me not hear you speak of Mortimer.'[1]
Zounds, I will speak of him, and let my soul
Want mercy if I do not join with him!
He will (forsooth) have all my prisoners;
And when I urged the ransom once again
Of my wife's brother, then his cheek looked pale,
And on my face he turned an eye of death,
Trembling even at the name of Mortimer.

WORCESTER

I cannot blame him. Was he not proclaimed
By Richard that dead is, the next of blood?

NORTHUMBERLAND

He was.

HOTSPUR

But soft, I pray you.

NORTHUMBERLAND

I heard the proclamation.

HOTSPUR

Did King Richard then
Proclaim my brother Edmund Mortimer
Heir to the throne?

WORCESTER

He did.

NORTHUMBERLAND

Myself did hear it.

HOTSPUR

But shall it be that you, that set the crown
Upon the head of this forgetful man,
Shall it for shame be spoken in these days,
Or fill up chronicles in time to come,
That men of your nobility and power
Did gage them both in an unjust behalf
(As both of you, God pardon it! have done)
To put down Richard, that sweet lovely rose,
And plant this thorn, this canker, Bolingbroke?

WORCESTER

Peace, cousin—

HOTSPUR

And shall it in more shame be further spoken
That you are fooled, discarded, and shook off
By him for whom these shames ye underwent?
Therefore I say—

WORCESTER

Peace, cousin, say no more.

HOTSPUR

By heaven, methinks it were an easy leap
To pluck bright honour from the pale-faced moon,
Or dive into the bottom of the deep,
Where fadom line could never touch the ground,
And pluck up drown'd honour by the locks,
So he that doth redeem her thence might wear
Without corrival all her dignities;

But out upon this half-faced fellowship!
Good cousin, give me audience for a while.[2]
I cry you mercy.

WORCESTER

Those same noble Scots
That are your prisoners—

HOTSPUR

I'll keep them all.
By God, he shall not have a Scot of them!

WORCESTER

Those prisoners you shall keep.

HOTSPUR

Nay, I will! That's flat!
He said he would not ransom Mortimer,
Forbade my tongue to speak of Mortimer,
But I will find him when he lies asleep,
And in his ear I'll hollo 'Mortimer.'
Nay, I'll have a starling shall be taught to speak
Nothing but 'Mortimer,' and give it him
To keep his anger still in motion.

WORCESTER

Hear you, cousin, a word.

HOTSPUR

All studies here I solemnly defy
Save how to gall and pinch this Bolingbroke;
And that sword-and-buckler Prince of Wales:
But that I think his father loves him not
And would be glad he met with some mischance,
I would have him poisoned with a pot of ale.

NORTHUMBERLAND

Brother, the king hath made your nephew mad.

WORCESTER

Farewell, kinsman.

HOTSPUR

Why, look you, I am whipped and scourged with rods—

WORCESTER

I will talk to you when you are better tempered to attend.

HOTSPUR

Nettled and stung with pismires when I hear
Of this vile politician, Bolingbroke.
In Richard's time—what do you call the place?

A plague upon it! it is in Gloucestershire;
'Twas where the madcap duke his uncle kept,
His uncle York—where I first bowed my knee
Unto this king of smiles, this Bolingbroke—
'Sblood! when you and he came back from Ravenspurgh—

NORTHUMBERLAND

At Berkeley Castle.

HOTSPUR

You say true.
Why, what a candy deal of courtesy
This fawning greyhound then did proffer me!
Look, 'when his infant fortune came of age,'
And 'gentle Harry Percy,' and 'kind cousin'—
O, the devil take such cozeners!—God forgive me!
Good uncle, tell your tale, for I have done.

WORCESTER

Nay.

HOTSPUR

I have done.

WORCESTER

If you have not, to it again.

HOTSPUR

I have done, i' faith.

WORCESTER

We will stay your leisure.
Then once more to your Scottish prisoners:
Deliver them up without their ransom straight.
                    (to Northumberland)
You, my lord,
Your son in Scotland being thus employed,
Shall secretly into the bosom creep
Of that same noble prelate well-beloved,
The archbishop.

HOTSPUR

Of York, is it not?

WORCESTER

True.

HOTSPUR

I smell it. Upon my life, it will do well.
And then the power of Scotland and of York
To join with Mortimer, ha?

WORCESTER

And so they shall.
When time is ripe, which will be suddenly,
I'll steal to Glendower and Lord Mortimer,
Where you and Douglas, and our pow'rs at once,
As I will fashion it, shall happily meet.

(*Exits.*)

NORTHUMBERLAND

Farewell, good brother.

HOTSPUR

Uncle, adieu.

NORTHUMBERLAND

We shall thrive, I trust.

(*Exits.*)

HOTSPUR

O, let the hours be short
Till fields and blows and groans applaud our sport!

(*Exits.*)

CHORUS

And so the Persies departed, minding nothing more than to depose king
Henrie from the high type of royaltie.[3]

(*Revolve.*)

Scene Eleven

Boar's Head Tavern.
Enter the Prince, Poins and Peto.

PRINCE

Got with much ease. The thieves are scattered, and possessed with fear so strongly
that they dare not meet each other.[1]

POINS

Each takes his fellow for an officer.[2]

PRINCE

Falstaff sweats to death and lards the lean earth as he walks along. Were't not
for laughing, I should pity him.

POINS

How the rogue roared!

(*Enter Falstaff, Bardolph, Gadshill and the Page.*)

POINS

Welcome, Jack. Where hast thou been?[3]

FALSTAFF

A plague of all cowards, I say, and a vengence too! Marry and amen! Boy, give me a cup of sack, boy. Is there no virtue extant?

(He drinks.)

Go thy ways, old Jack, die when thou wilt; if manhood, good manhood, be not forgotten upon the face of the earth, then I am a shotten herring. There lives not three good men unhanged in England; and one of them is fat, and grows old. God help the while! A bad world, I say. A plague of all cowards, I say still!

PRINCE

How now, woolsack? What mutter you?

FALSTAFF

A king's son! If I do not beat thee out of thy kingdom with a dagger of lath and drive all thy subjects afore thee like a flock of wild geese, I'll never wear hair on my face more.

PRINCE

Why, you whoreson round man!

FALSTAFF

You Prince of Wales!

PRINCE

What's the matter?

FALSTAFF

What's the matter? There be four of us here have ta'en a thousand pound this day morning.

PRINCE

Where is it, Jack?

POINS

Where is it?

FALSTAFF

Where is it? Taken from us it is. A hundred upon poor four of us!

PRINCE

What, a hundred, man?

FALSTAFF

I am a rogue if I were not at half-sword with a dozen of them two hours together. I have scaped by miracle. I am eight times thrust through the doublet, four through the hose; my buckler cut through and through; my sword hacked like a handsaw—ecce signum!

PRINCE

Speak, sirs. How was it?

BARDOLPH

We four set upon some dozen—[4]

FALSTAFF

Sixteen at least, my lord.

BARDOLPH

And bound them.[5]

PAGE

No, no, they were not bound.[6]

FALSTAFF

You rogue, they were bound, every man of them, or I am a Jew else—an Ebrew Jew.

BARDOLPH

As we were sharing, some six or seven fresh men set upon us—[7]

FALSTAFF

And unbound the rest.

PRINCE

What, fought you with all of them?

FALSTAFF

All? I know not what you call all, but if I fought not with fifty of them, I am a bunch of radish! If there were not two or three and fifty upon poor old Jack, then am I no two-legged creature.

PRINCE

Pray God you have not murd'red some of them.

FALSTAFF

Nay, that's past praying for. I have peppered two of them. Two I am sure I have paid, two rogues in buckram suits. I tell thee what, Hal—if I tell thee a lie, spit in my face. Here I lay, and thus I bore my point. Four rogues in buckram let drive at me.

PRINCE

What, four? Thou saidst but two even now.

FALSTAFF

Four, Hal. I told thee four.

POINS

Ay, ay, he said four.

FALSTAFF

These four came all afront and mainly thrust at me. I made no more ado but took all their seven points in my target, thus.

PRINCE

Seven? Why, there were but four even now.

FALSTAFF

In buckram?

POINS

Ay, four, in buckram suits.

FALSTAFF

Seven, by these hilts, or I am a villain else.

PRINCE

(aside to Poins)

Prithee let him alone. We shall have more anon.

FALSTAFF

Dost thou hear me, Hal?

PRINCE

Ay, and mark thee too, Jack.

FALSTAFF

Do so, for it is worth the list'ning to. These nine in buckram that I told thee of—

PRINCE

So, two more already.

FALSTAFF

Their points being broken—

POINS

Down fell their hose.

FALSTAFF

Began to give me ground; but I followed me close, came in, foot and hand, and with a thought seven of the eleven I paid.

PRINCE

O monstrous! Eleven buckram men grown out of two!

FALSTAFF

But, as the devil would have it, three misbegotten knaves in Kendal green came at my back and let drive at me; for it was so dark, Hal, that thou couldst not see thy hand.

PRINCE

These lies are like their father that begets them—gross as a mountain.

FALSTAFF

What?

PRINCE

Open. Palpable.

FALSTAFF

Art thou mad?

PRINCE

Why, thou clay-brained guts—

FALSTAFF

Art thou mad?

PRINCE

Thou knotty-pated fool, thou whoreson—

FALSTAFF

Is not the truth the truth?

PRINCE

Obscene, greasy tallow-catch—how couldst thou know these men in Kendal green when it was so dark thou couldst not see thy hand? Come, tell us your reason. What sayest thou to this?

POINS

Come, your reason, Jack, your reason.

FALSTAFF

What, upon compulsion? Zounds, give you a reason on compulsion? If reasons were as plentiful as blackberries, I would give no man a reason upon compulsion, I.

PRINCE

I'll be no longer guilty of this sin; this sanguine coward, this bed-presser, this horseback-breaker, this huge hill of flesh—

(The others react.)

FALSTAFF

'Sblood, you starveling, you eel-skin, you dried neat's-tongue, you bull's pizzle, you vile standing tuck—

PRINCE

Well breathe awhile. Clap to the doors.[8] Mark, we two saw you four set on four, and bound them and were masters of their wealth. Mark now how a plain tale shall put you down. Then did we two set on you four and, with a word, outfaced you from your prize, and have it; yea, and can show it you here in this house. And, Falstaff, you carried your guts away as nimbly, with as quick dexterity, and roared for mercy, and still run and roared, as ever I heard a bullcalf. What a slave art thou to hack thy sword as thou hast done, and then say it was in fight! What trick, what device, what starting hole canst thou now find out to hide thee from this open and apparent shame?

FALSTAFF

By the Lord, I knew ye as well as he that made ye. Why, hear you, my masters. Was it for me to kill the heir apparent? Should I turn upon the true prince? Why, thou knowest I am as valiant as Hercules, but beware instinct. The lion will not touch the true prince. Instinct is a great matter. I was no a coward on instinct.

I shall think the better of myself, and thee, during my life—I for a valiant lion, and thou for a true prince. But, by the Lord, lads, I am glad you have the money.

(Enter Mistress Quickly.)

MISTRESS QUICKLY

O Jesu!

PRINCE

How now, my lady the hostess?

MISTRESS QUICKLY

My lord the Prince!

PRINCE

What say'st thou to me?

MISTRESS QUICKLY

Marry, my lord, there is a noble man of the court at door would speak with you. He says he comes from your father.

PRINCE

Give him as much as will make him a royal man, and send him back again to my mother.

FALSTAFF

What manner of man is he?

MISTRESS QUICKLY

An old man.

FALSTAFF

What doth gravity out of his bed at midnight?

(Enter Bracy.)

BRACY

Your Grace!

FALSTAFF

Shall I give him his answer?

PRINCE

Prithee do, Jack.

FALSTAFF

Faith, and I'll send him packing.

(Exit Falstaff and Bracy.)

PRINCE

Now, sirs. By'r Lady, you fought fair; so did you, Bardolph. You are lions too, you ran away upon instinct, you will not touch the true prince; no—fie!

BARDOLPH

Faith, I ran when I saw the others run.

PRINCE

Faith, tell me now in earnest, how came Falstaff's sword so hacked?

PAGE

Why, he hacked it with his dagger, and said he would swear truth out of England but he would make you believe it was done in fight, and persuaded us to do the like.[9]

BARDOLPH

Yea, and to tickle our noses with speargrass to make them bleed, and then to beslubber our garments with it and swear it was the blood of true men. I blushed to hear his monstrous devices.

(Enter Falstaff.)

PRINCE

Here comes lean Jack.

POINS

Here comes bare-bone.[10]

PRINCE

How now, my sweet creature of bombast? How long is't ago, Jack, since thou sawest thine own knee?

FALSTAFF

My own knee? When I was about thy years, Hal, I was not an eagle's talent in the waist; I could have crept into any alderman's thumbring. A plague of sighing and grief! It blows a man up like a bladder. There's villainous news abroad. Here was Sir John Bracy from your father. You must to court in the morning. That same mad fellow of the north, Percy, and he of Wales that gave Amamon the bastinado, and made Lucifer cuckold, and swore the devil his true liegeman upon the cross of a Welsh hook—what a plague call you him?

POINS

Owen Glendower.

FALSTAFF

Owen, Owen—the same; and his son-in-law Mortimer, and old Northumberland, and that sprightly Scot of Scots, Douglas, that runs a-horseback up a hill perpendicular—

PRINCE

He that rides at high speed and with his pistol kills a sparrow flying.

FALSTAFF

You have hit it.

PRINCE

So did he never the sparrow.

FALSTAFF

Well, that rascal hath good metal in him; he will not run.

PRINCE

Why, what a rascal art thou then, to praise him so for running!

FALSTAFF

A-horseback, ye cuckoo! but afoot he will not budge a foot.

PRINCE

Yes, Jack, upon instinct.

FALSTAFF

I grant ye, upon instinct. Well, he is there too, and Worcester is stol'n away to-night; thy father's beard is turned white with the news; you may buy land now as cheap as stinking mack'rel.

PRINCE

Why then, it is like, if there come a hot June, and the civil buffeting hold, we shall buy maidenheads as they buy hobnails, by the hundreds.

FALSTAFF

By the mass, lad, thou sayest true; it is like we shall have good trading that way. But tell me, Hal, art thou not horrible afeard? Thou being heir apparent, could the world pick thee out three such enemies again as that fiend Douglas, that spirit Percy, and that devil Glendower? Art thou not horribly afraid? Doth not thy blood thrill at it?

PRINCE

Not a whit, i' faith. I lack some of thy instinct.

FALSTAFF

Well, thou wilt be horribly chid to-morrow when thou comest to thy father. If you love me, practice an answer.

BARDOLPH

Shall we have a play extempore?

FALSTAFF

Shall I? Content. Well, an the fire of grace be not quite out of thee, now shalt thou be moved.

BARDOLPH

Give me a cup of sack to make my eyes look red, that it might be thought I have wept; for I must speak in passion, and I will do it in King Cambyses' vein.[11]

(singing)

When good King Arthur ruled this land, He was a goodly King.
He stole three pecks of barley meal to make a big pudding.

A big pudding the King did make,
And stuffed it well with plums.
And in it put great lumps of fat
As big as my two thumbs.

The King and Queen did eat thereof,
And noble men beside.
And what they could not eat that night

The Queen next morning fried.

When good King Arthur ruled this land, He was a goodly King.

MISTRESS QUICKLY
O, the Father, how he holds his countenance!

FALSTAFF
For God's sake, lords, convey my tristful queen! For tears do stop the floodgates of her eyes.

MISTRESS QUICKLY
O Jesu, he doth it as like one of these harlotry players as ever I see!

FALSTAFF
Peace, good pintpot.

PRINCE
Peace, good tickle-brain. Stand aside, nobility. Well, here is my leg.[12]

FALSTAFF
And here is my speech. Harry, I do not only marvel where thou spendest thy time, but also how thou art accompanied. That thou art my son I have partly thy mother's word, partly my own opinion, but chiefly a villainous trick of thine eye and a foolish hanging of thy nether lip that doth warrant me. If then thou be son to me, here lies the point: why, being son to me, art thou so pointed at? Shall the blessed sun of heaven prove a micher and eat blackberries? A question not to be asked. Shall the son of England prove a thief and take purses? A question to be asked. There is a thing, Harry, which thou hast often heard of, and it is known to many in our land by the name of pitch. This pitch, as ancient writers do report, doth defile; so doth the company thou keepest. For, Harry, now I do not speak to thee in drink, but in tears; not in pleasure, but in passion; not in words only, but in woes also: and yet there is a virtuous man whom I have often noted in thy company, but I know not his name.

PRINCE
What manner of man, an it like your majesty?

FALSTAFF
A goodly portly man, i' faith and a corpulent; of a cheerful look, a pleasing eye, and a most noble carriage; and, as I think, his age some fifty, or, by'r Lady, inclining to threescore; and now I remember me, his name is Falstaff. If that man should be lewdly given, he deceiveth me; for Harry, I see virtue in his looks. If then the tree may be known by the fruit, as the fruit by the tree, then, peremptorily I speak it, there is virtue in that Falstaff. Him keep with, the rest banish. And tell me now, thou naughty varlet, tell me where thou hast been this month?

PRINCE
Dost thou speak like a king? Do thou stand for me, and I'll play my father.

FALSTAFF
Depose me? If thou dost it half so gravely, so majestically, both in word and matter, hang me up by the heels for a rabbit-sucker or a poulter's hare.

PRINCE
Well, here I am set.

FALSTAFF
And here I stand. Judge, my masters.

PRINCE
Now, Harry, whence come you?

FALSTAFF
My noble lord, from Eastcheap.

PRINCE
The complaints I hear of thee are grievous.

FALSTAFF
'Sblood, my lord, they are false!

PRINCE
Swearest thou, ungracious boy?

FALSTAFF
Nay, I'll tickle ye for a young prince, i' faith.

PRINCE
Henceforth ne'er look on me. Thou art violently carried away from grace. There is a devil haunts thee in the likeness of an old fat man; a tun of man is thy companion. Why dost thou converse with that trunk of humours, that bolting hutch of beastliness, that swoll'n parcel of dropsies, that huge bombast of sack, that stuffed cloakbag of guts, that roasted Manningtree ox with the pudding in his belly, that reverend vice, that grey iniquity, that father ruffian, that vanity in years? Wherein is he good, but to taste sack and drink it? wherein neat and cleanly, but to carve a capon and eat it? wherein cunning, but in craft? wherein crafty, but in villainy? wherein villainous, but in all things? wherein worthy, but in nothing?

FALSTAFF
I would your grace would take me with you. Whom means your grace?

PRINCE
That villainous abominable misleader of youth, Falstaff, that old white-bearded Satan.

FALSTAFF
My lord, the man I know.

PRINCE
I know thou dost.

FALSTAFF
But to say I know more harm in him than in myself were to say more than I

know. That he is old (the more the pity), his white hairs do witness it; but that he is (saving your reverence) a whoremaster, that I utterly deny. If sack and sugar be a fault, God help the wicked! If to be old and merry be a sin, then many an old host that I know is damned. If to be fat be to be hated, then Pharaoh's lean kine are to be loved. No, my good lord: banish Peto, banish Bardolph, banish Poins; but for sweet Jack Falstaff, kind Jack Falstaff, true Jack Falstaff, valiant Jack Falstaff, and therefore more valiant being, as he is, old Jack Falstaff, banish him not from thy Harry's company. Banish plump Jack, and banish all the world.

PRINCE

I do, I will.

> *(A knocking heard. Exit Bardolph. Enter Bardolph, running.)*

BARDOLPH

O, my lord, my lord! the Chief Justice with a most monstrous watch is at the door.

FALSTAFF

Out, ye rogue! Play out the play. I have much to say in behalf of that Falstaff.

BARDOLPH

The Chief Justice!

PRINCE

Go hide thee behind the arras. The rest walk up above. Now, my masters, for a true face and good conscience.

FALSTAFF

Both which I have had; but their date is out, and therefore I'll hide me.

> *(Exit all but the Prince. Enter Chief Justice, Carrier and Attendants.)*

PRINCE

Now, my lord.

CHIEF JUSTICE

Your grace.

PRINCE

What is your will with me?

CHIEF JUSTICE

A hue and cry
Hath followed certain men unto this house.

PRINCE

What men?

CHIEF JUSTICE

One of them is well known, my gracious lord—
A gross fat man.

CARRIER

As fat as butter.

PRINCE

The man, I do assure you, is not here,
For I myself at this time have employed him.
And, chief justice, I will engage my word to thee
That I will by to-morrow dinner time
Send him to answer thee, or any man,
For anything he shall be charged withal;
And so let me entreat you leave the house.

CHIEF JUSTICE

I will, my lord. There are two gentlemen
Have in this robbery lost three hundred marks.

PRINCE

It may be so. If he have robbed these men,
He shall be answerable; and so farewell.

CHIEF JUSTICE

Good night, my noble lord.

PRINCE

I think it is good morrow, is it not?

CHIEF JUSTICE

Indeed, my lord, I think it be two o'clock.

(Exit Chief Justice, Carrier and Attendants. Revolve.)

Scene Twelve

Alley.
Enter Prince and Peto.

PRINCE

This oily rascal is known as well as Paul's. Go call him forth.

PETO

Falstaff! Fast alseep behind the arras, and snorting like a horse.

PRINCE

Hark how hard he fetches breath. There let him sleep till day. I'll to the court in the morning. We must all to the wars, and thy place shall be honourable. I'll procure this fat rogue a charge of foot, and I know his death will be a march of twelve score. The money shall be paid back again with advantage. Be with me betimes in the morning, and so good morrow, Peto.

PETO

Good morrow, good my lord.

(Exit Prince over rise. Revolve.)

Scene Thirteen

Council room.
King Henry, the Prince and lords are discovered.

KING HENRY

Lords, give us leave: the Prince of Wales and I
Must have some private conference; but be near at hand,
For we shall presently have need of you.

(Exit lords.)

I know not whether God will have it so
For some displeasing service I have done,
That, in his secret doom, out of my blood
He'll breed revengement and a scourge for me;
But thou dost in thy passages of life
Make me believe that thou art only marked
For the hot vengence and the rod of heaven
To punish my mistreadings. Tell me else,
Could such inordinate and low desires,
Such poor, such bare, such lewd, such mean attempts,
Such barren pleasures, rude society,
As thou art matched withal and grafted to,
Accompany the greatness of thy blood
And hold their level with thy princely heart?
For all the world,
As thou art to this hour was Richard then
When I from France set foot at Ravenspurgh;
And even as I was then is Percy now.
Now, by my sceptre, and my soul to boot,
He hath more worthy interest to the state
Than thou, the shadow of succession;
For of no right, nor colour like to right,
He doth fill fields with harness in the realm,
Turns heads against the lion's arm'd jaws,
And, being no more in debt to years than thou,
Leads ancient lords and reverend bishops on
To bloody battles and bruising arms.
God pardon thee! Yet let me wonder, Harry,
At thy affections, which do hold a wing
Quite from the flight of all thy ancestors.
Thy place in council thou hast rudely lost,
And art almost an alien to the hearts
Of all the court and princes of my blood.
The hope and expectation of thy time
Is ruined, and the soul of every man

Prophetically do forethink thy fall.
Had I so lavish of my presence been,
So common-hackneyed in the eyes of men,
So stale and cheap to vulgar company,
Opinion, that did help me to the crown,
Had still kept loyal to possession
And left me in reputeless banishment,
A fellow of no mark nor liklihood.
The skipping king, he ambled up and down
With shallow jesters and rash bavin wits,
Mingled his royalty with cap'ring fools;
Grew a companion to the common streets,
So when he had occassion to be seen,
He was but as the cuckoo is in June,
Heard, not regarded—seen, but with such eyes
As, sick and blunted with community,
Afford no extraordinary gaze,
Such as is bent on sunlike majesty.
And in that very line, Harry, standest thou;
For thou hast lost thy princely privilege
With vile participation. Not an eye
But is aweary of thy common sight,
Save mine, which hath desired to see thee more.[1]

PRINCE
I shall hereafter, my thrice-gracious lord,
Be more myself.

KING HENRY
Percy, Northumberland,
The Archbishop's grace of York, Douglas, Mortimer
Capitulate against us and are up.
But wherefore do I tell these news to thee?
Thou that are like enough, through vassal fear,
To fight against me under Percy's pay,
To dog his heels and curtsey at his frowns,
To show how much thou art degenerate.

PRINCE
Do not think so. You shall not find it so.
And God forgive them that so much have swayed
Your majesty's good thoughts away from me.
I will redeem all this on Percy's head
And, in the closing of some glorious day,
Be bold to tell you that I am your son.
And that shall be the day, when'er it lights,
That this same child of honour and renown,

This gallant Hotspur, this all-prais'd knight,
And your unthought-of Harry chance to meet.
For every honour sitting on his helm,
Would they were multitudes, and on my head
My shames redoubled! For the time will come
That I shall make this northern youth exchange
His glorious deeds for my indignities.
This in the name of God I promise here;
I do beseech your majesty may salve
The long-grown wounds of my intemperance.
If not, the end of life cancels all bands,
And I will die a hundred thousand deaths
Ere break the smallest parcel of this vow.

KING HENRY

A hundred thousand rebels die in this!

(Revolve.)

Scene Fourteen

Alley.
Soldiers marching. Business only.

Scene Fifteen

Boar's Head Tavern
Falstaff and Page discovered.

FALSTAFF

Boy! A pox of this gout! Or a gout of this pox! For the one or the other plays
the rogue with my great toe. Boy!

PAGE

Sir!

FALSTAFF

What money is in my purse?

PAGE

Seven groats and two pence.

FALSTAFF

I can get no remedy against this consumption of the purse. Borrowing only
lingers and lingers it out, but the disease is incurable. Go bear this letter to my
Lord of Lancaster, this to the prince, this to the Earl of Westmoreland, and this
to old Mistress Ursala, whom I have weekly sworn to marry since I perceived
the first white hair of my chin about it! 'Tis no matter if I do halt; I have the
wars for my colour, and my pension shall seem the more reasonable. A good

wit will make use of anything. I will turn disease into commodity.[1]

(Falstaff and Page exit. Revolve.)

Scene Sixteen

London street.

Chief Justice and Attendants discovered. Enter Falstaff and Page.

CHIEF JUSTICE

Sir John Falstaff![1]

FALSTAFF

(to Page)
Wait close; I will not see him.

CHIEF JUSTICE

SIR JOHN FALSTAFF!

FALSTAFF

Boy, tell him I am deaf.

CHIEF JUSTICE

Sir John Fal—

PAGE

You must—

CHIEF JUSTICE

Sir John Falstaff, I must—

PAGE

You must—

CHIEF JUSTICE

I must speak with you.

PAGE

You must speak louder.

CHIEF JUSTICE

Louder!

PAGE

My master is deaf. My master is deaf.

CHIEF JUSTICE

Deaf! Go pluck him by the elbow—

PAGE

DEAF.

CHIEF JUSTICE

I am sure he is—deaf—I must speak with him—to the hearing of anything good.

FALSTAFF

About it! About it! What! A young knave, and begging! Is there not wars? Is there not employment? Doth not the king lack subjects? Do not the rebels need soldiers? About it, boy, you know where to find me.

CHIEF JUSTICE

PAGE

Sir John Falstaff.

You must speak louder.

(Exit Page.)

ATTENDANT

Sir John Falstaff!

CHIEF JUSTICE

Sir John!

FALSTAFF

(to Attendant)

Your lordship!

CHIEF JUSTICE

I sent for you. You would not come when I sent for you.

FALSTAFF

An't please your lordship, I hear his majesty is—

CHIEF JUSTICE

I talk not of his majesty.

FALSTAFF

And I hear, moreover, his highness is fallen into this some whoreson apoplexy.

CHIEF JUSTICE

Well, God mend him!

FALSTAFF

This apoplexy, as I take it, is a kind of lethargy.

CHIEF JUSTICE

I pray you.

FALSTAFF

An't please your lordship, a kind of sleeping in the blood.

CHIEF JUSTICE

Let me speak with you.

FALSTAFF

A whoreson tingling, a kind of deafness.

CHIEF JUSTICE

DEAFNESS! Deafness!

FALSTAFF

Deafness!

CHIEF JUSTICE

I think you are fallen into the disease, for you hear not what I say to you.

FALSTAFF

Very well, my lord, very well. Rather, an't please you, it is the disease of not listening, that I am troubled withal.

(to Attendant)

Pardon me my lord.

(to Chief Justice)

God give your lordship good time of day. I am glad to see your lordship abroad. I heard [say] your lordship was sick.

(to Attendant)

I hope his lordship goes abroad by advice. His lordship, though not clean past his youth, hath yet some smack of age in him, some relish of the saltness of age in him—

CHIEF JUSTICE

Well, the truth is, Sir John, you live in great infamy.

FALSTAFF

I most humbly beseech your lordship to have a reverent care of your health.

CHIEF JUSTICE

Your means are very slender and your waste is great.

FALSTAFF

I would it were otherwise. I would my means were greater and my waist slenderer. Ha!

CHIEF JUSTICE

What! You are as a candle, the better part burnt out.

FALSTAFF

A wassail candle, my lord, all tallow.

CHIEF JUSTICE

There is not a white hair in your face but should have his effect of gravity.

FALSTAFF

His effect of gravy, gravy, gravy.

CHIEF JUSTICE

What!

FALSTAFF

You that are old consider not the capacities of us that are young; you do measure the heat of our livers by the bitterness of your galls.

CHIEF JUSTICE

Do you set down your name in the scroll of youth, that are written down old with all the characters of age? Have you not a moist eye? A dry hand? A yellow cheek? A white beard? A decreasing leg? An increasing belly? Is not your voice broken? Your wind short? Your chin double? Your wit single? And every part about you blasted with antiquity? And will you yet call yourself young?

FALSTAFF

You must speak louder. My lord, I was born about three of the clock in the afternoon, with a white head and something of a round belly. For my voice, I have lost it with halloing and singing of anthems.

FALSTAFF
You follow the prince up and down like his ill angel.

FALSTAFF
I cannot rid my hands of him.

CHIEF JUSTICE
Well, the king hath severed you and Prince Harry. I hear you are going to the wars.

FALSTAFF
Yea. There is not a dangerous action can peep out his head but I am thrust upon it. Well, I cannot last forever. But it was always yet the trick of our English nation, if they have a good thing, to make it too common. I would to God my name were not so terrible to the enemy as it is. I were better to be eaten to death with a rust than to be scoured to nothing with perpetual motion.

CHIEF JUSTICE
Well, be honest, be honest, and God bless your expedition!

FALSTAFF
Will your lordship lend me a thousand pound to furnish me forth?

CHIEF JUSTICE
Not a penny, not a penny.

FALSTAFF
Not a penny?

CHIEF JUSTICE
Not a penny.

FALSTAFF
Fare you well.

CHIEF JUSTICE
Fare you well. God send the prince a better companion.

FALSTAFF
God send the companion a better prince!
> *(Revolve. Wooden curtain down.)*

Scene Seventeen

CHORUS
Now the Percies to make their part seeme good, devised certaine articles of such matters as it was supposed that not onlie the communaltie of the realme but also the nobilitie found themselves greeved with: which articles they sent abroad to

their freends further off, assuring them that for the redresse of such oppressions, they would shed the last drop of blood in their bodies, if need were.[1]

(Revolve.)

Scene Eighteen

Percy house.
Enter Hotspur, reading a letter.

HOTSPUR

'But, for mine own part, my lord, I could be well contented to be there, in respect of the love I bear your house.' He could be contented—why is he not then? In respect of the love he bears our house? He shows in this he loves his own barn better than our house. Let me see more.[1]

(Enter Lady Percy.)

How now, Kate?

LADY PERCY

O my good lord, why are you thus alone?

HOTSPUR

I must leave you within these two hours. 'The purpose you undertake is dangerous'—why, that's certain! 'Tis dangerous to take a cold, to sleep, to drink—[2]

LADY PERCY

For what offense have I this fortnight been
A banished woman from my Harry's bed?

HOTSPUR

But I tell you my lord fool—

LADY PERCY
(reading)

'The purpose you undertake is dangerous.'[3]

HOTSPUR

Out of this nettle, danger, we pluck this flower, safety.

LADY PERCY

Tell me, sweet lord, what is't that takes from thee
Thy stomach, pleasure, and thy golden sleep?

HOTSPUR

'...dangerous, the friends you have uncertain, the time itself unsorted, and your whole plot too light for the counterpoise of so great an opposition.'

LADY PERCY

Why hast thou lost the fresh blood in thy cheeks?

HOTSPUR

Say you so, say you so—

LADY PERCY

And given my treasures and my rights of thee
To thick-eyed musing and cursed melancholy?

HOTSPUR

I say unto you again, you are a shallow, cowardly hind, and you lie. What a lackbrain is this! By the Lord, our plot is a good plot as ever was laid; our friends true and constant: a good plot, good friends, and full of expectation.

LADY PERCY

In thy faint slumbers I by thee have watched,
And heard thee murmur tales of iron wars,
Speak terms of manage to thy bounding steed—

HOTSPUR

An excellent plot—

LADY PERCY

Cry 'Courage! to the field!'

HOTSPUR

Very good friends—

LADY PERCY

And thou hast talked
Of sallies and retires, of trenches, tents

LADY PERCY	HOTSPUR
Of palisadoes, frontiers,	What a frosty-spirited rogue is this?
Parapets, Of basiliks,	Zounds!
Of cannon, culverin,	
Of prisoners' ransom,	Ha!
And of soldiers slain,	
And all the currents of a heady fight.	

HOTSPUR

An I were now by this rascal, I could brain him with his lady's fan. What a pagan rascal is this! Is there not my father, my uncle, and myself?

LADY PERCY

O!

HOTSPUR

Hmmm.

LADY PERCY

What portents are these?

HOTSPUR

You shall see now, in very sincerity of fear and cold heart will he to the king and lay open all our proceedings. O, I could divide myself and go to buffets for moving such a dish of skim milk with so honourable an action! Hang him, let him tell the king! we are prepared. I must leave you within these two hours.

LADY PERCY
Such heavy business hath my lord in hand,
And I must know it, else he loves me not.

HOTSPUR
What, ho!

CARPENTER
(off-stage left)
My lord!

POSS
(off-stage right)
My lord!

(Enter Servants.)

HOTSPUR
Is Gilliams with the packet gone?

POSS
He is, my lord, an hour ago.[4]

HOTSPUR
Hath Butler brought those horses from the sheriff?

CARPENTER
One horse, my lord, he brought even now.[5]

HOTSPUR
What horse? A roan?

POSS
It is.

HOTSPUR
A crop-ear, is it not?

POSS
It is, my lord.

HOTSPUR
That roan shall be my throne. O, esperance!

(Exit Servants.)

Well, I will back him straight.
Bid Butler lead him forth into the park.

(Enter Servants.)

CARPENTER
Butler!

POSS
Butler!

(Exit Servants.)

LADY PERCY

But hear you, my lord.

HOTSPUR

What say'st thou, my lady?

LADY PERCY

What is it carries you away?

HOTSPUR

Why, my horse, my love—my horse!

LADY PERCY

Out, you mad-headed ape!
A weasel hath not such a deal of spleen
As you are tossed with. In faith,
I'll know your business, Harry; that I will!
I fear my brother Mortimer doth stir
About his title and hath sent for you
To line his enterprise; but if you go—

HOTSPUR

So far afoot, I shall be weary, love.

LADY PERCY

Come, come, you paraquito, answer me
Directly unto this question that I ask.

HOTSPUR

Away, away, you trifler!

LADY PERCY	HOTSPUR
In faith, I'll break thy little finger, Harry,	Love? I love thee not.
And if thou wilt not tell me all things true.	

HOTSPUR

I care not for thee, Kate. This is no world
To play with mammets and to tilt with lips.
We must have bloody noses and cracked crowns,
And pass them current too. Gods me, my horse!
What say'st thou, Kate? What wouldst thou have with me?

LADY PERCY

Do you not love me? do you not indeed?
Well, do not then; for since you love me not,
I will not love myself. Do you not love me?
Nay, tell me if you speak in jest or no.

HOTSPUR

Come, wilt thou see me ride?
And when I am a-horseback, I will swear
I love thee infinitely. But hark you, Kate:
I must not have you henceforth question me
Whither I go, nor reason whereabout.
Whither I must, I must, and to conclude,
This evening must I leave you, gentle Kate.
I know you wise, but yet no farther wise
Than Harry Percy's wife; constant you are,
But yet a woman; and for secrecy,
No lady closer, for I well believe
Thou wilt not utter what thou dost not know,
And so far will I trust thee, gentle Kate.

LADY PERCY

How? so far?

HOTSPUR

Not an inch further. I must leave you within these two hours.[6]

(Burlap down. Wooden curtain up.)

Scene Nineteen

Salisbury.
Enter Falstaff and army.

FALSTAFF

Boy, fill me a bottle of sack. Our soldiers shall march through. Lieutenant Peto, meet me at town's end.[1]

PETO

I will, captain. Farewell.[2]

(Exit Peto.)

PAGE

Will you give me some money, captain?[3]

FALSTAFF

Lay out, lay out.

(Exit Page.)

If I be not ashamed of my soldiers, I am a soused gurnet. I have misused the king's press damnably. I have got, in exchange of a hundred and fifty soldiers—

BARDOLPH

Three hundred odd pounds.[4]

FALSTAFF

I press me none but good householders and yoemen's sons; and they have bought out their services; and now my whole charge consists of discarded unjust serving men, younger sons to younger brothers, revolted ostlers, trade-fall'n; the cankers of a calm world and a long peace.

(Enter Shallow and Davy.)

SHALLOW
Davy, Davy, Davy, Davy, let me see, Davy. Let me see, Davy, let me see.[5]

FALSTAFF
Bardolph! Shallow!

SHALLOW
Some pidgeons, Davy, a couple of short-legged hens, a joint of mutton, and any pretty little tiny kickshaws, tell William cook.

BARDOLPH
I beseech you, which is Justice Shallow?[6]

SHALLOW
I am Robert Shallow, sir, a poor esquire of this county, and one of the king's justices of the peace.

BARDOLPH
My captain, sir, commends him to you, my captain, Sir John Falstaff—

SHALLOW
Sir John Falstaff!

BARDOLPH
A tall gentleman, by heaven, and a most gallant leader.

FALSTAFF
Master Robert Shallow!

SHALLOW
Jesu, Sir John. Give me your hand, give me your worship's good hand. By my troth, you like well and bear your years very well. Welcome, Sir John.

FALSTAFF
I am glad to see you well, good Master Robert Shallow. Have you provided me here half a dozen sufficient men?

SHALLOW
Marry, have we, sir. Will you sit! Where's the roll? Where's the roll? Where's the roll? Let me see, let me see, let me see. Davy!

DAVY
Here, sir.[7]

SHALLOW
You must stay to dinner, Sir John.

FALSTAFF
You must excuse me, Master Robert Shallow.

SHALLOW
I will not excuse you, you shall not be excused, excuses shall not be admitted.

DAVY

Doth the man of war stay all night, sir?

SHALLOW

Yea, Davy. About thy business, Davy.

FALSTAFF

Bardolph!

SHALLOW

By cock and pie, sir, you shall not away to-night.[8]

(Enter Silence with recruits.)

SILENCE

Master Robert Shallow![9]

SHALLOW

And how doth my good cousin Silence?

SILENCE

Good morrow, good cousin Shallow.

FALSTAFF

Master Surecard, as I think?

SHALLOW

No, Sir John, it is my cousin Silence, in commission with me.

FALSTAFF

Good Master Silence, it well befits you should be of the peace. Fie! This is hot weather, gentlemen.

SHALLOW

Jesu, the same, Sir John, the very same. I see him break Skogan's head at the court-gate, when 'a was a crack not thus high. And the very same day did I fight with one Sampson Stockfish, a fruiterer, behind Gray's Inn. Jesu, Jesu, the mad days that I have spent! And to see how many of my old acquaintance are dead![10]

SILENCE

We shall all follow, cousin.

SHALLOW

Certain, 'tis certain, very sure, very sure. Death, as the Psalmist saith, is certain to all, all shall die. How a good yoke of bullocks at Stamford fair?

SILENCE

By my troth, I was not there.

SHALLOW

Death is certain. Is old Double of your town living yet?

SILENCE

Dead, sir.

SHALLOW

Jesu, Jesu, dead! 'A drew a good bow, and dead! 'A shot a fine shoot. John a

Gaunt loved him well and betted much money on his head. Dead! How a score
of ewes now?

SILENCE

Thereafter as they be. A score of good ewes may be worth ten pounds.

SHALLOW

And is old Double dead? So, so, so, so, so, so.

FALSTAFF

Let me see the soldiers, I beseech you.

SHALLOW

Yea, marry, sir. Davy! The soldiers, Davy. Let them appear as I call, let them
do so, let them do so. I dare say my cousin William is become a good scholar.
He is at Oxford still, is he not?[11]

SILENCE

Indeed, sir, to my cost.

SHALLOW

'A must, then to the Inns o' Court shortly. I was once of Clement's Inn, where
I think they will talk of mad Shallow yet.

SILENCE

You were called 'lusty Shallow' then, cousin.

SHALLOW

By the mass, I was called anything. And I would have done anything indeed
too, and roundly too.

FALSTAFF

Let me see the soldiers—

SHALLOW

There was I, and little John Doit of Staffordshire, and black George Barnes,
and Francis Pickbone, and Will Squele, a Cotswold man; you had not four such
swinge-bucklers in all the Inns o' Court again. Then was Jack Falstaff, now Sir
John, a boy, and page to Thomas Mowbray, Duke of Norfolk.

SILENCE

Death is certain.[12]

SHALLOW

Let me see, where is Mouldy?

MOULDY

Here.

BULLCALF

An't please you.[13]

FALSTAFF

'Tis the more time thou wert used.

SHALLOW

Ha, ha, ha! most excellent, i' faith! Things that are mouldy lack use. Very singular good! In faith, well said, Sir John, very well said.

FALSTAFF

Prick him.

SHALLOW

O, Sir John, do you remember since we lay all night in the Windmill in Saint George's Field?

FALSTAFF

No more of that, good Master Shallow, no more of that.

SHALLOW

Ha! 'Twas a merry night. And is Jane Nightwork alive?

FALSTAFF

She lives, Master Shallow.

SHALLOW

Doth she hold her well?

FALSTAFF

Old, old, Master Shallow.

SHALLOW

Nay, she must be old. She cannot choose but be old. Certain she's old, and [had] Robin Nightwork by old Nightwork before I came to Clement's Inn.

FALSTAFF

That's fifty-five year ago.[14]

SHALLOW

Ha, cousin Silence, that thou hadst seen that that this knight and I have seen! Ha, Sir John, said I well?

FALSTAFF

We have heard the chimes at midnight, Master Shallow.

SHALLOW

That we have, that we have, that we have, in faith, Sir John, we have. The days that we have seen!

FALSTAFF

Prick Mouldy.

BULLCALF

He was pricked well enough before, an you could have let him alone. His old dame will be undone now for one to do her husbandry and her drudgery.[15]

MOULDY

You need not to have pricked me.

SILENCE

There are men fitter to go out than he.[16]

FALSTAFF

Go to. Peace, Mouldy, you shall go. Mouldy, it is time you were spent.

MOULDY

Spent!

SHALLOW

Peace, fellow, peace. Stand aside. Know you where you are? For the other, Sir John, let me see. Simon Shadow!

SILENCE

Simon Shadow!

FALSTAFF

Simon Shadow! Yea, marry, let me have him to sit under. Prick him.[17]

SHALLOW

Thomas Wart!

SILENCE

Thomas Wart!

DAVY

Tommy Wart!

BULLCALF

Tommy!

SHALLOW

Hello, Tommy.

SHALLOW

Shall I prick him, Sir John?

FALSTAFF

It were superfluous, for his apparel is built upon his back and the whole frame stands upon pins. Prick him no more.

SHALLOW

Francis Feeble! Ha, ha, ha! you can do it, sir, you can do it. I commend you well.

SILENCE

Francis Feeble!

DAVY

Francis Feeble!

FEEBLE

Here, sir.

SHALLOW

What trade art thou, Feeble?

FEEBLE

A woman's tailor, sir.

SHALLOW

Shall I prick him, sir?

FALSTAFF

You may. But if he had been a man's tailor, he'd a' pricked you. Wilt thou make as many holes in an enemy's battle as thou hast done in a woman's petticoat?

FEEBLE

I will do my good will, sir. You can have no more.

FALSTAFF

Very well said, good woman's tailor! Well said, courageous Feeble! Thou wilt be as valiant as the wrathful dove or most magnanimous mouse. Prick the woman's tailor well, Master Shallow, deep, Master Shallow.

FEEBLE

I would Wart might have gone, sir.

FALSTAFF

I would thou wert a man's tailor, that thou mightst mend him and make him fit to go. Ha! Let that suffice, most forcible Feeble.

FEEBLE

It shall suffice, sir.

FALSTAFF

Who is next?

SHALLOW

Peter Bullcalf o' the green!

FALSTAFF

Yea, marry, let's see Bullcalf.

DAVY

Peter Bullcalf!

BULLCALF

Here, sir.

FALSTAFF

'Fore God, a likely fellow! Come prick [me] Bullcalf till he roar again.

BULLCALF

O Lord! good my lord captain—

FALSTAFF

What, dost thou roar before thou art pricked?

BULLCALF

O Lord, sir! I am a diseased man.

FALSTAFF

What disease hast thou?

BULLCALF

A whoreson cold, sir, which I caught with ringing in the king's affairs upon his coronation day, sir.

FALSTAFF

Is here all?

SHALLOW

Here is two more called than your number. You must have but four here, sir.

FALSTAFF

Come, sir, which men shall I have?

SHALLOW

Four of which you please.

BULLCALF

Good Master Corporate Bardolph, stand my friend, and here's four Harry ten shillings in French crowns for you.

MOULDY

And, good master corporal captain, for my old dame's sake, stand my friend. She is old, and cannot help herself. You shall have forty, sir.

BARDOLPH

Go to, stand aside.

BARDOLPH

(to Falstaff)

Sir, a word with you. I have three pounds to free Mouldy and Bullcalf.

SHALLOW

Come, Sir John, which four will you have?

FALSTAFF

(to Bardolph)

Go to, well.

(to Mouldy and Bullcalf)

Mouldy, stay at home till you are past service. Bullcalf, grow till you come unto it. I will none of you.

SHALLOW

Sir John, Sir John, do not yourself wrong. They are your likeliest men.

FALSTAFF

Will you tell me, Master Shallow, how to choose a man? Care I for the limb, the thews, the stature, bulk and big assemblance of a man? Give me the spirit, Master Shallow. Here's Wart. You see what a ragged appearance it is. 'A shall charge you and discharge you with the motion of a pewterer's hammer. And this same half-faced fellow, Shadow. Give me this man. He presents no mark to the enemy; the foeman may with as great aim level at the edge of a penknife. How swiftly will this Feeble the woman's tailor run off! O, give me the spare men, and spare me the great ones. These fellows will do well, Master Shallow. Bardolph, give the soldiers coats. God keep you, Master Silence. I will not use many words with you. I must a dozen mile to-night.

BARDOLPH

Hup!

(Exit Bardolph and the recruits.)

FALSTAFF

Fare you well, gentle gentlemen.

SHALLOW

Sir John, the Lord bless you! God prosper your affairs! God send us peace! At your return, visit our house, let our old acquaintance be renewed.

FALSTAFF

I thank you.

SHALLOW

Peradventure I will with ye to the court.

(Exit Falstaff.)

Davy, I will use him well. A friend i' th' court is better than a penny in purse. Use his men well, Davy, for they are arrant knaves and will backbite.[18]

DAVY

No worse than they are backbitten, sir, for they have marvellous foul linen.

SHALLOW

Well conceited, Davy.

(Exit Davy.)

Come, Master Silence.

SILENCE

Death is certain.[19]

(Revolve.)

Scene Twenty

Salisbury.
Hotspur and lords discovered.
Enter Messenger.

MESSENGER

These letters come from your father.[1]

HOTSPUR

Letters from him? Why comes he not himself?

MESSENGER

He cannot come, my lord; he is grievous sick.

HOTSPUR

Zounds! how has he the leisure to be sick in such a justling time?

MESSENGER

His letters bear his mind, not I, my lord.

WORCESTER

I prithee tell me, doth he keep his bed?

MESSENGER

He did, my lord, four days ere I set forth,
He was much feared by his physicians.

HOTSPUR

Sick now? droop now? This sickness doth infect
The very lifeblood of our enterprise.
'Tis catching hither, even to our camp.

(Enter Sir Richard Vernon.)

My cousin Vernon! welcome, by my soul.

VERNON

The Earl of Westmoreland, seven thousand strong,
Is marching hitherwards; with him Prince John.

HOTSPUR

No harm. What more?

VERNON

And further, I have learned
The king himself in person is set forth.

HOTSPUR

He is welcome too. Where is his son,
The nimble-footed madcap Prince of Wales,
And his comrades, that daffed the world aside
And bid it pass?

VERNON

All furnished, all in arms;
All plumed like estridges that with the wind
Bated like eagles having lately bathed;
Glittering in golden coats like images;
As full of spirit as the month of May
And gorgeous as the sun at midsummer;
Wanton as youthful goats, wild as young bulls.
I saw young Harry with his beaver on,
He cushes on his thighs, gallantly armed,
Rise from the ground like feathered Mercury,
And vaulted with such ease into his seat
As if an angel dropped down from the clouds
To turn and wind a fiery Pegasus
And witch the world with noble horsemanship.

HOTSPUR

No more, no more! Worse than the sun in March,
This praise doth nourish agues. Let them come.
They come like sacrifices in their trim,
And to the fire-eyed maid of smoky war
All hot and bleeding will we offer them.
The mail'd Mars shall on his alter sit
Up to the ears in blood. I am on fire

To hear this rich reprisal is so nigh,
And yet not ours. Come, let me taste my horse,
Who is to bear me like a thunderbolt
Against the bosom of the Prince of Wales.
Harry to Harry shall, hot horse to horse,
Meet, and ne'er part till one drop down a corse.
What may the king's whole battle reach unto?

VERNON

To thirty thousand.

HOTSPUR

Forty let it be.
My father and Glendower being both away,
The powers of us may serve so great a day.
Come, let us take a muster speedily.
Doomsday is near. Die all, die merrily.

(Enter another Messenger.)

MESSENGER

My lord, here are letters for you.[2]

HOTSPUR

I cannot read them now.—
O gentlemen, the time of life is short!
To spend that shortness basely were too long
If life did ride upon a dial's point,
Still ending at the arrival of an hour.
An if we live, we live to tread on kings;
If die, brave death, when princes die with us!

(Enter another Messenger.)

MESSENGER

My lord, prepare. The king comes on apace.

HOTSPUR

I thank him that he cuts me from my tale,
For I profess not talking. Only this—
Let each man do his best; and here draw I
A sword whose temper I intend to stain
With the best blood that I can meet withal
In the adventure of this perilous day.
Now, Esperancè! Percy! and set on.
Sound all the lofty instruments of war,
And by that music let us all embrace;
For, heaven to earth, some of us shall never
A second time do such a courtesy.

(Revolve.)

Scene Twenty-one

Salisbury.
Falstaff discovered. Enter Prince and lords.

PRINCE

How now, blown Jack? How now, quilt?[1]

FALSTAFF

What, Hal? How now, mad wag? My good Lord of Westmoreland, I thought your honour had already been at Shrewsbury.

WESTMORELAND

Faith, Sir John, 'tis more than time that I were there, and you too, but my powers are there already.

CLARENCE

The king, I can tell you, looks for us all.[2]

PRINCE

Jack, whose fellows are these that come after?

FALSTAFF

Mine, Hal, mine. Tut, tut! food for powder, food for powder.

WESTMORELAND

Ay, but, Sir John, methinks they are exceedingly poor and bare—too beggarly.

FALSTAFF

Faith, for their poverty, I know not where they had that, and for their bareness, I am sure they never learned that of me.

CLARENCE

No, I'll be sworn.[3]

(Enter Gloucester.)

GLOUCESTER

Sirrah, make haste. Percy is already in the field.[4]

FALSTAFF

What, is the king encamped?

WESTMORELAND

He is, Sir John. I fear we shall stay too long.

(Exit lords.)

FALSTAFF

I would 'twere bedtime, Hal, and all well.[5]

PRINCE

Why, thou owest God a death.

(Exit Prince.)

FALSTAFF

'Tis not due yet: I would be loath to pay him before his day. What need I be so forward with him that calls not on me? Well, 'tis no matter; honour pricks me on. Yea, but how if honour prick me off when I come on? How then? Can honour set to a leg? No. Or an arm? No. Or take away the grief of a wound? No. Honour hath no skill in surgery then? No. What is honour? A word. What is that word honour? Air—a trim reckoning! Who hath it? He that died a Wednesday. Doth he feel it? No. Doth he hear it? No. 'Tis insensible then? Yea, to the dead. But will it not live with the living? No. Why? Detraction will not suffer it. Therefore I'll none of it. Honour is a mere scutcheon—and so ends my catechism.

(Falstaff exits. Revolve.)

Scene Twenty-two

Salisbury.
Prince discovered. Enter Hotspur.

HOTSPUR
If I mistake not, thou art Harry Monmouth.[1]

PRINCE
Thou speak'st as if I would deny my name.

HOTSPUR
My name is Harry Percy.

PRINCE
Why, then I see
A very valiant rebel of the name.
I am the Prince of Wales, and think not, Percy,
To share with me in glory and more.
Two stars keep not their motion in one sphere,
Nor can one England brook a double reign
Of Harry Percy and the Prince of Wales.

HOTSPUR
Nor shall it, Harry, for the hour is come
To end the one of us.

(They fight. The Prince kills Percy.)

O Harry, thou hast robbed me of my youth!
I better brook the loss of brittle life
Than those proud titles thou hast won of me.
They wound my thoughts worse than thy sword my flesh.
But thoughts the slaves of life, and life time's fool,
And time, that takes survey of all the world,
Must have a stop. O, I could prophesy,
But that the earthy and cold hand of death

Lies on my tongue. No, Percy, thou are dust,
And food for—

> *(Percy dies.)*

PRINCE

For worms, brave Percy. Fare thee well, great heart.
Ill-weaved ambition, how much art thou shrunk!
When that this body did contain a spirit,
A kingdom for it was too small a bound;
But now two paces of the vilest earth
Is room enough. This earth that bears thee dead
Bears not alive so stout a gentleman.
If thou wert sensible of courtesy,
I should not make so dear a show of zeal.
But let my favours hide thy mangled face;
And, even in thy behalf, I'll thank myself
For doing these fair rites of tenderness.
Adieu, and take thy praise with thee to heaven.
Thy ignominy sleep with thee in the grave,
But not rememb'red in thy epitaph.

> *END OF ACT ONE*

ACT TWO

Scene One

> *King's bedchamber.*
> *King Henry and Attendant discovered.*

KING HENRY

Go call the Earls of Surrey and of Warwick.
But, ere they come, bid them o'erread these letters
And well consider of them. Make good speed.

> *(Exit Attendant.)*

How many thousand of my poorest subjects
Are at this hour asleep! O sleep, O gentle sleep,
Nature's soft nurse, how have I frighted thee,
That thou no more wilt weigh my eyelids down
And steep my senses in forgetfulness?
Why rather, sleep, liest thou in smoky cribs,
Upon uneasy pallets stretching thee
And hushed with buzzing night-flies to thy slumber,
Than in the perfumed chambers of the great,
Under the canopies of costly state,

And lulled with sound of sweetest melody?
Wilt thou upon the high and giddy mast
Seal up the ship-boy's eyes, and rock his brains
In cradle of the rude imperious surge
And in the visitation of the winds,
Who take the ruffian billows by the top,
Curling their monstrous heads and hanging them
With deafening clamour in the slippery clouds,
That, with the hurly, death itself awakes?
Canst thou, O partial sleep, give thy repose
To the wet sea-son in an hour so rude,
And in the calmest and most stillest night,
Deny it to a king? Then happy low, lie down!
Uneasy lies the head that wears a crown.[1]

(Enter Warwick, Ely and Westmoreland.)

WARWICK

Many good morrows to your majesty!

KING HENRY

Is it good morrow, lords?

WARWICK

'Tis one o'clock, and past.

KING HENRY

Why, then, good morrow to you all, my lords.
Have you read o'er the letters that I sent you?

WESTMORELAND

We have, my liege.[2]

KING HENRY

Then you perceive the body of our kingdom
How foul it is, what rank diseases grow,
And with what danger, near the heart of it.

WESTMORELAND

It is but as a body yet distempered,
Which to his former strength may be restored
With good advice and little medicine.[3]

WARWICK

My Lord Northumberland will soon be cooled.

KING HENRY

O God! that one might read the book of fate,
And see the revolution of the times
Make mountains level, and the continent,
Weary of solid firmness, melt itself
Into the sea! O, if this were seen,

The happiest youth, viewing his progress through,
What perils past, what crosses to ensue,
Would shut the book, and sit him down and die.
'Tis not ten years gone
Since Richard and Northumberland, great friends,
Did feast together, and in two years after
Were they at wars. It is but eight years since
This Percy was the man nearest my soul,
Who like a brother toiled in my affairs
And laid his love and life under my foot,
Yea, for my sake, even to the eyes of Richard
Gave him defiance. But which of you was by—

       (to Warwick)

You, cousin Nevil, as I remember—
When Richard, with his eye brimful of tears,
Did speak these words, now proved a prophecy?
'Northumberland, thou ladder by the which
My cousin Bolingbroke ascends my throne,
The time shall come,' thus did he follow it,
'The time will come that foul sin, gathering head,
Shall break into corruption.' So went on,
Foretelling this same time's condition
And the division of our amity.

WARWICK

There is a history in all men's lives,
Figuring the nature of the times deceased,
The which observed, a man may prophesy,
With a near aim, of the main chance of things
As yet not come to life, which in their seeds,
And weak beginnings lie intreasur'd.
Such things become the hatch and brood of time,
And by the necessary form of this
King Richard might create a perfect guess
That great Northumberland, then false to him,
Would of that seed grow to a greater falseness,
Which should not find a ground to root upon,
Unless on you.

KING HENRY

Are these things then necessities?
Then let us meet them like necessities.

ELY

Please it your grace to go to bed.[4]

WARWICK

Upon my soul, my lord,
The powers that you already have sent forth
Shall bring this prize in very easily.

WESTMORELAND

To comfort you the more, I have received
A certain instance that Glendower is dead.[5]

WARWICK

Your majesty hath been this fortnight ill,
And these unseasoned hours perforce must add
Unto your sickness.

KING HENRY

I will take your counsel.

(Exit lords. Revolve.)

Scene Two

London street.
Enter Prince and Poins.

PRINCE

Before God, I am exceeding weary.[1]

POINS

Is't come to that? I had thought weariness durst not have attached one of so high
blood.

PRINCE

Faith, it doth me, though it discolours the complexion of my greatness to acknowledge it. Doth it not show vilely in me to desire small beer?

POINS

How ill it follows, after you have laboured so hard, you should talk so idly!
Tell me, how many good young princes would do so, their fathers being so sick
as yours at this time is?

PRINCE

Shall I tell thee one thing, Poins?

POINS

Yes, faith, and let it be an excellent good thing.

PRINCE

It shall serve among wits of no higher breeding than thine.

POINS

Go to. I stand the push of your one thing that you will tell.

PRINCE

Marry, I tell thee, it is not meet that I should be sad, now my father is sick.

Albeit I could tell to thee, as to one it pleases me, for fault of a better, to call
my friend, I could be sad, and sad indeed too.

POINS

By the mass, Bardolph.

(Enter Bardolph and Page.)

BARDOLPH

Your grace! There's a letter for you.

PRINCE

And how doth thy master, Bardolph?

BARDOLPH

In bodily health, sir.

PAGE

Well, my lord.

BARDOLPH

He heard of your grace's coming to town.

POINS

Look you how he writes.

(reads)

'Sir John Falstaff, knight, to the son of the king, nearest his father, Harry Prince
of Wales, greeting. I will imitate the honourable Romans in brevity.'[2]

PRINCE

(reads)

'I commend me to thee, I commend thee, and I leave thee. Be not too familiar
with Poins. Repent at idle times as thou mayest, and so farewell.

   'Thine, by yea and no, which is as much as to say, as thou usest him, Jack
     Falstaff with all my familiars, John with my brothers and sisters, and Sir
     John with all Europe.'

POINS

My lord, I'll steep this letter in sack and make him eat it.

PRINCE

Is your master here in London?

BARDOLPH

Yea, my lord.

PRINCE

Where sups he?

BARDOLPH

At the old place, my lord.

POINS

What company? Sup any women with him?[3]

PAGE

None, my lord, but old Mistress Quickly and Mistress Doll Tearsheet.

PRINCE

What pagan may that be?

BARDOLPH

A proper gentlewoman, sir.[4]

PAGE

And a kinswoman of my master's.

PRINCE

Even such kin as the parish heifers are to the town bull. Sirrah, you boy, and
Bardolph, no word to your master that I am yet come to town. There's for your
silence.

BARDOLPH

I have no tongue, sir.

PAGE

And for mine, sir, I will govern it.

PRINCE

Fare you well; go.

(Exit Bardolph and Page.)

I tell thee, my heart bleeds inwardly that my father is so sick. And keeping such
vile company as thou art hath in reason taken from me all ostentation of sorrow.[5]

POINS

The reason?

PRINCE

What wouldst thou think of me if I should weep?

POINS

I would think thee a most princely hypocrite.

PRINCE

It would be every man's thought, and thou art a blessed fellow to think as every
man thinks. Never a man's thought in the world keeps the roadway better than
thine. Every man would think me a hypocrite indeed. By this hand, thou thinkest
me as far in the devil's book as thou and Falstaff for obduracy and persistency.
Let the end try the man.

(Revolve.)

Scene Three

Boar's Head Tavern.
Falstaff and Bardolph discovered.

FALSTAFF

Bardolph, am I not fall'n away vilely since this last action? Do I not bate? Do
I not dwindle? Why, my skin hangs about me like an old lady's loose gown! I
am withered like an old apple-john. Well, I'll repent. And I have not forgotten

what the inside of a church is made of, I am a brewer's horse. Company, villainous company, hath been the spoil of me.[1]

BARDOLPH
Sir John, you are so fretful you cannot live long.

FALSTAFF
Why, there it is! Come, sing me a bawdy song and make me merry. I was as virtuously given as a gentleman need to be, virtuous enough: swore little, diced not above seven times a week, visited a bawdy house not above once in a quarter of an hour, paid money that I borrowed three or four times, lived well, and in good compass; and now I live out of all order and out of all compass.

BARDOLPH
Why, you are so fat, Sir John, that you must needs be out of all compass—out of all reasonable compass, Sir John.

FALSTAFF
Do thou amend thy face, and I'll amend my life. I never see thy face but I think upon hellfire.

(Enter Page, Doll Tearsheet and Mistress Quickly.)

FALSTAFF
How now, Mistress Doll![2]

PAGE
The music is come, sir.

FALSTAFF
Let them play. How now!

(Exit Page.)

MISTRESS QUICKLY
Sick of a calm, yea, good faith.

FALSTAFF
So is all her sect. An they be once in a calm, they are sick.

DOLL TEARSHEET
You muddy rascal, is that all the comfort you give me?

FALSTAFF
You make fat rascals, Mistress Doll.

DOLL TEARSHEET
I make them! Gluttony and diseases make them; I make them not.

FALSTAFF
If the cook help to make the gluttony, you help to make the diseases, Doll. We catch of you, Doll, we catch of you. Grant that, my poor virtue, grant that.

DOLL TEARSHEET
Yea, joy, our chains and our jewels.

FALSTAFF

'Your brooches, pearls, and ouches.' For to serve bravely is to come halting off, you know. To come off the breach with his pike bent bravely, and to surgery bravely; to venture upon the charged chambers bravely—

DOLL TEARSHEET

Hang yourself, you muddy conger, hang yourself!

MISTRESS QUICKLY

By my troth, this is the old fashion. You two never meet but you fall to some discord. What the good-year!

(Orchestra enters.)

One must bear, and that must be you.

(to Doll)

You are the weaker vessel, as they say, the emptier vessel.

DOLL TEARSHEET

Can a weak empty vessel bear such a huge full hogshead? There's a whole merchant's venture of Bordeaux stuff in him; you have not seen a hulk better stuffed in the hold.

FALSTAFF

(to orchestra)

Play, sirs.

DOLL TEARSHEET

Come, I'll be friends with thee, Jack. Thou art going back to the wars, and whether I shall ever see thee again or no, there is nobody cares.

(Enter Page.)

PAGE

Sir, Ancient Pistol's without and would speak with you.

(Enter Pistol.)

PISTOL

'Si fortune me tormente, sperato me contento.' God save you, Sir John![3]

FALSTAFF

Ancient Pistol, I would not have you go off here. Discharge yourself of our company, Pistol.

MISTRESS QUICKLY

No, good captain, not here, sweet captain.

PISTOL

Sweet knight, I kiss thy neif.

MISTRESS QUICKLY	PISTOL
Good Captain Peesel, be quiet; 'tis very late, i' faith.	What! We have seen the seven stars.

BARDOLPH

I pray thee, go down, good ancient.

PISTOL

[Then] feed, and be fat, my fair Calipolis.

DOLL TEARSHEET

For God's sake, be quiet.[4]

PISTOL

Fear we broadsides?

DOLL TEARSHEET

Hang him, swaggering rascal![5]

MISTRESS QUICKLY

Swagger, swagger—if he swaggers, let him not come here.

MISTRESS QUICKLY	PISTOL
I must live among my neighbors, I'll no swaggerers. I'm in a good name and fame with the very best. There comes no swaggerers here.	Shall pack horses and hollow pampered jades of Asia, which cannot go but thirty mile a-day, compare with Caesars, and with Cannibals, and Trojan Greeks?

DOLL TEARSHEET

For God's sake, thrust him outdoors.

MISTRESS QUICKLY

I have not lived all this while to have swaggering now.

FALSTAFF

He's no swaggerer, hostess; a tame cheater, i' faith.

PISTOL

Nay, rather damn them with King Cerberus, and let the welkin roar. Shall we fall foul for toys?

FALSTAFF

You may stroke him as gently as a puppy greyhound.

PISTOL

No, let the fiend give fire.

BARDOLPH

Be gone, good Pistol. This will grow to a brawl anon.

PISTOL

And, sweetheart, lie thou there.

(He lays down his sword.)

FALSTAFF

Here, Pistol, I charge you with a cup of sack. Do you discharge upon my hostess?

PISTOL

I will discharge upon her, Sir John, with two bullets.

FALSTAFF

She is pistol-proof, sir; you shall hardly offend her.

PISTOL

Then to you, Mistress Dorothy; I will charge you.

FALSTAFF

Pistol—

DOLL TEARSHEET

Charge me!

FALSTAFF	DOLL TEARSHEET
I would be quiet.	What! You poor, base, rascally, cheating, lack-linen mate! Away, you mouldy rogue!

PISTOL

I know you, Mistress Dorothy.

DOLL TEARSHEET

Away, you cut-purse rascal! You filthy bung, away!

PISTOL

What! shall we have incision? Shall we imbrue?

DOLL TEARSHEET

By this wine, I'll thrust my knife into your mouldy chaps, an you play the saucy cuttle with me.

PISTOL

God let me not live but I will murder your ruff for this.

PISTOL	FALSTAFF	M. QUICKLY
I'll see her damned first, to Pluto's damned lake, by this hand, to the infernal deep, with Erebus and tortures vile also. Hold hook and line, say I. Down, dogs, down!	Pistol, I would be quiet.	Good Captain Peesel.
		DOLL TEARSHEET
		Captain! Thou abominable damned cheater, art thou not ashamed to be called captain? You a captain! For what? For tearing a poor whore's ruff in a bawdy-house?

BARDOLPH	PAGE
Prithee, go down, good ancient.	Prithee, go down

FALSTAFF

Give me my rapier, boy.

DOLL TEARSHEET

I pray thee, Jack, I pray thee, do not draw.

FALSTAFF	MISTRESS QUICKLY
(draws his sword)	Put up your naked weapons, put
Get you outdoors.	up your naked weapons.

PISTOL

(snatches up his sword)

Then death rock me asleep, abridge my doleful days!
Why, then, let grievous, ghastly, gaping wounds
Untwine the Sisters Three! Come, Atropos, I say!

(Falstaff drives Pistol out. Exit Pistol and Bardolph.)

DOLL TEARSHEET

Ah, you sweet little rogue, you! Alas, poor ape, how thou sweatest! Come, let me wipe thy face; come on, you whoreson chops. Ah, rogue! i' faith, I love thee. Thou art as valourous as Hector of Troy, worth five of Agamemnon, and ten times better than the Nine Worthies. Ah, villain!

FALSTAFF

A rascally slave! I will toss the rogue in a blanket.

DOLL TEARSHEET

Do, an thou darest for thy heart. And thou dost, I'll canvass thee between a pair of sheets.

FALSTAFF

A rascal bragging slave! The rogue fled from me like quicksilver.

DOLL TEARSHEET

I' faith, and thou followedst him like a church. Thou whoreson little tidy Bartholomew boar-pig, when wilt thou leave fighting o' days and foining o' nights, and begin to patch up thine old body for heaven?

FALSTAFF

Peace, good Doll! Do not speak like a death's-head. Do not bid me remember mine end. Kiss me, Doll.

DOLL TEARSHEET

By my troth, I kiss thee with a most constant heart.

FALSTAFF

I am old, I am old.

DOLL TEARSHEET

I love thee better than I love e'er a scurvy young boy of them all.

FALSTAFF

What stuff wilt have a kirtle of? I shall receive money o' Thursday. Shalt have a cap to-morrow. A merry song, come. It grows late; we'll to bed. Thou'lt forget me when I am gone.

DOLL TEARSHEET

By my troth, thou'lt set me a-weeping, an thou sayest so. Prove that ever I dress myself handsome till thy return. Well, hearken a' th' end.

FALSTAFF

Now comes in the sweetest morsel of the night, and we must hence and leave it unpicked.

(Knocking within.)

Knocking at the door.

(Enter Bardolph.)

How now! What's the matter?

BARDOLPH

You must away to court, sir, presently. A dozen captains stay at door for you.

FALSTAFF
(to the Page)

Pay the musicians, sirrah. Farewell, hostess. Farewell, Doll. You see, my good wenches, how men of merit are sought after. The undeserver may sleep when the man of action is called on.

MISTRESS QUICKLY

Fare thee well.

FALSTAFF

Farewell, good wenches.

(Exit Falstaff, Page and Bardolph.)

MISTRESS QUICKLY

Well, fare thee well. I have known thee these twenty-nine years, come peascod-time, but an honester and truer-hearted man—well, fare thee well.

DOLL TEARSHEET

I cannot speak. If my heart be not ready to burst—well, sweet Jack, have a care of thyself.

BARDOLPH
(within)

Mistress Tearsheet!

MISTRESS QUICKLY

What's the matter?

BARDOLPH

Bid Mistress Tearsheet come to my master.

MISTRESS QUICKLY

O, run, Doll. Run, good Doll. Come.
(to Bardolph, within)

She comes blubbered.
(to Doll)

Yea, will you come, Doll?

(Exit Doll. Revolve.)

Scene Four

London street.
Business only.[1]

Scene Five

King's bedchamber.
King Henry is in bed. Clarence, Gloucester and lords
also discovered.

WARWICK

Health to my sovereign, and new happiness.[1]

WESTMORELAND

Added to that that I am to deliver.
Mowbray, the Bishop Scroop, Hastings and all
Are brought to the correction of your law.
There is not now a rebel's sword unsheathed,
But Peace puts forward her olive everywhere.

KING HENRY

O Westmoreland, thou art a summer bird,
Which ever in the haunch of winter sings
The lifting up of day.
I should rejoice now at this happy news.
Humphrey, my son of Gloucester,
Where is the prince your brother?[2]

GLOUCESTER

I think he's gone to hunt, my lord, at Windsor.

KING HENRY

And how accompanied?

GLOUCESTER

I do not know, my lord.

KING HENRY

Why art thou not at Windsor with him, Thomas?

CLARENCE

He is not there, my lord.

GLOUCESTER

He dines in London.[3]

KING HENRY

And how accompanied? Canst thou tell that?

CLARENCE

With Poins and his other continual followers.

KING HENRY

Most subject is the fattest soil to weeds,
And he, the noble image of my youth,
Is overspread with them. Therefore my grief
Stretches itself beyond the hour of death.
The blood weeps from my heart when I do shape

In forms imaginary the unguided days
And rotten times that you shall look upon.

GLOUCESTER

Comfort, your majesty!

CLARENCE

O my royal father!

GLOUCESTER

His eye is hollow, and he changes much.[4]

WESTMORELAND

Stand from him, give him air.[5]

WARWICK

This apoplexy will certain be his end.[6]

GLOUCESTER

The people fear me, for they do observe
Unfathered heirs and loathly births of nature.
The seasons change their manners, as the year
Had found some months asleep and leaped over them.

CLARENCE

The river hath thrice flowed, no ebb between,
And the old folk, time's doting chronicles,
Say it did so a little time before
That our great-grandsire, Edward, sicked and died.

KING HENRY

Set me the crown upon my pillow here.
Let there be no noise made, my gentle friends,
Unless some dull and favourable hand
Will whisper music to my weary spirit.[7]

WARWICK

Call for the music in the other room.

(Enter Prince.)

PRINCE

Who saw the Duke of Clarence?

CLARENCE

I am here, brother.

PRINCE

How doth the king?

GLOUCESTER

Let us withdraw into the other room.[8]

PRINCE

I will sit and watch here by the king.

(Exit all but the Prince and King Henry, who is asleep.)

Why doth the crown lie there upon his pillow,
Being so troublesome a bedfellow?
O polished perturbation! Golden care!
That keep'st the ports of slumber open wide
To many a watchful night! Sleep with it now!
Yet not so sound and half so deeply sweet
As he whose brow with homely biggen bound
Snores out the watch of night. O majesty!
When thou dost pinch thy bearer, thou dost sit
Like a rich armour worn in the heat of day,
That scald'st with safety.
My gracious lord! my father!
This sleep is sound indeed. This is a sleep
That from this golden rigol hath divorced
So many English kings. Thy due from me
Is tears and heavy sorrows of the blood,
Which nature, love, and filial tenderness
Shall, O dear father, pay thee plenteously.
My due from thee is this imperial crown.

(Puts on crown. Exit Prince.)

KING HENRY
(waking)

Warwick! Gloucester! Clarence!

(Enter all.)

CLARENCE

Doth the king call?

WARWICK

What would your majesty? How fares your grace?

KING HENRY

Why did you leave me here alone, my lords?

GLOUCESTER

We left the prince my brother here, my liege,
Who undertook to sit and watch by you.[9]

KING HENRY

The Prince of Wales! Where is he? Let me see him. He is not here.

WARWICK

He is gone this way.

CLARENCE

He came not through the chamber where we stayed.[10]

KING HENRY

Where is the crown? Who took it from my pillow?

WARWICK
When we withdrew, my liege, we left it here.

KING HENRY
The prince hath ta'en it hence. Go, seek him out.
Is he so hasty that he doth suppose
My sleep my death?
Find him, my Lord of Warwick, chide him hither.

(Exit Warwick.)

KING HENRY
This part of his conjoins with my disease
And helps to end me. See, sons, what things you are!
How quickly nature falls into revolt
When gold becomes her object!
For this the foolish overcareful fathers
Have broke their sleep with thoughts, their brains with care,
Their bones with industry.
For this they have engrossed and pil'd up
The cankered heaps of strange-achiev'd gold;
For this they have been thoughtful to invest
Their sons with arts and martial exercises.
When, like the bee, tolling from every flower,
Our thighs packed with wax, our mouths with honey,
We bring it to the hive, and, like the bees,
Are murdered for our pains.

(Enter Warwick.)

WARWICK
My lord, I found the prince in the next room.

KING HENRY
But wherefore did he take away the crown?

(Enter Prince.)

PRINCE
I never thought to hear you speak again.

KING HENRY
Thy wish was father, Harry, to that thought.
I stay too long by thee, I weary thee.
Dost thou so hunger for mine empty chair
That thou wilt needs invest thee with my honours
Before thy hour is ripe?
Depart the chamber, leave us here alone.

(Exit all but the Prince.)

O foolish youth!
Thou seek'st the greatness that will overwhelm thee.

Stay but a little, for my cloud of dignity
Is held from falling with so weak a wind
That it will quickly drop. My day is dim.
Thou hast stolen that which after some few hours
Were thine without offense, and at my death
Thou hast sealed up my expectation.
Thy life did manifest thou lovedst me not,
And thou wilt have me die assured of it.
Thou hidest a thousand daggers in thy thoughts,
Which thou hast whetted on thy stony heart,
To stab at half an hour of my life.
What! Canst thou not forbear me half an hour?
Then get thee gone and dig my grave thyself,
And bid the merry bells ring to thine ear
That thou are crown'd, not that I am dead.
Let all the tears that should bedew my hearse
Be drops of balm to sanctify thy head.
Only compound me with forgotten dust;
Give that which gave thee life unto the worms.
Pluck down my officers, break my decrees,
For now a time is come to mock at form.
Harry the Fifth is crowned. Up, vanity!
Down, royal state! All you sage counsellors, hence!
And to the English court assemble now,
From every region, apes of idleness!
Now, neighbour confines, purge you of your scum.
Have you a ruffian that will swear, drink, dance,
Revel the night, rob, murder, and commit
The oldest sins the newest kind of ways?
Be happy, he will trouble you no more.
England shall double gild his treble guilt,
England shall give him office, honour, might,
For the fifth Harry from curbed license plucks
The muzzle of restraint, and the wild dog
Shall flesh his tooth on every innocent.
O my poor kingdom, sick with civil blows!
When that my care could not withhold thy riots,
What wilt thou do when riot is thy care?
O, thou wilt be a wilderness again,
Peopled with wolves, thy old inhabitants.

PRINCE

O, pardon me, my liege! There is your crown,
And He that wears the crown immortally
Long guard it yours.

God witness with me, when I here came in,
And found no course of breath within your majesty,
How cold it struck my heart. If I do feign,
O, let me in my present wildness die
And never live to show the incredulous world
The noble change that I have purpos'd.
Coming to look on you, thinking you dead,
I spake unto this crown as having sense,
And thus upbraided it: 'The care on thee depending
Hath fed upon the body of my father.
Therefore, thou best of gold art worst of gold.
Other, less fine in carat, is more precious,
Preserving life in medicine potable,
But thou, most fine, most honoured, most renowned,
Hast eat thy bearer up.' Thus, my royal liege,
Accusing it, I put it on my head,
To try with it, as with an enemy
That had before my face murdered my father,
The quarrel of a true inheritor.
But if it did infect my blood with joy,
Or swell my thoughts to any strain of pride,
If any rebel or vain spirit of mine
Did with the least affection of a welcome
Give entertainment to the might of it,
Let God for ever keep it from my head.

KING HENRY

Come hither, Harry, sit thou by my bed,
And hear, I think, the very latest counsel
That ever I shall breathe. [O my son,]
God put it in thy mind to take it hence,
That thou mightst win the more thy father's love,
Pleading so wisely in excuse of it!
God knows, my son,
By what bypaths and indirect crooked ways
I met this crown, and I myself know well
How troublesome it sat upon my head.
To thee it shall descend with better quiet,
Better opinion, better confirmation,
For all the soil of the achievement goes
With me into the earth. It seemed in me
But as an honour snatched with boisterous hand,
And I had many living to upbraid
My gain of it by their assistances,
Which daily grew to quarrel and to bloodshed,

Wounding suppos'd peace. All these bold fears
Thou seest with peril I have answer'd,
For all my reign hath been but as a scene
Acting that argument. And now my death
Changes the mode, for what in me was purchased
Falls upon thee in a more fairer sort,
So thou the garland wear'st successively.
Yet, though thou stand'st more sure than I do,
Thou art not firm enough, since griefs are green.
And all my friends, which thou must make thy friends,
Have but their stings and teeth newly ta'en out,
By whose fell working I was first advanced
And by whose power I well might lodge a fear
To be again displaced. Which to avoid,
I cut them off, and had a purpose now
To lead out many to the Holy Land,
Let rest and lying still might make them look
Too near unto my state. Therefore, my Harry,
Be it thy course to busy giddy minds
With foreign quarrels, that action, hence borne out,
May waste the memory of the former days.
More would I, but my lungs are wasted so
That strength of speech is utterly denied me.
How I came by the crown, O God forgive,
And grant it may with thee in true peace live!

PRINCE

[My gracious liege,]
You won it, wore it, kept it, gave it me.
Then plain and right must my possession be,
Which I with more than with a common pain
'Gainst all the world will rightfully maintain.

(Revolve.)

Scene Six

Shallow's house.
Falstaff, Bardolph, Shallow, others discovered.

SILENCE

(singing)
'Be merry, be merry, my wife has all—'[1]

SHALLOW

Davy!

SILENCE

For women are shrews, both short and tall.'

DAVY

Sweet sir, most sweet sir, master page, good master page, sit.

FALSTAFF

Davy!

DAVY

I'll be with *you* anon.

SHALLOW

Davy! Give Master Bardolph some wine, Davy. Be merry, Master Bardolph, and, my little soldier there, be merry.

DAVY

There's a dish of leather coats for you—

SHALLOW

Davy!

FALSTAFF

This Davy serves you for good uses. He is both your serving-man and your husband.

SHALLOW

Hmmmm?

BARDOLPH

This Davy serves you for good uses. He is both your serving-man and your husband.

SHALLOW

A good varlet, a good varlet, a very good varlet, Sir John. By the mass, I have drunk too much sack at supper. A very good varlet.

FALSTAFF

'Fore God, you have here a goodly dwelling and a rich.[2]

SHALLOW

Hmmmm?

BARDOLPH

You have here a goodly dwelling and a rich.

SHALLOW

Beggars all, beggars all, beggars all.

BARDOLPH

Beggars all, Sir John.

FALSTAFF

Rich, rich, rich.

SHALLOW

Beggars all, Sir John. Nay, you shall see my orchard, where, in an arbour, we will eat a last year's pippin of my own graffing, with a dish of caraways, and so forth.

SILENCE

(singing)

'Welcome, merry Shrove-tide.'

FALSTAFF

I did not think Master Silence had been a man of this mettle.

SILENCE

Who I? I have been merry twice and once ere now.

SILENCE/DAVY/BARDOLPH

(singing)

'Do nothing but eat, and make good cheer,
And praise God for the merry year,
When flesh is cheap and females dear,
And lusty lads roam here and there
So merrily, and ever among so merrily.'

DAVY

A cup of wine, sir?

SILENCE/PAGE/BARDOLPH

(singing)

'A cup of wine that's brisk and fine,
And drink unto the leman mine,
And a merry heart lives long-a.'

SHALLOW

Brisk and fine.

BARDOLPH

Brisk.

FALSTAFF

Well said.

SHALLOW

Honest Bardolph.

FALSTAFF

Master Silence.

DAVY/PAGE/SILENCE

Bardolph!

SILENCE

Silence! An we shall be merry, now comes in the sweet o' the night.

BARDOLPH

The sweet o' the night.

SHALLOW

Honest Bardolph. If thou want'st
anything, and wilt not call, beshrew
thy heart.
(to the Page)
My little tiny thief! I'll drink to
Master Bardolph, and to all the
cabileros about London.

SILENCE
(singing)
'Fill the cup, and let it come, And
pledge me a mile to the bottom.'

DAVY

I hope to see London ere I die.
(Enter Pistol.)

SILENCE
(singing)
'And Robin Hood, Scarlet, and John.'

PISTOL

Shall dunghill curs confront the Helicons?
And shall good news be baffled?

SHALLOW

Honest gentleman, I know not your breeding.

PISTOL

Why then, lament therefore.

DAVY

An't please your worship, there's one Pistol come from the court.

SHALLOW

Give me pardon, sir. If, sir, you come with news from the court, I take it there's
but two ways, either to utter them, or to conceal them. I am, sir, under the king,
in some authority.

PISTOL

Under which king, Besonian? Speak, or die.

SHALLOW

Under King Harry.

PISTOL

Harry the Fourth? or Fifth?

SHALLOW

Harry the Fourth.

PISTOL

A foutra for thine office!
Sir John, thy tender lambkin now is king.
Harry the Fifth's the man. I speak the truth.

When Pistol lies, do this, and fig me, like
The bragging Spaniard.

FALSTAFF

What, is the old king dead?

PISTOL

As nail in door. The things I speak are just.

FALSTAFF

Pistol, I will double-charge you with dignities. Master Shallow, choose what office thou wilt in the land, 'tis thine Master Shallow. My Lord Shallow—be what thou wilt, I am fortune's steward—get on thy boots. We'll ride all night.

BARDOLPH

O!!!

DAVY	PAGE
London!	Harry the Fifth!

BARDOLPH

Joyful day!

FALSTAFF

Saddle my horse.

PAGE

Saddle my horse.

BARDOLPH

I would not take a knighthood for my fortune. Saddle my horse!

FALSTAFF	PISTOL	PAGE
Pistol!	What?	Whose horse?

PISTOL	FALSTAFF	SHALLOW
I do bring good news.	Utter no more to me!	Boot, boot—

FALSTAFF

And withal, devise something to do thyself good. Boot!

SHALLOW

Boot!

FALSTAFF

Boot, Master Shallow. I know the young king is sick for me. Saddle my—let us take any man's horses; the laws of England are at my commandment. Blessed are they that have been my friends, and woe to my lord chief justice!

(Exit Falstaff.)

BARDOLPH	PAGE
Harry the Fifth!	Harry the Fifth!
Harry the Fifth!	Harry the Fifth's the man!

PAGE

Up, Harry!

BARDOLPH

Harry the Fifth!

ALL

The Fifth!

SILENCE

(singing)
'Fill the cup, and let it come . . .)
(Complete revolve.)

Scene Seven

London Gate.[1]

Scene Eight

Castle exterior.

Scene Nine

London street.
Henry V and his train pass across the stage.
Enter Falstaff, Pistol, Bardolph, Shallow, Page, others.

FALSTAFF

Stand here by me, Master Robert Shallow, I will make the king do you grace.
I will leer upon him as a' comes by, and do but mark the countenance that he
will give me.[1]

PISTOL

God bless thy lungs, good knight.

FALSTAFF

Come here, Pistol, stand behind me. O, if I had had time to have made new
liveries, I would have bestowed the thousand pound I borrowed of you. But 'tis
no matter; this poor show doth better. This doth infer the zeal I had to see him.

PISTOL

It doth so.[2]

FALSTAFF

It shows my earnestness of affection—

PISTOL

It doth so.

FALSTAFF

My devotion—

PISTOL

It doth, it doth, it doth.

FALSTAFF

As it were, to ride day and night, and not to deliberate, not to remember, not to have patience to shift me—

SHALLOW

It is best, certain.

FALSTAFF

But to stand stained with travel, and sweating with desire to see him, thinking of nothing else, putting all affairs else in oblivion, as if there were nothing else to be done but to see him.

PISTOL

'Tis 'semper idem,' for 'obsque hoc nihil est.' 'Tis all in every part. There roared the sea, and trumpet-clangor sounds.

(Enter Henry V and his train, the Lord Chief Justice among them.)

FALSTAFF

God save thy grace, King Hal, my royal Hal!

PISTOL

The heavens thee guard and keep, most royal imp of fame!

FALSTAFF

God save thee, my sweet boy!

HENRY V

My lord chief justice, speak to that vain man.

CHIEF JUSTICE

Have you your wits? Know you what 'tis you speak?

FALSTAFF

My king! My Jove! I speak to thee, my heart!

HENRY V

I know thee not, old man. Fall to thy prayers.
How ill white hairs become a fool and jester!
I have long dreamed of such a kind of man,
So surfeit-swelled, so old, and so profane,
But, being awaked, I do despise my dream.
Make less thy body hence, and more thy grace.
Leave gormandizing. Know the grave doth gape
For thee thrice wider than for other men.
Reply not to me with a fool-born jest.
Presume not that I am the thing I was,
For God doth know, so shall the world perceive,
That I have turned away my former self.
So will I those that kept me company.

When thou dost hear I am as I have been,
Approach me, and thou shalt be as thou wast,
The tutor and feeder of my riots.
Till then, I banish thee, on pain of death,
As I have done the rest of my misleaders,
Not to come near our person by ten mile.
For competence of life I will allow you,
That lack of means enforce you not to evils.
And, as we hear you do reform yourselves,
We will, according to your strengths and qualities,
Give you advancement. Be it your charge, my lord,
To see performed the tenour of our word.
Set on.

(Exit Henry V and his train.)

FALSTAFF

Master Shallow, I owe you a thousand pound.

SHALLOW

Yea, marry, Sir John, which I beseech you to let me have home with me.

FALSTAFF

That can hardly be, Master Shallow. Do not you grieve at this. I shall be sent for in private to him. Look you, he must seem thus to the world. Fear not your advancements; I will be the man yet that shall make you great.

SHALLOW

I cannot [well] perceive how, unless you should give me your doublet and stuff me out with straw. I beseech you, good Sir John, let me have five hundred of my thousand.

FALSTAFF

Sir, I will be as good as my word. This that you heard was but a colour.

SHALLOW

A colour that I fear you will die in, Sir John.

FALSTAFF

Fear no colours. Go with me to dinner. Come, Lieutenant Pistol, come, Bardolph. I shall be sent for soon at night.

END OF ACT TWO

ACT THREE

Scene One

CHORUS

In the second yeare of his reigne, king Henrie called his high court of parlement, the last daie of Aprill in the towne of Leicester, in which manie petitions mooved.

Among which, one was a bill, the effect of which supplication was, that the temporall lands devoutlie given, and disordinatlie spent by religious, and other spirituall persons, should be seized into the kings hands, with the same might suffice to mainteine, to the honor of the king, and defense of the realme, fifteene earles [and] fifteene hundred almesse-houses for reliefe onelie of the poore, impotent, and needie persons. This bill was much noted, and more feared among the religious sort, whom suerlie it touched verie neere, and therefore to find remedie against it, they determined to assaie all waies to put by and overthrow this bill.[1]

(Exit Chorus. Enter the Archbishop of Canterbury and the Bishop of Ely.)

ELY

This would drink deep.[2]

CANTERBURY

'Twould drink the cup and all.

ELY

But how, my lord, shall we resist it now?

CANTERBURY

It must be thought on.
For all the temporal lands which men devout
By testament have given to the Church
Would they strip from us.

ELY

As much as would maintain, to the king's honour,
Full fifteen earls and fifteen hundred knights,
Six thousand and two hundred good esquires.[3]

CANTERBURY

And to relief of lazars, and weak age
Of indigent faint souls, past corporal toil,
A hundred almshouses right well supplied;
And to the coffers of the king beside,
A thousand pounds by th' year.

ELY

Thus runs the bill.[4]

CANTERBURY

We lose the better half of our possession.

ELY

But what prevention?

CANTERBURY

The king is full of grace and fair regard.

ELY

And a true lover of the holy Church. But, my good lord,

How now for mitigation of this bill?
Doth his majesty incline to it, or not?

CANTERBURY

He seems indifferent;
But I have made an offer to his majesty —
And in regard of causes now in hand,
As touching France—to give a greater sum
Than ever at one time the clergy yet
Did to his predecessors part withal.

ELY

How did this offer seem received, my lord?

CANTERBURY

With good acceptance of his majesty;
Save that there was not time enough to hear.
The French ambassador upon that instant
Craved audience; and the hour I think is come
To give him hearing.

(Enter Henry V, lords and attendants.)

WESTMORELAND

Shall we call in th' ambassador, my liege?[5]

HENRY V

No yet, my cousin.

CANTERBURY
(aside to Ely)

Is it four o'clock?

ELY

It is.

CANTERBURY
(to the king)

God and his angels guard your sacred throne
And make you long become it!

HENRY V
(to Westmoreland)

We would be resolved,
Before we hear him, of some things of weight
That task our thoughts concerning us and France.
(to Canterbury)
My learn'd lord, we pray you to proceed
And justly and religiously unfold
Why the Law Salique, that they have in France,
Or should or should not bar us in our claim.
And God forbid, my dear and faithful lord,

That you should fashion, wrest, or bow your reading;
For God doth know how many now in health
Shall drop their blood in approbation
Of what your reverence shall incite us to.
Therefore take heed how you impawn our person,
How you awake the sleeping sword of war.
We charge you in the name of God, take heed.
Under this conjuration speak, my lord;
For we will hear, note, and believe in heart
That what you speak is in your conscience washed
As pure as sin with baptism.

CANTERBURY

There is no bar
To make against your highness' claim to France—

HENRY V

But this which they produce from Pharamond:
'In terram Salicam mulieres ne succedant;'
'No woman shall succeed in Salique land'—[6]

CANTERBURY

Which Salique land the French unjustly gloze
To be the realm of France, and Pharamond
The founder of this law and female bar.

ELY

Yet their own authors faithfully affirm
That the land Salique is in Germany.[7]

CANTERBURY

Then doth it well appear the Salique Law
Was not devis'd for the realm of France.

WORCESTER

Nor did the French possess the Salique land—[8]

CANTERBURY

Until four hundred one and twenty years
After defunction of King Pharamond.

HENRY V

May I with right and conscience make this claim?

CANTERBURY

The sin upon my head, dread sovereign!
For in the Book of Numbers is it writ:
When the son dies, let the inheritance
Descend unto the daughter. Gracious lord,

Stand for your own, unwind your bloody flag,
Look back into your mighty ancestors;
Go, my dread lord, to your great-grandsire's tomb,
From whom you claim; invoke his warlike spirit,
And your great-uncle's, Edward the Black Prince,
Who on the French ground played a tragedy,
Making defeat on the full power of France,
Whiles his most mighty father on a hill
Stood smiling to behold his lion's whelp
Forage in blood of French nobility.

ELY

Awake remembrance of these valiant dead
And with your puissant arm renew their feats.
You are their heir; you sit upon their throne;
The blood and courage that renown'd them
Runs in your veins; and my thrice-puissant liege
Is in the very May-morn of his youth,
Ripe for exploits and mighty enterprises.

WARWICK

Your brother kings and monarchs of the earth
Do all expect that you should rouse yourself,
As did the former lions of your blood.[9]

CANTERBURY

In aid whereof we of the spirituality
Will raise your highness such a mighty sum
As never did the clergy at one time
Bring in to any of your ancestors.

HENRY V

We must not only arm t' invade the French,
But lay down our proportions to defend
Against the Scot, who will make road upon us
With all advantages.

CANTERBURY

They of those marches, gracious sovereign,
Shall be a wall sufficient to defend
Your England from the pilfering borderers.

HENRY V

We do not mean the coursing snatchers only,
But fear the main intendment of the Scot.
For government, though high, and low, and lower,
Put into parts, doth keep in one consent,
Congreeing in a full and natural close,
Like music.

CANTERBURY

True. Therefore doth heaven divide
The state of man in divers functions,
Setting endeavour in continual motion;
To which is fix'd as an aim or butt
Obedience; for so work the honeybees,
Creatures that by a rule in nature teach
The act of order to a peopled kingdom.
They have a king, and officers of sorts,
Where some like magistrates correct at home,
Others like merchants venture trade abroad,
Others like soldiers arm'd in their stings
Make boot upon the summer's velvet buds,
Which pillage they with merry march bring home
To the tent-royal of their emporer,
Who, busied in his majesty, surveys
The singing masons building roofs of gold,
The civil citizens kneading up the honey,
The poor mechanic porters crowding in
Their heavy burdens at his narrow gate,
The sad-eyed justice, with his surly hum,
Delivering o'er to executors pale
The lazy yawning drone. I this infer,
That many things having full reference
To one consent may work contrariously,
As many arrows loos'd several ways
Come to one mark, as many ways meet in one town;
So may a thousand actions, once afoot,
End in one purpose, and be all well borne
Without defeat.

HENRY V

Call in the messengers sent from the Dauphin.

CANTERBURY

Therefore to France, my liege!
Divide your happy England into four,
Whereof take you one quarter into France,
And you withal shall make all Gallia shake.
If we, with thrice such powers left at home,
Cannot defend our own doors from the dog,
Let us be worried, and our nation lose
The name of hardiness and policy.

(Exit several attendants.)

HENRY V

Now are we well resolved.

(Enter Montjoy, Ambassador of France, attended.)
Now are we well prepared to know the pleasure
Of our fair cousin Dauphin; for we hear
Your greeting is from him, not from the king.

MONTJOY

May't please your majesty to give us leave
Freely to render what we have in charge;
Or shall we sparingly show you far off
The Dauphin's meaning, and our embassy?

HENRY V

Tell us the Dauphin's mind.

MONTJOY

Thus then, in few:
Your highness, lately sending into France,
Did claim some certain dukedoms, in the right
Of your great predecessor, King Edward the Third.
In answer of which claim, the prince our master
Says that you savour too much of your youth,
And bids you be advised: There's naught in France
That can be with a nimble galliard won;
You cannot revel into dukedoms there.
He therefore sends you, meeter for your spirit,
This tun of treasure; and in lieu of this,
Desires you let the dukedoms that you claim
Hear no more of you. This the Dauphin speaks.

HENRY V

What treasure, uncle?

WARWICK

Tennis balls, my liege.[10]

HENRY V

We are glad the Dauphin is so pleasant with us.
His present and your pains we thank you for.
When we have matched our rackets to these balls,
We will in France (by God's grace) play a set
Shall strike his father's crown into the hazard.
Tell him he hath made a match with such a wrangler
That all the courts of France will be disturbed
With chaces. And we understand him well,
How he comes o'er us with our wilder days,
Not measuring what use we made of them.
And tell the pleasant prince this mock of his
Hath turned his balls to gunstones, and his soul
Shall stand sore charg'd for the wasteful vengence

That shall fly with them; for many a thousand widows
Shall this his mock mock out of their dear husbands,
Mock mothers from their sons, mock castles down;
And some are yet ungotten and unborn
That shall have cause to curse the Dauphin's scorn.
Convey them with safe conduct. Fare you well.

(Exit Montjoy and attendants.)

WARWICK

This was a merry message.[11]

HENRY V

We hope to make the slender blush at it.
Therefore, my lords, omit no happy hour
That may give furth'rance to our expedition.

(Enter Chorus.)

CHORUS

When the archbishop had ended his prepared tale, all the companie began to
crie, Warre, warre; France, France.

HENRY V

For we have now no thought in us but France.

CHORUS

Hereby the bill for dissolving of religious houses was cleerlie set aside, and
nothing thought on but onlie the recovering of France, according as the archbishop
had moved.[12]

(Revolve.)

Scene Two

Boar's Head Tavern.
Pistol, Mistress Pistol, Page and Bardolph discovered.

PISTOL

Bardolph, be blithe; wife, rouse thy vaunting veins;
Boy, bristle thy courage up; for Falstaff he is dead,
And we must yearn therefore.[1]

MISTRESS PISTOL

'A made a finer end, and went away an it had been any christom child. 'A parted
ev'n just between twelve and one, ev'n at the turning o' th' tide. For after I saw
him fumble with the sheets, and play with flowers, and smile upon his finger's
end, I knew there was but one way; for his nose was as sharp as a pen, and 'a
babbled of green fields. 'How now, Sir John?' quoth I. 'What, man? be o' good
cheer.' So 'a cried out 'God, God, God!' three or four times. Now I, to comfort
him, bid him 'a should not think of God; I hoped there was no need to trouble
himself with any such thoughts yet. So 'a bade me lay more clothes on his feet.

I put my hand into the bed and felt them, and they were as cold as any stone. Then I felt to his knees, and so upward and upward, and all was as cold as any stone.

PAGE

They say he cried out of sack.[2]

MISTRESS PISTOL

Ay, that 'a did.

BARDOLPH

And of women.

MISTRESS PISTOL

Nay, that 'a did not.

PAGE

Yes, that 'a did; 'a said once the devil would have him about women.

MISTRESS PISTOL

'A did in some sort, indeed, handle women; but then he was rheumatic, and talked of the Whore of Babylon.

PAGE

Do you not remember 'a saw a flea stick upon Bardolph's nose, and 'a said it was a black soul burning in hell-fire?

BARDOLPH

Well, the fuel is gone that maintained that fire. That's all the riches I got in his service.

PAGE

Shall we shog? The king will be gone from Southampton.[3]

PISTOL

Come, let's away. My love, give me thy lips.
Look to my chattels and my moveables.
Trust none;
For oaths are straws, men's faiths are wafer-cakes,
And Hold-fast is the only dog, my duck.
Yoke-fellows in arms, let us to France.

BARDOLPH

Would I were with him, wheresome'er he is, either in heaven or in hell![4]

MISTRESS PISTOL

Nay sure, he's not in hell! He's in Arthur's bosom, if ever man went to Arthur's bosom.

(Curtain.)

Scene Three

London street.
Business only.[1]

Scene Four

CHORUS

Now all the youth of England are on fire,
And silken dalliance in the wardrobe lies.
Now thrive the armourers, and honour's thought
Reigns solely in the breast of every man.
They sell the pasture now to buy the horse,
Following the mirror of all Christian kings
With wing'd heels, as English Mercuries.
For now sits Expectation in the air
And hides a sword, from hilts unto the point,
With crowns imperial, crowns, and coronets
Promised to Harry and his followers.[1]
Thus with imagined wing our swift scene flies,
In motion of no less celerity
Than that of thought. Suppose that you have seen
The well-appointed king at Hampton pier
Embark his royalty; and his brave fleet
With silken streamers the young Phoebus fanning.
Play with your fancies, and in them behold
Upon the hempen tackle shipboys climbing;
Hear the shrill whistle which doth order give
To sounds confused; behold the threaden sails,
Borne with th' invisible and creeping wind,
Draw the huge bottoms through the furrowed sea,
Breasting the lofty surge. O, do but think
You stand upon the rivage and behold
A city on th' inconstant billows dancing;
For so appears this fleet majestical,
Holding due course to Harfleur. Follow, follow!
Grapple your minds to sternage of this navy,
And leave your England as dead midnight still,
Guarded with grandsires, babies, and old women;
For who is he whose chin is but enriched
With one appearing hair that will not follow
These culled and choice-drawn cavaliers to France?
Work, work your thoughts, and therein see a siege:
Behold the ordinance on their carriages,
With fatal mouths gaping at Harfleur.
Suppose th' ambassador from the French comes back;
Tells Harry that the king doth offer him
Katherine his daughter, and with her to dowry
Some petty and unprofitable dukedoms.
The offer likes not; and the nimbler gunner

With linstock now the devilish cannon touches,

(Alarum, and chambers go off.)

And down goes all before them. Still be kind,
And eke out our performance with your mind.[2]

(Complete revolve.)

Scene Five

Enter Henry V and his army.

HENRY V

Once more into the breach, dear friends, once more,
Or close the wall up with our English dead!
In peace there's nothing so becomes a man
As modest stillness and humility,
But when the blast of war blows in our ears,
Then imitate the action of the tiger:
Stiffen the sinews, summon up the blood,
Disguise fair nature with hard-favoured rage;
Then lend the eye a terrible aspect:
Let it cry through the portage of the head
Like the brass cannon; let the brow o'erwhelm it
As fearfully as doth a gall'd rock
O'erhang and jutty his confounded base,
Swilled with the wild and wasteful ocean.
Now set the teeth and stretch the nostril wide,
Hold hard the breath and bend up every spirit
To his full height! On, on, you noble English,
Dishonour not your mothers; now attest
That those whom you called fathers did beget you!
Be copy now to men of grosser blood
And teach them how to war! And you, good yoemen,
Whose limbs were made in England, show us here
The mettle of your pasture. Let us swear
That you are worthy of your breeding; which I doubt not,
For there is none of you so mean and base
That hath not noble lustre in your eyes.
I see you stand like greyhounds in the slips,
Straining upon the start. The game's afoot!
Follow your spirit; and upon this charge
Cry 'God for Harry! England and Saint George!'[1]

(Exit Henry V and his army. Alarum, and chambers go off. Revolve.)

Scene Six

Fluellen discovered.
Drum and colours. Enter Henry V, Gloucester, and
lords.

FLUELLEN

God pless your majesty!¹

FLUELLEN

God pless your majesty![1]

HENRY V

How now, Fluellen? Cam'st thou from the bridge?

FLUELLEN

Ay, so please your majesty. The Duke of Exeter has very gallantly maintained the pridge.

HENRY V

What men have you lost, Fluellen?

FLUELLEN

Marry, for my part, I think the duke hath lost never a man but one that is like to be executed for robbing a church—one Bardolph, if your majesty know the man.

HENRY V

We would have all such offenders so cut off.

(Enter Montjoy.)

MONTJOY

You know me by my habit.

HENRY V

Well then, I know thee. What shall I know of thee?

MONTJOY

My master's mind.

HENRY V

Unfold it.

MONTJOY

Thus says my king: Say thou to Harry of England: Though we seemed dead, we did but slumber. Now we speak upon our cue, and our voice is imperial. England shall repent his folly, see his weakness, and admire our sufferance. So far my king and master; so much my office.

HENRY V

Thou dost thy office fairly. Turn thee back,
And tell thy king I do not seek him now,
But could be willing to march on to Calais
Without impeachment: for, to say the sooth,
[Though] 'tis no wisdom to confess so much,
My people are with sickness much enfeebled,

My numbers lessened, and those few I have
Almost no better than so many French.
Go therefore tell thy master here I am;
My ransom is this frail and worthless body;
My army but a weak and sickly guard;
Yet, God before, tell him we will come on,
Though France himself and such another neighbour
Stand in our way. So tell thy master.

MONTJOY
I shall deliver so. Thanks to your highness.

(Exit Montjoy.)

GLOUCESTER
I hope they will not come upon us now.

HENRY V
We are in God's hand, brother, not in theirs.
March to the bridge. It now draws toward night.
Beyond the river we'll encamp ourselves,
And on to-morrow bid them march away.

(Exit Henry V, Gloucester, Fluellen and lords. Revolve.)

Scene Seven

CHORUS
On the two and twentith day of October, the duke of Yorke that led the vauntgard mounted up to the heigth of an hill with his people, and sent out scowts to discover the countrie, the which upon their returne advertised him, that a great armie of Frenchmen was at hand, approching towards them. The king thereupon, incontinentlie rode foorth to view his adversaries, and that doone, returned to his people, and with cheerefull countenance caused them to be put in order of battell, and so kept them still in that order till night was come, and then determined to seeke a place to incampe and lodge his armie in for the night. There was not one amongst them that knew any certeine place whither to go, in that unknowne countrie: but by chance they happened upon a little village, where they were refreshed with meat and drinke somewhat more plenteouslie than they had beene diverse daies before. The French nobilitie came and pitched down their standards and banners in the countrie of saint Paule, within the territorie of Agincourt, having in their armie (as some write) to the number of threescore thousand horssemen, besides footmen, wagoners and other. They were lodged even in the waie by which the Englishmen must needs passe towards Calis, and all that night after their comming thither, made great game. The Englishmen also for their parts were of good comfort, and nothing abashed of the matter, and yet they were both hungrie, wearie, sore travelled, and vexed with manie cold diseases. The daie following was the five and twentith of October in the

yeare 1415, being then fridaie, and the feast of Crispine and Crispinian.[1]
Now entertain conjecture of a time
When creeping murmur and the poring dark
Fills the wide vessel of the universe.
From camp to camp, through the foul womb of night,
The hum of either army stilly sounds,
That the fixed sentinels almost receive
The secret whispers of each other's watch.
Fire answers fire, and through their paly flames
Each battle sees the other's umbered face.
Steed threatens steed, in high and boastful neighs
Piercing the night's dull ear; and from the tents
The armourers accomplishing the knights,
With busy hammers closing rivets up,
Give dreadful note of preparation.
The country cocks do crow, the clocks do toll
And the third hour of drowsy morning name.
Proud of their numbers and secure in soul,
The confident and over-lusty French
Do the low-rated English play at dice;
And chide the cripple tardy-gaited night
Who like a foul and ugly witch doth limp
So tediously away. The poor condemn'd English,
Like sacrifices, by their watchful fires
Sit patiently and inly ruminate
The morning's danger; and their gesture sad,
Investing lank-lean cheeks and war-worn coats,
Presenteth them unto the gazing moon
So many horrid ghosts. O, now, who will behold
The royal captain of this ruined band
Walking from watch to watch, from tent to tent?
For forth he goes and visits all his host,
Bids them good morrow with a modest smile
And calls them brothers, friends, and countrymen.
Upon his royal face there is no note
How dread an army hath enrounded him;
Nor doth he dedicate one jot of colour
Unto the weary and all-watch'd night,
But freshly looks, and overbears attaint
With cheerful semblance and sweet majesty;
That every wretch, pining and pale before,
Beholding him, plucks comfort from his looks.
A largess universal, like the sun,
His liberal eye doth give to every one,

Thawing cold fear, that mean and gentle all
Behold, as may unworthiness define,
A little touch of Harry in the night.[2]

> *(Revolve.)*

Scene Eight

Henry V discovered, in disguise.
Enter Pistol.

PISTOL

Qui va là?[1]

HENRY V

A friend.

PISTOL

Discuss unto me, art thou officer;
Or art thou base, common, and popular?

HENRY V

I am a gentleman of a company. What are you?

PISTOL

As good a gentleman as the emporer.

HENRY V

Then you are a better than the king.

PISTOL

The king's a bawcock, and a heart of gold,
A lad of life, an imp of fame,
Of parents good, of fist most valiant.
I kiss his dirty shoe, and from heartstring
I love the lovely bully. What is thy name?

HENRY V

Harry le Roy.

PISTOL

Le Roy? A Cornish name. Art thou of Cornish crew?

HENRY V

No, I am a Welshman. God be with you!

PISTOL

My name is Pistol called.

HENRY V

It sorts well with your fierceness.

> *(Exit Pistol.)*

Scene Nine

Enter three soldiers, John Bates, Alexander Court and Michael Williams.

WILLIAMS

Who goes there?

HENRY V

A friend.

BATES

Under what captain serve you?

HENRY V

Under Sir Thomas Erpingham.

COURT

A good commander and a most kind gentleman. Brother John Bates, is not that the morning which breaks yonder?[1]

BATES

I think it be; but we have no great cause to desire the approach of day.

WILLIAMS

We see yonder the beginning of the day, but I think we shall never see the end of it. I pray you, what thinks Sir Thomas of our estate?

HENRY V

Even as men wracked upon a sand, that look to be washed off the next tide.

BATES

He hath not told his thought to the king?

HENRY V

No; nor is it meet he should. For though I speak it to you, I think the king is but a man, as I am. The violet smells to him as it doth to me; the element shows to him as it doth to me; all his senses have but human conditions. His ceremonies laid by, in his nakedness he appears but a man. Yet, in reason, no man should possess him with any appearance of fear, lest he, by showing it, should dishearten his army.

COURT

He may show what outward courage he will; but I believe, as cold a night as 'tis, he could wish himself in Thames up to the neck; and so I would he were, and I by him, so we were quit here.[2]

HENRY V

By my troth, I will speak my conscience of the king: I think he would not wish himself anywhere but where he is.

BATES

Then I would he were here alone. So should he be sure to be ransomed, and a many poor men's lives saved.

HENRY V

Methinks I could not die anywhere so contented as in the king's company, his cause being just and his quarrel honourable.

WILLIAMS

That's more than we know.

BATES

Ay, or more than we should seek after.

COURT

We know enough if we know we are the king's subjects.[3]

WILLIAMS

But if the cause be not good, the king himself hath a heavy reckoning to make when all those legs and arms and heads, chopped off in a battle, shall join together at the latter day and cry all, 'We died at such a place,' some swearing, some crying for a surgeon, some upon their wives left poor behind them, some upon the debts they owe, some upon their children rawly left. I am afeared there are few die well that die in a battle; for how can they charitably dispose of anything when blood is their argument? Now, if these men do not die well, it will be a black matter for the king that led them to it.

HENRY V

The king is not bound to answer the particular endings of his soldiers.

WILLIAMS

'Tis certain, every man that dies ill, the ill upon his own head—the king is not to answer it.

BATES

I do not desire he should answer for me, and yet I determine to fight lustily for him.

HENRY V

I myself heard the king say he would not be ransomed.

WILLIAMS

Ay, he said so, to make us fight cheerfully; but when our throats are cut, he may be ransomed, and we ne'er the wiser.

HENRY V

If I live to see it, I will never trust his word after.

WILLIAMS

You pay him then! You'll never trust his word after!

HENRY V

I should be angry with you if the time were convenient.

WILLIAMS

Let it be a quarrel between us if you live.

HENRY V

I embrace it.

WILLIAMS
How shall I know thee again?

HENRY V
Give me any gage of thine, and I will wear it in my bonnet. Then, if ever thou dar'st acknowledge it, I will make it my quarrel.

WILLIAMS
Here's my glove. Give me another of thine.

HENRY V
There.

WILLIAMS
This will I also wear in my cap. If ever thou come to me and say, after to-morrow, 'This is my glove,' by this hand, I will take thee a box on the ear.

HENRY V
If ever I live to see it, I will challenge it.

WILLIAMS
Thou dar'st as well be hanged.

HENRY V
Well, I will do it, though I take thee in the king's company.

WILLIAMS
Keep thy word.

BATES
Be friends, you English fools, be friends! We have French quarrels enow, if you could tell how to reckon.

(Exit soldiers.)

Scene Ten

HENRY V
(removes disguise)
O God of battles, steel my soldiers' hearts,
Possess them not with fear! Take from them now
The sense of reck'ning, if th' oppos'd numbers
Pluck their hearts from them. Not to-day, O Lord,
O, not to-day, think not upon the fault
My father made in compassing the crown!
I Richard's body have interr'd new;
And on it have bestowed more contrite tears
Than from it issued forc'd drops of blood.
Five hundred poor I have in yearly pay,
Who twice a day their withered hands hold up
Toward heaven, to pardon blood;
And I have built two chantries,

Where the sad and solemn priests sing still
For Richard's soul. More will I do:
Though all that I can do is nothing worth,
Since that my penitence comes after all,
Imploring pardon.[1]

(Revolve.)

Scene Eleven

Enter Henry V, lords and Chief Justice.

WESTMORELAND

Of fighting men they have full three-score thousand.[1]

WARWICK

There's five to one; besides, they are all fresh.[2]

CHIEF JUSTICE

God's arm strike with us! 'Tis a fearful odds.[3]

(Enter Gloucester.)

GLOUCESTER

My lord, my lord, the army stays upon your presence.

WESTMORELAND

O that we now had here
But one ten thousand of those men in England
That do no work to-day!

HENRY V

What's he that wishes so?
My cousin Westmoreland? No, my fair cousin.
If we are marked to die, we are enow
To do our country loss; and if to live,
The fewer men, the greater share of honour.
God's will! I pray thee wish not one man more.
By Jove, I am not covetous for gold,
Nor care I who doth feed upon my cost;
It yearns me not if men my garments wear;
Such outward things dwell not in my desires:
But if it is a sin to covet honour,
I am the most offending soul alive.
No, faith, my coz, wish not a man from England.
God's peace! I would not lose so great an honour
As one man more methinks would share from me
For the best hope I have. O, do not wish one more!
Rather proclaim it, Westmoreland, through my host,
That he which hath no stomach to this fight,

Let him depart; his passport shall be made,
And crowns for convoy put into his purse.
We would not die in that man's company
That fears his fellowship to die with us.
This day is called the Feast of Crispian.
He that outlives this day, and comes safe home,
Will stand a-tiptoe when this day is named
And rouse him at the name of Crispian.
He that shall live this day, and see old age,
Will yearly on the vigil feast his neighbours
And say, 'To-morrow is Saint Crispian.'
Then will he strip his sleeve and show his scars,
[And say, 'These wounds I had on Crispin's day.']
Old men forget; yet all shall be forgot,
But he'll remember, with advantages,
What feats he did that day. Then shall our names,
Familiar in his mouth as household words—
Harry the King, Bedford and Exeter,
Warwick and Talbot, Salisbury and Gloucester—
Be in their flowing cups freshly rememb'red.
This story shall the good man teach his son;
And Crispin Crispian shall ne'er go by,
From this day to the ending of the world,
But we in it shall be remembered—
We few, we happy few, we band of brothers;
For he to-day that sheds his blood with me
Shall be my brother. Be he ne'er so base,
This day shall gentle his condition;
And gentlemen in England now abed
Shall think themselves accursed they were not here,
And hold their manhoods cheap whiles any speaks
That fought with us upon Saint Crispin's day.

(Enter Salisbury.)

SALISBURY

My sovereign lord, bestow yourself with speed.
The French are bravely in their battles set
And will with all expedience charge on us.

HENRY V

All things are ready, if our minds be so.

WESTMORELAND

Perish the man whose mind is backward now!

WARWICK

Thou dost not wish more help from England, coz?⁴

WESTMORELAND

God's will, my liege! would you and I alone,
Without more help, could fight this royal battle!

HENRY V

Why, now thou hast unwished five thousand men!
Which likes me better than to wish us one.
God be with you all.

(Exit all. Enter Chorus.)

CHORUS

The Frenchmen being ordered under their standards and banners, made a great shew: for suerlie they were esteemed in number six times as manie or more, than was the whole companie of the Englishmen, with wagoners, pages and all. They rested themselves, waiting for the bloudie blast of the terrible trumpet, till the houre betweene nine and ten of the clocke of the same date. The Frenchmen in the meane while, as though they had beene sure of victorie, made great triumph, for the capteins had determined before, how to divide the spoile. The noble men had devised a chariot, wherein they might triumphantlie conveie the king captive to the citie of Paris, crieng to their soldiers; Haste you to the spoile, glorie and honour; little weening (God wot) how soone their brags should be blowne awaie.[5]

(Revolve.)

Scene Twelve

Enter Pistol, Page and French Soldier.

PISTOL

Yield, cur![1]

FRENCH SOLDIER

Je pense que vous êtes le gentilhomme de bonne qualité.

PISTOL

Qualtitie calmie custure! Art thou a gentleman? What is thy name? Discuss.

FRENCH SOLDIER

O Seigneur Dieu!

PISTOL

O Signieur Dew should be a gentleman.
Perpend my words, O Signieur Dew, and mark.
O Signieur Dew, thou diest on point of fox,
Except, O signieur, thou do give to me
Egregious ransom.

FRENCH SOLDIER

O, prenez miséricorde! ayez pitié de moi!

PISTOL

Moy shall not serve. I will have forty moys,
Or I will fetch thy rim out at thy throat
In drops of crimson blood.
Boy, ask me this slave in French
What is his name.

PAGE

Ecoutez. Comment êtes-vous appelé?

FRENCH SOLDIER

Monsieur le Fer.

PAGE

He says his name is Master Fer.

PISTOL

Master Fer? I'll fer him, and firk him, and ferret him! Discuss the same in French
unto him.

PAGE

I do not know the French for 'fer,' and 'ferret,' and 'firk.'

PISTOL

Bid him prepare, for I will cut his throat.

FRENCH SOLDIER

O, je vous supplie, pour l'amour de Dieu, me pardonner! Je suis gentilhomme
de bonne maison. Gardez ma vie, et je vous donnerai deux cents écus.

PISTOL

What are his words?

PAGE

He prays you to save his life. He is a gentleman of a good house, and for his
ransom he will give you two hundred crowns.

PISTOL

Tell him my fury shall abate, and I
The crowns will take.

FRENCH SOLDIER

Petit monsieur, que dit-il?

PAGE

Encore qu'il contre son jurement de pardonner aucun prisonnier; néanmoins,
pour les écus que vous l'avez promis, il est content de vous donner la liberté,
le franchisement.

FRENCH SOLDIER

Sur mes genoux je vous donne mille remercîments; et je m'estime heureux que
le suis tombé entre les mains d'un chevalier, je pense, le plus brave, vaillant,
et très-distingué seigneur d'Angleterre.

PISTOL

Expound unto me, boy.

PAGE

He gives you, upon his knees, a thousand thanks; and he esteems himself happy
that he hath fall'n into the hands of one (as he thinks) the most brave, valourous,
and thrice-worthy signieur of England.

PISTOL

As I suck blood, I will some mercy show!
Follow me.

PAGE

Suivez-vous le grand capitaine.

> *(Exit Pistol, Page and French Soldier. Revolve.)*

Scene Thirteen

> *Henry V, Fluellen, lords and attendants discovered.*
> *Enter Montjoy.*

MONTJOY

Great king,
I come to thee for charitable license
That we may wander o'er this bloody field
To book our dead, and then to bury them.[1]

HENRY V

I tell thee truly,
I know not if the day be ours or no.

MONTJOY

The day is yours.[2]

HENRY V

What is this castle called that stands hard by?

MONTJOY

They call it Agincourt.[3]

HENRY V

Then call we this the field of Agincourt,
Fought on the day of Crispin Crispianus.

FLUELLEN

Your grandfather of famous memory, an't please your majesty, and your great-
uncle Edward the Plack Prince of Wales, as I have read in the chronicles, fought
a most prave pattle here in France.

HENRY V

They did, Fluellen.

FLUELLEN

Your majesty says very true. By Jeshu, I am your majesty's countryman, I care

not who know it! I will confess it to all the orld. I need not to be ashamed of
your majesty, praised be God, so long as your majesty is an honest man.

HENRY V

God keep me so!

(Enter Williams.)

Our heralds go with him.
Bring me just notice of the numbers dead
On both our parts.

(Exit Montjoy with attendants.)

WARWICK

(to Williams)

Soldier, you must come to the king.[4]

HENRY V

Soldier, why wear'st thou that glove in thy cap?

WILLIAMS

An't please your majesty, 'tis the gage of one that I should fight withal, if he
be alive.

HENRY V

An Englishman?

WILLIAMS

An't please your majesty, a rascal that swaggered with me last night; who, if
'a live and ever dare to challenge this glove, I have sworn to take him a box o'
th' ear.

HENRY V

Give me thy glove, soldier. Look, here is the fellow of it.
'Twas I indeed thou promis'd to strike;
And thou hast given me most bitter terms.[5]

FLUELLEN

An please your majesty, let his neck answer for it, if there is any martial law
in the world.

HENRY V

How canst thou make me satisfaction?

WILLIAMS

All offenses, my lord, come from the heart. Never came any from mine that
might offend your majesty.

HENRY V

It was ourself thou didst abuse.

WILLIAMS

Your majesty came not like yourself. You appeared to me but as a common
man. And what your highness suffered under that shape, I beseech you take it
for your own fault, and not mine; for had you been as I took you for, I made
no offense. Therefore I beseech your majesty pardon me.

HENRY V
(to Fluellen)

Fill this glove with crowns
And give it to this fellow. Keep it, fellow,
And wear it for an honour in thy cap
Till I do challenge it. Give him the crowns;
And, captain, you must needs be friends with him.

FLUELLEN

Hold, soldier, there is twelve pence for you; and I pray you to serve God, and
keep you out of prawls and prabbles.

WILLIAMS

I will none of your money, sir.

FLUELLEN

It is with a good will. I can tell you it will serve you to mend your shoes. Come,
your shoes is not so good. 'Tis [a] good silling, I warrant you, or I will change
it.

(Enter an English Herald.)

HENRY V

Now, herald, are the dead numb'red?

HERALD
(giving him the paper)

Here is the numbered of slaught'red French.

HENRY V

This note doth tell me of ten thousand French
That in the field lie slain.
Where is the number of our English dead?

(Herald gives him another paper.)

Edward the Duke of York, the Earl of Suffolk,
None else of name; and of all other men
But five-and-twenty.
Was ever known so great and little loss
On one part and on th' other? Take it, God!

WARWICK

'Tis wonderful![6]

HENRY V

And be it death proclaim'd through our host
To boast of this, or take that praise from God
Which is his only.

FLUELLEN

Is it not lawful, an please your majesty, to tell how many is killed?

HENRY V

Yes, captain; but with this adknowledgment,
That God fought for us.

FLUELLEN

Yes, my conscience, he did us great good.

(Revolve.)

Scene Fourteen

CHORUS

And so about foure of the clocke in the after noone, the king when he saw no
appearance of enimies, caused the retreit to be blowen; and gathering his armie
togither, gave thanks to almightie God for so happie a victorie, causing his
prelats and chapleins to sing this psalme: In exitu Israel de Aegypto, non nobis
Domine, non nobis, sed nomini tuo da gloriam. Which doone, he caused Te
Deum, with certeine anthems to be soong, giving laud and praise to God, without
boasting of his owne force or anie humane power. When the king of England
had well refreshed himselfe, and his souldiers, that had taken the spoile of such
as were slaine, he with his prisoners in good order returned to his towne of
Calis.[1]

(Exit Chorus.)

Scene Fifteen

French court.
Katherine and Alice discovered.

KATHERINE

Alice, tu as été en Angleterre, et tu parles bien le langage.[1]

ALICE

Un peu, madame.

KATHERINE

Je te prie m'enseigner; il faut que j'apprenne à parler. Comment appelez-vous
la main en Anglais?

ALICE

La main? Elle est appelée de hand.

KATHERINE

De hand. Et les doigts?

ALICE

Les doigts? Ma foi, j'oublie les doigts; mais je me souviendrai. Les doigts? Je
pense qu'ils sont appelés de fingres; oui, de fingres.

KATHERINE

La main, de hand; les doigts, le fingres. Je pense que je suis le bon écolier; j'ai gagné deux mots d'Anglais vitement. Comment appelez-vous les ongles?

ALICE

Les ongles? De nails.

KATHERINE

De nails. Ecoutez; dites-moi si je parle bien: de hand, de fingres, et de nails.

ALICE

C'est bien dit, madame; il est fort bon Anglais.

KATHERINE

Dites-moi l'Anglais pour le bras.

ALICE

De arm, madame.

KATHERINE

Et le coude.

ALICE

D'elbow.

KATHERINE

D'elbow. Je m'en fais la répétition de tous les mots que vous m'avez appris dès à présent.

ALICE

Il est trop difficile, madame, comme je pense.

KATHERINE

Excusez-moi, Alice; écoutez: d'hand, de fingre, de nails, d'arma, de bilbow.

ALICE

D'elbow, madame.

KATHERINE

O Seigneur Dieu, je m'en oublie! d'elbow. Comment appelez-vous le col?

ALICE

De nick, madame.

KATHERINE

De nick. Et le menton?

ALICE

De chin.

KATHERINE

De sin. Le col, de nick; le menton, de sin.

ALICE

Oui. Sauf votre honneur, en vérité, vous pronouncez les mots aussi droit que les natifs d'Angleterre.

KATHERINE

Je ne doute point d'apprendre, par la grace de Dieu, et en peu de temps.

ALICE

N'avez-vous pas déjà oublié ce que je vous ai enseigné?

KATHERINE

Non, je réciterai à vous promptement: d'hand, de fingre, de mails—

ALICE

De nails, madame.

KATHERINE

De nails, de arm, de ilbow—

ALICE

Sauf votre honneur, d'elbow.

KATHERINE

Ainsi dis-je; d'elbow, de nick, et de sin. Comment appelez-vous le pied et la robe?

ALICE

Le foot, madame; et le count.

KATHERINE

Le foot et le count! O Seigneur Dieu! ils sont les mots de son mauvais, corruptible, gros, et impudique, et non pour les dames d'honneur d'user: je ne voudrais pronouncer ces mots devant les seigneurs de France pour tout le monde. Foh! le foot et le count! Néanmoins, je réciterai une autre fois ma leçon ensemble: d'hand, de fingre, de nails, d'arm, d'elbow, de nick, de sin, de foot, le count.

ALICE

Excellent, madame!

KATHERINE

C'est assez une fois: allons-nous à diner.

(Enter Henry V.)

HENRY V

Fair Katherine, and most fair!
You will vouchsafe to teach a soldier terms
Such as will enter at a lady's ear
And plead his love suit to her gentle heart?[2]

KATHERINE

Your majesty shall mock at me. I cannot speak your England.

HENRY V

O fair Katherine, if you will love me soundly with your French heart, I will be glad to hear you confess it brokenly with your English tongue. Do you like me, Kate?

KATHERINE
Pardonnez-moi?

HENRY V
Do you like me?

KATHERINE
I cannot tell wat is 'like me.'

HENRY V
An angel is like you, Kate, and you are like an angel.

KATHERINE
Que dit-il? Que je suis semblable à les anges?

ALICE
Oui, vraiment, sauf votre grâce, ainsi dit-il.

HENRY V
I said so, dear Katherine, and I must not blush to affirm it.

KATHERINE
O bon Dieu! les langues des hommes sont pleines de tromperies.

HENRY V
What says she, fair one? that the tongues of men are full of deceits?

ALICE
Oui, dat de tongues of de mans is be full of deceits. Dat is de princesse.

HENRY V
The princess is the better Englishwoman. I' faith, Kate, my wooing is fit for thy understanding. I am glad thou canst speak no better English; for if thou couldst, thou wouldst find me such a plain king that thou wouldst think I had sold my farm to buy my crown. I know no ways to mince it in love but directly to say, 'I love you.' Then, if you urge me farther than to say, 'Do you in faith?' I wear out my suit. Give me your answer, i' faith, do: and so clap hands and a bargain. How say you, lady?

KATHERINE
Sauf votre honneur, me understand well.

HENRY V
Marry, if you would put me to verses or to dance for your sake, Kate, why, you undid me. If I could win a lady at leapfrog, or by vaulting into my saddle with my armour on my back, under the correction of bragging be it spoken, I should quickly leap into a wife. But, before God, Kate, I cannot look greenly nor gasp out my eloquence. If thou canst love a fellow of this temper, Kate, whose face is not worth sunburning, that never looks in his glass for love of anything he sees there, let thine eye be thy cook. And while thou liv'st, dear Kate, take a fellow of plain and uncoined constancy, for he perforce must do thee right, because he hath not the gift to woo in other places. For these fellows of infinite tongue that can rhyme themselves into ladies' favours, they do always

reason themselves out again. What! A speaker is but a prater; a rhyme is but a ballad. A good leg will fall, a straight back will stoop, a black beard will turn white, a curled pate will grow bald, a fair face will wither, a full eye will—

KATHERINE

Eye—

HENRY V

Will wax hollow; but a good heart, Kate, is the sun and the moon. If thou wouldst have such a one, take me; and take me, take a soldier; take a soldier, take a king. And what say'st thou then to my love? Speak, my fair—and fairly, I pray thee.

KATHERINE

Is it possible dat I sould love de ennemie of France?

HENRY V

No, it is not possible you should love the enemy of France, Kate; but in loving me you should love the friend of France, for I love France so well that I will not part with a village of it—I will have it all mine. And, Kate, when France is mine and I am yours, then yours is France and you are mine.

KATHERINE

I cannot tell wat is dat.

HENRY V

No, Kate? I will tell thee in French, which I am sure will hang upon my tongue like a new-married wife about her husband's neck, hardly to be shook off. Je quand sur le possession de France, et quand vous avez le possession de moi (let me see, what then? Saint Denis be my speed!), donc votre est France et vous êtes mienne. It is as easy for me, Kate, to conquer the kingdom as to speak so much more French. I shall never move thee in French, unless it be to laugh at me.

KATHERINE

Sauf votre honneur, le Français que vous parlez, il est meilleur que l'Anglais lequel je parle.

HENRY V

Kate, dost thou understand thus much English? Canst thou love me?

KATHERINE

I cannot tell.

HENRY V

If ever thou beest mine, Kate—as I have a saving faith within me tells me thou shalt—thou must therefore prove a good soldier-breeder. Shall not thou and I, between Saint Denis and Saint George, compound a boy, half French, half English, that shall go to Constantinople and take the Turk by the beard?

KATHERINE

Beard—

HENRY V

Shall we not? What say'st thou, my fair flower-de-luce?

KATHERINE

I do not know dat.

HENRY V

No; 'tis hereafter to know, but now to promise. Do but now promise, you will endeavour for your French part of such a boy, and for my English moiety take the word of a king and a bachelor. How answer you, la plus belle Katherine du monde, mon très-cher et devin déesse?

KATHERINE

Your majestee ave fausse French enough to deceive de most sage demoiselle dat is en France.

HENRY V

Now, fie upon my false French! By mine honour in true English, I love thee, Kate; by which honour I dare not swear thou lovest me; yet my blood begins to flatter me that thou dost. Now beshrew my father's ambition! He was thinking of civil wars when he got me; therefore was I created with a stubborn outside, with an aspect of iron, that when I come to woo ladies, I fright them. But in faith, Kate, the elder I wax the better I shall appear. My comfort is that old age, that ill layer-up of beauty, can do no more spoil upon my face. Thou hast me, if thou hast me, at the worst; and thou shalt wear me, if thou wear me, better and better; and therefore tell me, most fair Katherine, will you have me? Put off your maiden blushes; avouch the thoughts of your heart with the looks of an empress; take me by the hand—

KATHERINE

Hand—

HENRY V

And say, 'Harry—

KATHERINE

Harry—

HENRY V

Of England, I am thine!' which word thou shalt no sooner bless mine ear withal but I will tell thee aloud, 'England is thine, Ireland is thine, France is thine, and Henry—

KATHERINE

Henry—

HENRY V

Plantagenet is thine'; who, though I speak it before his face, if he be not fellow with the best king, thou shalt find the best king of good fellows. Come, your answer in broken music! therefore, queen of all, Katherine, break thy mind to me in broken English. Wilt thou have me?

KATHERINE

Dat is as it sall please de roi mon pere.

HENRY V

Nay, it will please him well, Kate; it shall please him, Kate.

KATHERINE

Den it sall also content me.

HENRY V

Upon that I kiss your hand and I call you my queen.

KATHERINE

Laissez, mon seigneur, laissez, laissez! Ma foi, je ne veux point que vous abaissiez votre grandeur en baisant la main d'une de votre seigneurie indigne serviteur. Excusez-moi, je vous supplie, mon très-puissant seigneur.

HENRY V

Then I will kiss your lips, Kate.

KATHERINE

Les dames et demoiselles pour être baisées devant leur noces, il n'est pas la coutume de France.

HENRY V

Madam my interpreter, what says she?

ALICE

Dat it is not be de fashon pour le ladies of France—I cannot tell wat is 'baiser' en Anglish.

HENRY V

To kiss.

ALICE

Your majestee entendre bettre que moi.

HENRY V

It is not a fashion for the maids in France to kiss before they are married, would she say?

ALICE

Oui, vraiment.

HENRY V

O Kate, nice customs curtsy to great kings. Dear Kate, you and I cannot be confined within the weak list of a country's fashion. We are the makers of manners, Kate; and the liberty that follows our places stops the mouth of all findfaults, as I will do yours for upholding the nice fashion of your country in denying me a kiss. Therefore patiently, and yielding.

(kisses her)

You have witchcraft in your lips, Kate. There is more eloquence in a sugar touch of them than in the tongues of the French Council, and they should sooner persuade Harry of England than a general petition of monarchs. Here comes your father.

(Enter the King of France, his Queen, Burgundy, and the English Lords.)

BURGUNDY
God save your majesty! My royal cousin, teach you our princess English?

HENRY V
I would have her learn, my fair cousin, how perfectly I love her, and that is good English. Shall Kate be my wife?

FRANCE
So please you. We have consented to all terms of reason.

HENRY V
Is't so, my lords of England?

WESTMORELAND
The king hath granted every article:
His daughter first; and in sequel, all,
According to their firm propos'd natures.

FRANCE
Take her, fair son, and from her blood raise up
Issue to me, that the contending kingdoms
Of France and England, whose very shores look pale
With envy of each other's happiness,
May cease their hatred, and this dear conjunction
Plant neighbourhood and Christian-like accord
In their sweet bosoms, that never war advance
His bleeding sword 'twixt England and fair France.

ALL
Amen!

HENRY V
Now, welcome, Kate; and bear me witness all
That here I kiss her as my sovereign queen.

(Kisses her. Flourish.)

Scene Sixteen

Enter Chorus, downstage.

CHORUS
Thus far, with rough and all-unable pen,
  Our bending author hath pursued the story,
In little room confining mighty men,

Mangling by starts the full course of their glory.
Small time; but in that small most greatly lived
This Star of England. Fortune made his sword,
By which the world's best garden he achieved,
And of it left his son imperial lord.
Henry the Sixth, in infant bands crowned King
Of France and England, did this king succeed;
Whose state so many had the managing
That they lost France and made his England bleed:
Which oft our stage hath shown; and for their sake,
In your fair minds let this acceptance take.[1]

THE END

NOTES

1,i

1. *Henry V*, Prologue, 1–34

1,ii

1. *I Henry IV*, I,i,1–16
2. *Richard II*, V,vi,30–33
3. Holinshed, vol. 2, p. 865

I,iii

1. II Henry IV, II, ii,69–135

I,iv

1. 146.
2. II,iv,272/274
3. Mistress Quickly, 273
4. 31/I,ii,1
5. Doll Tearsheet, II,iv,219
6. 220/*I Henry IV*, II,ii,15–18
7. Doll, *II Henry IV*, II,iv,222
8. 275–76/*I Henry IV*, I,ii,74–75
9. *II Henry IV*, II,iv,296
10. *I Henry IV*, III,iii,110
11. Prince, 120
12. I,ii,2–12
13. Poins, 139
14. Ibid., 158
15. Ibid., 160
16. Ibid., 167–69
17. Ibid., 150

I,v

1. *Richard II*, V,iii,1–12

I,vi

1. *I Henry IV*, II,ii,4
2. Prince, 29–30
3. Gadshill, 49
4. Ibid., 50
5. Peto, 58
6. Gadshill, 59

I,vii

1. Holinshed, vol. 3, p. 22

I,viii

1. Hotspur, Worcester, and Northumberland come downstage and exit through the door in the palace exterior.

I,ix

1. *I Henry IV*, I,i,91–95
2. Westmoreland, 96
3. I,iii,1–6
4. King Henry, 78
5. Ibid., 79–80
6. Ibid.
7. Hotspur, 94–95
8. King Henry, 114
9. Ibid., 116–17
10. Ibid., 118

I,x

1. King Henry, 119
2. Worcester, 211
3. Holinshed, vol. 3, p. 22

I,xi

1. II,ii,96/98
2. Prince, 97
3. II,iv,107
4. Gadshill, 165
5. Ibid., 167
6. Peto, 168
7. Gadshill, 171–72
8. 236/Falstaff, 261
9. Peto, 290–92
10. Prince, 310
11. Falstaff, 366–69
12. Ibid., 379/371

I,xiii

1. III,ii. For all of his reordering of these several speeches of the king, the only notable omission is line 33 with its reference to Hal's younger brother, Prince John, who did not figure into Welles's text.

I,xv

1. *II Henry IV*, I,ii,220–35

I,xvi

1. Attendant, I,ii,62

I,xvii

1. Holinshed, vol. 3, p. 23

I,xviii

1. *I Henry IV*, II,iii,1–6
2. 83/6–8
3. Hotspur, 6
4. Stanley Poss, a Mercury extra
5. Francis Carpenter, who played Davy, doubled as Hotspur's other servant.
6. 110/33

I,xix

1. IV,ii,1–2/9
2. Bardolph, 10
3. Ibid., 4
4. Falstaff, 14
5. *II Henry IV*, V,i,8–9
6. III,ii,53
7. V,i,7
8. 1
9. Falstaff, III,ii,82
10. 27–32
11. 95–96/8–9
12. Shallow, 38
13. Mouldy, 97
14. Silence, 199
15. Mouldy, 108–10
16. Ibid., 111
17. 120/107
18. 275–76/V,i,27–29
19. Shallow, III,ii,38

I,xx

1. *I Henry IV*, IV,i,14
2. V,ii,79

I,xxi

1. IV,ii,46
2. Westmoreland, 53
3. Prince, 70
4. Ibid., 71–72
5. V,i,125

I,xxii

1. V,iv,57

II,i

1. *II Henry IV*, III,i,1–31
2. Warwick, 37
3. Ibid., 41–43
4. Ibid., 98–99
5. Ibid., 102–3

II,ii

1. II,ii,1
2. Prince, 100/108–11/113–14
3. Ibid., 138/140
4. Page, 144
5. 43–6.

II,iii

1. *I Henry IV*, III,iii,1–10
2. *II Henry IV*, II,iv,33
3. 165/101
4. Mistress Quickly, 162
5. 65.

II,iv

1. Falstaff and Bardolph walk out of Boar's Head and exit up the street.

II,v

1. Westmoreland, IV,iv,81
2. 91–93/109/11–12
3. Clarence, 51
4. Ibid., IV,v,6
5. Warwick, IV,iv,116
6. Gloucester, 130
7. IV,v,5/1–3
8. Clarence, 17
9. Ibid., 51–52
10. Gloucester, 56

II,vi

1. V,iii,32–33
2. 5–6.

II,vii

1. The business of this and the following scene (II,viii), while uncertain, involved crowds passing across the stage to attend Henry's coronation.

II,ix

1. V,v,5–8
2. Shallow, 15

III,i

1. Holinshed, vol. 3, p. 65
2. *Henry V*, I,i,19
3. Canterbury, 12–14
4. Ibid., 19
5. I,ii,3
6. Canterbury, 37–39
7. Ibid., 43–44
8. Ibid., 56
9. Exeter, 122–24
10. Ibid., 258
11. Ibid., 298
12. Holinshed, vol. 3, p. 66

III,ii

1. II,iii,4–6
2. Nym, 25
3. Ibid., 40
4. 7–8

III,iii

1. Soldiers on their way to join Henry's cause pass across the stage.

III,iv

1. Prologue, II,1–11
2. Prologue, III,1–35

III,v

1. III,i,1–34

III,vi

1. III,vi,85

III,vii

1. Holinshed, vol. 3, pp. 77–78
2. Prologue, IV, 1–47

III,viii

1. IV,i,35

III,ix

1. Williams, 92/84
2. Bates, 108–11
3. Ibid., 123–24

III,x

1. 275–92

III,xi

1. IV,iii,3
2. Exeter, 4
3. Salisbury, 5
4. Henry V, 73
5. Holinshed, vol. 3, pp. 78, 80

III,xii

1. IV,iv,1

III,xiii

1. Herald, IV,vii,65–67
2. Ibid., 82
3. Ibid., 84
4. Exeter, 113
5. IV,viii,36–39
6. Exeter, 107

III,xiv

1. Holinshed, vol. 3, p. 82

III,xv

1. III,iv,1–2
2. V,ii,98–101

III,xvi

1. Epilogue, 1–14

Selected Bibliography*

Adubato, Robert A. "A History of the WPA's Negro Theatre Project in New York City, 1935–1939." Unpublished dissertation, 1978.

Artaud, Antonin. *The Theatre and Its Double*. Translated by Mary C. Richards. New York, 1958.

Bazin, Andre. *Orson Welles*. Translated by Jonathan Rosenbaum. New York, 1978.

Bessy, Maurice. *Orson Welles*. Paris, 1982.

Buttita, Tony, and Barry Witham. *Uncle Sam Presents: A Memoir of the Federal Theatre, 1935–1939*. Philadelphia, 1982.

Cahiers du Cinema. Special Series, 12 (1982).

Carringer, Robert L. *The Making of Citizen Kane*. Berkeley, 1985.

Clurman, Harold. *The Fervent Years*. New York, 1957.

Cobos, Juan, and Miguel Rubio. "Welles and Falstaff." *Sight and Sound* (Autumn 1966).

Craig, E. Quitta. *Black Drama of the Federal Theatre Era*. Amherst, 1980.

Crowl, Samuel. "The Long Goodbye: Welles and Falstaff." *Shakespeare Quarterly* (Autumn 1980).

Eckert, Charles, ed. *Focus on Shakespearean Films*. Englewood Cliffs, N.J., 1972.

Flanagan, Hallie, *Arena*. New York, 1940.

France, Richard. *The Theatre of Orson Welles*. Bucknell, Penn., 1977.

Gerstle, Gary L. "Mission from Moscow: American Communism in the 1930's." *Reviews in American History* 12 (1984).

Goldstein, Malcolm. *The Political Stage*. New York, 1974.

Gorelik, Mordecai. "Legacy of the New Deal Drama." *Drama Survey* 4 (Spring 1965).

Greene, Naomi. *Antonin Artaud: Poet Without Words*. New York, 1974.

Himelstein, Morgan Y. *Drama Was a Weapon: The Left-Wing Theatre in New York*. New Brunswick, N.J., 1963.

---

*I have deliberately omitted the recent Brady, Leaming, and Higham biographies, as well as the special issue of *Persistence of Vision* (no. 7, 1989), as they add nothing of substance to the study of Orson Welles.

————. "Theory and Performance in the Depression Theatre." *Modern Drama* 14 (February 1971).

Houseman, John. "The Birth of the Mercury Theatre." *Educational Theatre Journal* (March 1972).

————. "A Director Remembers." Sound recording. Los Angeles, 1977.

————. Run-Through, New York, 1972.

Isaacs, Edith J. R. *The Negro in the American Theatre*. New York, 1947.

Johnson, William. "Orson Welles: Of Time and Loss." *Film Quarterly* (1968).

Jorgens, Jack. *Shakespeare on Film*. Bloomington, Ind., 1977.

Kael, Pauline. *The Citizen Kane Book*. Boston, 1972.

Klehr, Harvey. *The Heyday of American Communism: The Depression Decade*. New York, 1984.

Koval, Francis. "An Interview with Orson Welles." *Sight and Sound* (Spring 1950).

Levine, Ira A. *Left-Wing Dramatic Theory in American Theatre*. Ann Arbor, Mich., 1985.

Lyons, Bridget G., ed. *Chimes at Midnight*. New Brunswick, N.J., 1988.

Maltby, Richard. *Passing Parade: A History of Popular Culture in the Twentieth Century*. New York, 1989.

Matthews, Jane deHart. *The Federal Theatre*. Princeton, N.J., 1967.

McBride, Joseph. *Orson Welles*. New York, 1972.

McCloskey, Susan. "Shakespeare, Orson Welles, and the 'Voodoo' *Macbeth*." *Shakespeare Quarterly* (Winter 1985).

McDermott, Douglas. "Propaganda and Art: Dramatic Theory and the American Depression." *Modern Drama* 12 (May 1968).

McLean, Andrew M. "Orson Welles and Shakespeare." *Literature/Film Quarterly* (1983).

Melosh, Barbara. "The New Deal's Federal Theatre Project." *Medical Heritage* 2 (1986).

Mullin, Michael. "*Macbeth* on Film." *Literature/Film Quarterly* (1973).

Naremore, James. *The Magic World of Orson Welles*. New York, 1978.

————. "The Walking Shadow: Welles' Expressionist *Macbeth*." *Literature/Film Quarterly* (1973).

O'Connor, John S. "But Was It Shakespeare?" *Theatre Journal* (October 1980).

O'Connor, John S., and Lorraine Brown, eds. *Free, Adult, Uncensored: The Living History of the Federal Theatre Project*. Washington, D.C., 1978.

Parra, Danièle, and Jacques Zimmer. *Orson Welles*. Paris, 1985.

Peeler, David P. *Hope Among Us: Social Criticism and Social Solace in Depression America*. Athens, Ga., 1987.

Pells, Richard H. *Radical Visions and American Dreams: Culture and Social Thought in the Depression Years*. Middletown, Conn., 1973.

Rabkin, Gerald. *Drama and Commitment: Politics in the American Theatre of the Thirties*. Bloomington, Ind., 1964.

Rabkin, Norman, ed. *Reinterpretations of Elizabethan Drama*. New York, 1969.

Rosenthal, Jean. "Five Kings." *Theatre Arts Magazine* (June 1939).

————. *The Magic of Light*. New York, 1972.

Ross, Ronald. "The Role of Blacks in the Federal Theatre." *Journal of Negro History* 59 (January 1974).

Ross, Theophil W. "Conflicting Concepts of the Federal Theatre Project: A Critical History." Unpublished dissertation, 1981.

Simon, Rita James, ed. *As We Saw the Thirties: Essays on Social and Political Movements of a Decade.* Chicago, 1967.

Smirnov, A. A. *Shakespeare: A Marxist Interpretation.* New York, 1936.

Sokel, Walter H. *The Writer in Extremis.* Stanford, Calif. 1959.

Scott, William. *Documentary Expression and Thirties America.* Chicago, 1973.

Susman, Warren, ed. *Culture and Commitment, 1929–1945.* New York, 1973.

Taylor, Karen Malpede. *People's Theatre in Amerika.* New York, 1972.

Thomson, Virgil. *Virgil Thomson.* New York, 1966.

Vacha, J. E. "The Case of the Runaway Opera: The Federal Theatre and Marc Blitzstein's *The Cradle Will Rock.*" *New York History* 62 (April 1981).

Warshow, Robert. *The Immediate Experience.* New York, 1970.

Welles, Orson. "Welles on Falstaff." *Cahiers du Cinema* (December 1967).

Whittler, Clarence J. *Some Social Trends in W.P.A. Drama.* New York, 1939.

Willett, John. *Expressionism.* New York, 1970.

Williams, Jay. *Stage Left.* New York, 1974.

Wilson, Garff. B. *A History of American Acting.* Bloomington, Ind., 1966.

About the Editor

RICHARD FRANCE teaches at the University of Southern California. His many plays include *The Image of Elmo Doyle,* contained in the *Best Short Plays of 1979;* the dramatization of *One Day in the Life of Ivan Denisovich,* and *Station J,* winner of the 1982 Silver PEN award. He has previously taught at Brown University and Lawrence University and his book *The Theatre of Orson Welles* was a *Choice* selection for Most Outstanding Academic Books of 1978.